Where Have All the Liberals Gone?

Race, Class, and Ideals in America

JAMES R. FLYNN

CAMBRIDGE
UNIVERSITY PRESS

CAMBRIDGE UNIVERSITY PRESS

Cambridge, New York, Melbourne, Madrid, Cape Town, Singapore, São Paulo, Delhi

Cambridge University Press
The Edinburgh Building, Cambridge CB2 8RU, UK

Published in the United States of America by Cambridge University Press, New York

www.cambridge.org
Information on this title: www.cambridge.org/9780521494311

First published 2008

Printed in the United States of America

A catalogue record for this publication is available from the British Library

ISBN   978-0-521-49431-1 hardback

In memoriam:

Don Anderson

If Jefferson was wrong, America was wrong.
>   (James Parton, 1874)

I don't see color.
>   (Beatrice Hugeley, black member of the
>   Congress of Racial Equality, 1961)

We now hear that she [Spain] is well rid of her colonies
and that, if she will devote her energies to her internal
development . . . she may be regenerated.
>   (William Graham Sumner, 1899)

Here I stand.
>   (Martin Luther, at the Diet of Worms, April 18, 1521)

Contents

Figures and maps

Tables

Boxes

Acknowledgments

Chapter 2 owes much to William T. Dickens and Charles Baschnagel of the Brookings Institution and to Jeffrey S. Passel of the Pew Hispanic Center. They complied with my many requests for data from the March 2005 Current Population Survey with great patience. Also to Charles Murray of the American Enterprise Institution for data (specified in the text) from the National Longitudinal Survey of Youth. I wish to thank the University of Nebraska Press for permission to use sections of my book, James R. Flynn, *How To Defend Humane Ideals: Substitutes for Objectivity* (2000). These appear, revised and updated, in chapters 4, 5, 8, and 9. Finally, thanks to Ashgate for permission to reprint "The America who would be king" from David B. MacDonald, Robert G. Patman, and Betty Mason-Parker (eds.), *The Ethics of Foreign Policy* (Aldershot: Ashgate, 2007).

Prologue

The best lack all conviction, while the worst
Are full of passionate intensity.
(William Butler Yeats, 1920)

As the title of this book indicates, I believe that what passes for
public debate in America is barren because of the failure of will and
a poverty of ideals among American liberals. I am not a liberal but
a Social Democrat. However, if there is to be any hope of a Social
Democratic America there must first be a liberal America, so our
fates are conjoined. The spokespeople for conservatism are articulate
and spirited. But much of their success is due to the fact that liberals have been so feeble in criticizing their agenda and suggesting real
alternatives. No one ever won a political debate by endless repetition
of the refrain "but everything is going wrong."

I believe that the entire center of American politics, both
Republicans and Democrats, has lost touch with reality and the ideals
on which the Republic was founded. Debate on race, class, foreign
policy, how to safeguard Israel, how to live a good life, is obscured as
if some great dark cloud of self-imposed censorship had descended
on our minds. And yet, America has a great political tradition given
definitive expression by our patron saint, Thomas Jefferson. Perhaps
the first step toward clarity is to recall what America was supposed to
be all about.

I will offer an account of the Jeffersonian tradition from the
perspective of the Social Democratic left. When I propose alternatives to current American policies, the substance of these will reflect

Democratic Socialism. However, I hope that readers from any part of the political spectrum will find some profit herein. For example, most conservatives will reject my views on affirmative action, the welfare state, and even what I make of the Jeffersonian tradition. But I see no reason they should not resonate with my views about what is going on in black America, US foreign policy, and thinking about morality.

I will discuss four things as preeminent in terms of blighting what the American experiment was all about: **race**, particularly the fact that black Americans are handicapped by their skin color even in an era of declining prejudice; **class**, particularly the notion that it has become correlated with genes and that a large number of Americans are trapped in a marginalized underclass; **military power** driven by moral arrogance, so that America becomes a cause of despair (rather than hope) for the rest of the world; **morality** clouded by confusion, so that Americans lose sight of what it is to be fully human.

The list could be extended to include other things, environmental degradation, water scarcity, too much sugar in the tomato sauce, but I lack the expertise to say anything helpful about these. Surely, even in this age of prophets of doom, four disasters lurking on the horizon are enough for one book.

Given the centrality of America on the world scene, others have an interest in its fate. English readers in particular should identify with these themes. Their John Locke was the philosophical father of Jefferson and his ideals, they have a black minority, the development of an underclass is supposed to be their fate as well, their government seems obsessed with being an accessory to American foreign policy, and these are prey to similar moral confusions.

The Jeffersonian ideal constitutes the closest thing America has to a public philosophy, that is, a shared set of values that bind its people together. Part I consists of an introductory chapter in which I will describe what we are in danger of losing. It talks about Jefferson, the problems he foresaw, the problems he did not, and a few of those who have walked in his moral and political footsteps, some of them sadly taking wrong turns. The remainder of the book is divided into three parts, dealing respectively with black America, trends in American society and foreign policy, and fundamental moral issues. That is a wider range of topics than convention dictates. But I have never cared much about convention because it makes you a slave of your time rather than its master.

To justify the topics that dominate various chapters:

1 Most whites and many blacks lack a clear vision of the greatest problem that confronts American society, at least in terms of social justice, that is, the state of black America;
2 No one can discuss this problem without a frank and open discussion of the contention that American blacks, on average, have inferior genes for intelligence;
3 The case for affirmative action has never been properly put;
4 We must acknowledge the debt owed to *The Bell Curve* for making us rethink how we can achieve the American dream;
5 Whether we can salvage something from the dangerous mess that is American foreign policy;
6 The absence of what should be the principal issue of American politics, namely, the shift of resources away from military spending toward social purposes;
7 Overcoming moral confusion, particularly notions such as that we can give no reasoned defense of certain ideals versus others, and that we are creatures of circumstance that cannot be judged for what we do.

I make no apology for including some moral philosophy. Poverty of thinking about ethics can do as much to distract us from good living as the material poverty that makes keeping our bodies alive an all-consuming task. When people think their ideals are mere preferences or no more worthy of regard than any other, it saps their moral idealism. When they lose sight of what it is to be a responsible moral agent, it weakens the judgments they pass on themselves and others. The warning by Yeats issued in 1920, the danger that the best will lack all conviction, has if anything greater relevance today than it did three generations ago. The chapters on morality are the foundation on which all else rests. I suspect that they will be particularly interesting to those who, like myself, were students of Leo Strauss.

References to *The Bell Curve* will be conspicuous because it is the most impressive work to present a picture of America that contrasts with my own. I will criticize the "meritocracy thesis" (in chapter 5), which, to my mind, is the most troubling of its contents. I know of no one else who has done so. *The Bell Curve* was not about race, but since it was about America it could not ignore race. I think some readers will appreciate the alternative view I offer.

This book is particularly for the young. I suspect that most of them want something better than a foreign and military policy that provokes disgust, a domestic politics with neither the vision nor the resources to provide for the common good, and a foolish moral relativism that reduces all ideals to the lowest common denominator. My message is this: your idealism will fade unless a life of political activism is accompanied by a life of the mind. The problems herein are those I could not get out of my mind during sixty-two years of political activism. Perhaps an old agitator can keep those whose youthfully ardent desire for social justice has flared into existence from having to reinvent the wheel.

Well, then, we begin a journey that tries to answer a question that dominates everything else: does American idealism have a future? Particularly the kind of idealism that has characterized the American left. Can men and women enlist in its ranks bathed in the bright light of everything reason has to say about the contemporary world?

PART I

St. Thomas Jefferson

1   Something beautiful is vanished

But when the dream departs
It takes something from our hearts
Something beautiful is vanished
And it never comes again
          (Richard Henry Stoddard, 1825–1903)

At the end of *The Bell Curve*, Herrnstein and Murray attempt to square their view of America with that of Thomas Jefferson. Their endeavors come as no surprise. In 1776, Jefferson wrote the Declaration of Independence and penned these words: "We hold these truths to be self-evident, that all men are created equal, that they are endowed by their Creator with certain unalienable rights, that among these are life, liberty and the pursuit of happiness." In doing so, he struck a chord that has reverberated throughout American history. Virtually every major political actor on the American scene has quoted Jefferson's words and claimed to be a Jeffersonian, no matter how vigorously they disputed what his legacy entails.

But words can be mere words. If Americans have taken Jefferson seriously, we would expect to find some at least who have risked much to stand by his ideals. We would also expect periodic warnings about policies and developments that might prevent their realization in practice. Jefferson and his successors compiled a list of threats with imperialism, class, intolerance, and race most prominent. I have selected four giants to develop these themes. Their lives and thoughts are worth recounting for another reason: faced with a

---

Box 1

Some may find my sketch of American political history more than a little idiosyncratic. I had a kindred experience as a young lecturer at Wisconsin State. While sitting in a reading room, I found myself surrounded. Through one wall came the voice of a colleague and friend (we were friends for the time being although he said that, eventually, I would have to be eliminated). He was a member of the John Birch Society and was reading from a text he had written for the high schools. Through the other wall came a patriotic song sung by a girls' choir as if providing a musical accompaniment. With so little time, he could only note the most important events of American history, such as the founding of the first college fraternity and the frustration of two American boys having to fight in Korea under "a strange blue flag" (that of the United Nations). I have always hoped to buy a copy but fear it was never published.

---

dismal present, it is good to call to mind just what wonderful people the American political tradition has produced (see Box 1).

Only Jefferson himself invites us to examine the philosophical foundation of egalitarian ideals and to underline the fact that fervor is often a function of why we believe in something. However, William Graham Sumner will prove useful on imperialism, Eugene Victor Debs on class, and Carey Estes Kefauver on civil liberties. Kefauver also exemplifies how a principled man of great courage can be blind about the gulf between black and white.

Jefferson and God

Thomas Jefferson (1743–1826) said that his ethical premises were self-evident. He did not mean to imply that no justifying argument lay behind them, but rather that the argument was so obviously valid that no rational person would reject it. The question of whether he was more influenced by Locke or Lord Kames (who was himself a

Lockean) is irrelevant in that the liberal thinkers of the time all shared much the same notions.

They appealed to the concept of man as he came unsullied from nature. At that point, convention (what man does to himself) had not distorted nature's handiwork. People were obviously equal at birth, helpless needy creatures, and dependent on their parents whom nature had endowed with a parental instinct as a sign that they were obliged to care for their children. None was born with a visible title to preferment, no child was born with a scepter in his hand, and all had free will, signs that the divine right of kings was bankrupt and that men were meant to freely consent to whatever government they chose.

All men have an instinct for self-preservation, a sign that the lives of all were precious and that murder and suicide were wrong. No one can contract to be a slave because that gives to another a power you do not yourself possess, namely, the right to take your life when you wish. Nature did not present the earth divided up by property boundaries, so property was to be acquired by mixing one's labor with it. All of these arguments are in Locke's early unpublished work on the *Laws of Nature*, circa 1660, and Kant repeated many of them in Jefferson's own day (Kant, *Metaphysics of Morals*, AK, 420–468; Locke, 1954).

Lying behind this view of nature was the hand of God. In his old age, Jefferson wrote a treatise on Christianity designed to extract the true teachings of Christ from the rubbish in which they were buried (Matthews, 1984). All of Christ's teachings tend towards the happiness of man and they are summarized in the Sermon on the Mount. True Christianity involves only three propositions:

1 that there is only one God, and he all perfect
2 that there is a future state of rewards and punishments
3 that to love God with all thy heart and thy neighbor as thyself is the sum of religion.

The aging Jefferson took great satisfaction that his fellow Americans shared his reverence for the ethical foundations of the Republic's political ideals. In 1824, two years before his death, he wrote: "Nothing then is unchangeable but the inherent and inalienable rights of man" (Hofstadter, 1962, p. 43).

An ideal in search of a foundation

But when belief in God departs, the foundations collapse. As early as the 1850s, Mill composed his brilliant essay on *Nature*, published posthumously in 1874. Although his target is Locke what he says applies equally to Jefferson. Jefferson rejected the divinity of Christ but never doubted that Christ was God's exemplar as to how to live. He knew what he was expected to find in nature: benevolence and that the meek were as precious as the most high. His ethical ideals served as a sieve that filtered out the cruel face of nature and left a benevolent residue.

Mill was an atheist and looked at nature with an unprejudiced eye. As he says, only someone with a pre-existing humane ethic could overlook its brutality with whole cities buried by earthquakes and people stricken by meaningless diseases. An ethics truly derived from nature would make us worse than the Borgias. He goes on to ask, what do we mean by nature anyway? If we mean the whole of nature as governed by laws, every human act is good: the laws of biology are just as much obeyed when you poison someone as when you feed the needy. If you mean nature as untouched by human beings, every human act is bad: every time I exhale I alter the composition of the atmosphere in my immediate vicinity. Both conclusions are equally absurd (Mill, 1958).

With the original foundation of our ideals swept away, what is left? It has taken a long time for the rootlessness of ethics to dominate the popular consciousness but, except for the believers, the process is now complete. Allan Bloom's (1987) account of his students applies to my own: The self-evidence of humane moral principles has been replaced by a lazy set of "self-evident" notions clustering around the concept of cultural relativism. No one can defend his or her ideals as more rational than any others, so all ideals and the people who hold them are equal and all should be allowed to live as they please without censure. Bloom asks them about Hitler's ideals and female circumcision. I prod them on an equally sensitive point. Most liberal-minded students in New Zealand believe that the indigenous Polynesians (the Maori) have been badly treated. I ask them whether it is legitimate for us to cross cultural lines and accuse Maori of sexism (most tribes do not allow women to speak at public meetings). And if that is not legitimate, is it not wrong for Maori to accuse white New Zealanders of injustice.

It may be said that as long as there is a popular ideology that supports a belief in equality and liberty, that is enough, no matter how muddled it may be. But the current ideology suffers from two defects. First, it is so contradictory that no intelligent person, certainly no one like Jefferson, can take it seriously. It winnows out the best, namely, those with any critical intelligence, and when they see through it, they have nothing. Second, it destroys passionate dedication to ideals. Passion requires believing that certain ideals are better than all others, not that all ideals are equally arbitrary. The tolerance that arises from a muddled cultural relativism is not a passionate attachment to civil liberties and a willingness to die in a ditch for them. It is a tepid thing, based on the reduction of all ideals to mere preferences in life style, culminating in the absurd admonition of "don't be judgmental."

Nietzsche accuses modern intellectuals of "soul superstition." He ridicules those who do not believe in God but cling to a morality that makes sense only for believers. Love for mankind in general makes some sort of sense if everyone has a soul dear to God, but love of mankind without this is simply stupidity and brutishness. How could anyone love ordinary people, with their pettiness, ignorance, dearth of anything interesting to say or do, without some concept to sanctify them? Nietzsche tells us that we should ask ourselves whether we would *really* be committed to egalitarian ideals were our minds not infected by a disreputable metaphysical residue. It is a fair question.

In Part IV, I will explore three alternatives. First, the possibility that I have been unfair to the current ideology, which has its roots in thinkers as distinguished as William James and Ruth Benedict. Perhaps "relativism" makes more sense as a foundation for the good life than first appears. Second, the solution of the followers of Leo Strauss. They see relativism as the chief enemy of all that is good and have designed an elaborate and subtle strategy to contain it. Finding these two options vulnerable, inevitably I will suggest my own solution. This consists of openly accepting the truth of ethical skepticism and seeing what justification of our ideals remains.

Jefferson on entangling alliances

Untroubled by philosophical doubt, Jefferson believed that the principal threats to his ideals were political and social. He addressed the problems of American foreign policy and, thanks to his preeminence, everyone from isolationists to internationalists has tried to hitch Jefferson to their star (Peterson, 1998, pp. 266–271, 345, 416, 437–439, 448–452).

This is absurd, because broad ideals like life, liberty, and the pursuit of happiness cannot dictate foreign policy without being adapted to the political realities of the day and this last puts so heavy a weight in the scale that it transforms everything. Humane ideals certainly dictate that foreign policy cannot be amoral, as even my old professor Hans Morgenthau, the paradigm political realist, used to acknowledge (see *Scientific Man versus Power Politics*: 1946). But what they imply alters dramatically as we go from Jefferson's day, where the problem was to save the fledgling Republic from extinction by some great power, to our day, where the problem is how a nation of predominate power can do good rather than harm to the global community.

When Jefferson gave advice about the conduct of foreign policy, he always emphasized America's peculiar advantage. Its separation from the nations of Europe by oceans allowed America to live in peace, just so long as it was not foolish enough to gratuitously involve itself in their quarrels by making "entangling alliances." From his addresses and letters, there emerge three great objectives.

(1) The preservation of the Republic

War beyond the water is universal and must be kept out of our island. We must not pursue fantastic honor, unallied to virtue or happiness, or be swayed by angry passions. Leave Europeans to act out their follies and crimes among themselves. However, this did not forbid political realism. Jefferson wanted to buy the Louisiana territory from France to open up land for farmers. But he stressed that its peaceful acquisition had become urgent because it had passed from Spain into the hands of France. Spain was too weak to have aggressive aims. France was a great power and a common border would inevitably lead to war.

(2) The eventual pacification of the world

Jefferson thought that the main contribution America could make was to hope that its example might edify the nations of Europe and mitigate their war-like tendencies. One nation at least could be seen to have a "Quaker" foreign policy of good will toward all. The principles of humanity, the precepts of the gospel, and the general wish of the American people dictate friendship to all nations.

(3) "Regime change" or the spread of Republican government

Jefferson hoped that all nations would eventually enjoy Republican government and its blessings. Given America's peripheral position and influence, this had to be pursued indirectly. America must not waste the energies of its people in war and destruction, even in support of principles that excite its admiration. To take sides in Europe, even with those who claim to champion Republican

13

principles, is to become entangled with nations who will have many other interests different from ours (Cunningham, 1987, pp. 259–264; Matthews, 1984).

Jefferson stated objectives to which all Americans pay homage. But all with any sense will recognize that his policy of "isolation" was dictated by circumstances that have altered. What separates American policy from Jefferson today is a failure to match his political realism. I will argue that our cardinal error is to put his third objective ahead of his second, that is, to put regime change ahead of pacifying the global society. I claim no knowledge of what priorities Jefferson himself would have set were he transported 200 years from his time into ours. As Philip Wylie once said, there is more debate about what Jefferson would have thought about interstate commerce than a sane man can stand.

Jefferson and class: the earth belongs to the living

In January 1790, Jefferson gave Madison a fascinating paper. It stated a general principle that, like the rights of man, had universal application. The earth belongs always to the living in the sense that one generation cannot compromise the autonomy or freedom of the next. He had before his eyes the corrupt way in which property was distributed in royal France: lands given to the nobility, churches, and universities in perpetuity; hereditary offices, authorities, and titles; and monopolies in commerce, the arts, and the sciences. Such a system can be overturned at any time.

America was fortunate to lack such a feudal past. Nonetheless it was subject to the same principle: "The portion [of the earth] occupied by any individual ceases to be his when he himself ceases to be, and reverts to the society." He has no *natural right* (italics Jefferson's) to dictate who inherits it. Society may adopt rules of inheritance, allowing property to go to the wife, children, or creditors. But these laws like all others (including constitutions) are subject to amendment and revision. At this point, Jefferson goes a bit berserk using actuarial tables. A man aged 24 has a life expectancy of 55 years, and therefore can lease his lands for no more than 31 years, a man of 54 for no more than one year. Jefferson calculated that a generation's span was nineteen years and argued that no government should incur a debt that could not be repaid within that time. The arithmetic makes sense: a child had less than a 50/50 chance of reaching maturity but someone who did could expect another thirty-one years (Washington, 1861).

Jefferson thought of taxes as something that privileged classes used to burden ordinary people. Further, the bulk of taxpayers of his day were small farmers whose income came from their own toil. In a letter to James Milligan in April 1816, he says that it would be unjust to take the fruits of someone's labor, or what someone has inherited from a parent's labor, and transfer that wealth to another person less skilled and industrious. However, he recognizes that an individual's wealth can become "overgrown" to the point that this is a danger to the state and recommends new laws of inheritance as a corrective: they would compel equal inheritance by all heirs (Hofstadter, 1962, p. 37). While this might be a corrective for property in land, it would do little to disperse other forms of wealth less important in Jefferson's day, that is, a radically unequal distribution of wealth in terms of cash and stock.

Against Jefferson's egalitarianism, it has been stressed that while he claimed he had always supported universal manhood suffrage, his 1776 draft of a constitution of Virginia included a property requirement. But he also proposed that every mature free male be granted 50 acres of land, thus making suffrage virtually universal (Hofstadter, 1962, p. 31). This brings us to the heart of Jefferson's egalitarianism: he wanted a society in which everyone was a free man, that is, owned sufficient land to be autonomous and provide a good life. But he could not imagine how this would be possible for anyone but a farmer who owned his own farm. Merchants were money obsessed and corrupt. Wage workers were at the mercy of their employers and could only hope to better themselves by becoming employers who reduced others to dependence. Like everyone in his time, he merely accepted that life was to some degree a lottery: disease carried off infants and indeed those of all ages; accidents crippled; harvests failed. The concept of the welfare state simply did not have currency in his day (Cunningham, 1987).

Jefferson's own Presidency had a supreme irony. His embargo act attempted to maintain neutrality between France and Britain by curtailing imports from both. This forced America to attempt to be self-sufficient for manufactured goods. It spurred the kind of economic development that was fatal for Jefferson's ideal of a farming society with industry at a minimum. He had no solution to the problem of how a good society could be maintained as the labor force contained fewer and fewer who had the capacity to be free (farmers) and more and more who were crippled and deformed by their dependency (wage workers).

Sooner or later, the problem of how wage workers could approximate the autonomy, security of tenure, and dignity of farmers had to be faced. The obvious solutions were strong trade unions, popular control of the government, and the welfare state. As Jefferson's America faded, Debs and Social Democracy were waiting in the wings.

Jefferson on Native Americans and blacks

In his second inaugural address to Congress on March 4, 1805, Jefferson included a long passage that set out his views on America's "aboriginal inhabitants." They were endowed with the same rights of man as Europeans, the same faculties, and had an ardent love of liberty. But now they were being overwhelmed by a flood of white population.

Jefferson, and in this he was of course correct, could not see how they could survive unless they compromised their cultures to learn agriculture and the domestic arts and advanced under the rule of reason. His administration had liberally supplied them with implements and instruction but had met "powerful obstacles." Jefferson never wavered from his views on "Indians" expressed in 1780 in reply to Buffon's case for their innate inferiority. He says the Spanish only observed the Indians of South America after they had been degraded by ten generations of slavery. If they had studied the Indians of North America they would have seen "they were formed in mind as well as in body, on the same module with the 'Homo sapiens Europaeus'." He challenged anyone to find a speech by Logan, a Mingo chief, inferior to any delivered by Demosthenes or Cicero (Cunningham, 1987, pp. 276–277; Matthews, 1984, pp. 54–57).

Jefferson's views on blacks were: that the opinion that they are inferior in reason is one he endorses as a suspicion only; that it cannot be justified without "many observations" (he welcomed contrary evidence throughout his life); that blacks are equal in that they possess a moral sense and qualify for the rights of man; and that slavery is wrong. His first draft of the Declaration of Independence contained the following: "[The king] has waged cruel war against human nature itself, violating its most sacred rights of life and liberty in the persons of a distant people who never offended him, captivating and carrying them into slavery . . . determined to keep open a market where *Men* should be bought and sold." Jefferson was angry that he was forced to delete this passage. He had to face the fact that most Americans were unwilled to divest themselves of their slaves (Matthews, 1984, pp. 66–67).

Jefferson has been indicted for not freeing his own slaves. This overlooks the barriers Southern states had erected. Virginia law stated that if slaves were freed, anyone who found them could take possession. Jefferson was not willing to see his slaves fall into the hands of someone less benevolent. He would have to pay to transport them outside the boundaries of the South, and provide each with ample funds to get established, and even this would not ensure their survival given what they would face in eighteenth-century America. Jefferson was crippled by his own generosity. He borrowed funds to give to beggars and, in his last years, suffered from underwriting the note of a neighbor in need. Still in debt, he managed to free a few slaves upon his death (Hofstadter, 1962, p. 22; Matthews, 1984, pp. 67–68).

Sumner and the Spanish-American War

Fourteen years after Jefferson's death, William Graham Sumner (1840–1910) was born. As he watched America evolve from a rural into an industrialized society and from a small isolated nation into a world power, he became alarmed.

Sumner is remembered as America's leading Social Darwinist and her first Professor of Sociology. But his greatest contribution was a prescient analysis of how imperialism might corrupt America, although whether or not the disease would overwhelm the patient was in doubt for almost a century. The era of isolationism from 1918 to 1940 showed that some at least were resistant. Hitler's Germany and Stalin's Russia presented challenges that virtually coerced America into the role of a dominant global power between 1940 and the end of the Cold War in 1987. Those forty-seven years taught her bad habits. Today, the departures from America's traditional ideals Sumner lamented are no longer even seen for what they are. They enjoy bi-partisan support as if they were a rational policy of national security.

On January 16, 1899, Sumner (1899) delivered a speech to the Phi Beta Kappa Society of Yale University. He spoke about the Spanish-American War, which he called "The conquest of the United States by Spain." Sumner meant of course that while America had won the test of arms, Spain had won the battle of ideas. He advised the citizens of the Republic to think carefully about jettisoning America's traditional regard for liberty and self-government in favor of the imperialist mentality of Spain. If only someone of similar stature had delivered a similar address prior to America's invasion of Iraq. Sumner's points are of such obvious relevance that little comment is needed to render them contemporary.

Manipulation of public opinion

"It was necessary to make appeals to the public . . . [and] such appeals were found in sensational assertions which we had no means to verify, in phrases of alleged patriotism, in statements which we now know to have been entirely untrue." In one respect, deception fell short of that perpetrated before Iraq. The American public was given the impression that the sinking of the US battleship *Maine* in Havana Harbor was due to a Spanish mine when in fact it was either an accident or done by the Cuban rebels acting as agents provocateurs. But it was at least possible to suspect Spain at the time. The Bush administration managed to convince a majority of Americans that Saddam Hussein had destroyed the Twin Towers even though it knew that those who had done so were his sworn enemies. That the administration did this by indirection does not mitigate the fact that they fostered the misapprehension and took no effective steps to correct it.

Unexpected consequences

"A statesman could not be expected to know in advance that we should come out of the war with the Philippines on our hands, but it belongs to his education to warn him that a policy of adventure and of gratuitous enterprise would be sure to entail embarrassments of some kind." Applied to Iraq, Sumner's comments are too kind. The fact that Hussein's Sunni supporters would fight rather than be subjected to Shiite domination was only too predictable.

Taking control

"It is impossible to improvise a colonial system . . . It depends on a large body of trained men, acting under traditions which have become well established, and with a firm esprit de corps." We have lamented our failure to bring order out of the chaos of post-invasion Iraq as if it were a mere failure to plan, to anticipate, to prepare a detailed blueprint as to how to get the electricity running. Nation building where there is no national identity (as there was in post-war Germany and Japan) is an almost impossible task without tyranny. But even a chance of success would have required the creation of a cadre with years of training and experience (to be gained where?) behind them.

Reassurance that one's objectives are not imperialistic

"Senator Foraker has told us that we are not to keep the Philippines longer than is necessary to teach the people self-government." In Iraq we are not even willing to give an assurance that we mean to withdraw our troops. Our bases seem designed to be permanent and we will probably have to be forced to withdraw them because of the political instability or violence they engender.

American exceptionalism

"There is not a nation which does not talk about its civilizing mission just as grandly as we do. The English . . . talk least about it, but the Phariseeism with which they correct and instruct other peoples has made them hated all over the globe." Also: "We assume that what we like and practice, and what we think better, must come as a welcome blessing to Filipinos. This is grossly and obviously untrue. They hate our ways. They are hostile to our ideas. Our religion, language, institutions and manners offended them . . . The most important thing we shall inherit from the Spaniards will be the task of suppressing rebellions." Enough said.

Temptations of empire

"[Spain] saw her resources spent on interests that were foreign to her, but she could talk about an empire on which the sun never set and boast of her colonies, her gold mines, her fleets and armies and debts. She had glory and pride, mixed, of course, with defeat and disaster, such as must be experienced by any nation on that course of policy." Sumner here speaks of that most deadly of sins, pride. History is full of examples of nations who planted their flag throughout the world simply because they could, and demonstrated their power as if they were involved in some kind of display to attract a mate. That America has gone down that road since 1987 will be argued in detail. Sumner expresses his admiration for "hard-headed old Benjamin Franklin" who talked about the pest of glory: "The thirst for glory is an epidemic which robs a people of their judgment, seduces their vanity, cheats them of their interests, and corrupts their consciences."

At this point, Sumner digresses to lecture his audience on the benefits of free trade. But who has ever been so wise in so few words? He closes with a warning against military interests: "It is militarism which is eating up all of the products of science, and art, defeating the energy of the population and wasting its savings. It is militarism which forbids the people to give their attention to the problems of their welfare and to give their strength to the education and comfort of their children."

Sumner and race

In the same speech, Sumner makes some forthright comments about how America hides from the conflict between its public philosophy and its attitudes towards race: "Americans have been committed from the outset to the doctrine that all men are equal. We have elevated it into an absolute doctrine as a part of the theory of our social and political fabric and . . . it has always stood in glaring contradiction to the facts about Indians and Negroes and to our legislation about the Chinese."

He was equally blunt about the politics of race after the Civil War: "For thirty years the Negro has been in fashion. He has had political value and has been petted. Now we have made friends with the Southerners. They and we are hugging one another. We are all united. The Negro's day is over. He is out of fashion." And as to what this meant: "Americans cannot assure life, liberty, and the pursuit of happiness to Negroes inside of the United States. When the Negro postmaster's house was set on fire in the night in South Carolina, and not only he, but his wife and children were murdered as they came out . . . this incident passed without legal investigation or punishment." For all his merits, another great American, Estes Kefauver, lacked Sumner's realism about what it meant to leave blacks to the mercy of Southern justice.

Sumner and class

Therefore, it is odd that Sumner showed so little sensitivity as to what it meant to leave ordinary Americans to the mercy of industrialization. The Civil War (1861–65) helped change the face of America. She evolved from a developing nation in which the vulnerability of its citizens was a matter of nature's impact on agriculture and restrictions on the terms of trade into a modern industrial economy in which one class had no protection against another. As a great pioneer sociologist, Sumner was well aware of the rise of the "plutocracy" and an industrial working class. But he seems quite unable to appreciate how the struggle of the latter to live a decent life was circumscribed by factors outside their control, namely, periodic recessions and the helplessness of unorganized workers in the face of an industrial elite that could use armed force and starvation to reduce them to serfs with no guarantee of tenure.

According to Sumner, late nineteenth-century capitalism had divided society primarily into two groups. There were the winners who enjoyed middle-class security and comfort primarily because they exhibited the Calvinist virtues of thrift and hard work, decent family men who put money aside in a postal savings account. And there were the losers who were negligent, idle, extravagant, shiftless, and criminal. He goes so far as to say that any slum dweller can by modest effort make his or her way to where conditions are easier, culminating in this: "In general, there is no man who is honest and industrious who cannot put himself in a way to maintain himself and his family, misfortune apart, in a condition of substantial comfort" (Persons, 1963, pp. 84, 118, 134, 158–159).

The reality was somewhat different. As for the winners, what traits did they actually exhibit? Veblen (1899) describes hollow men seeking prestige by conspicuous display and wasteful consumption of material goods. Like Kwakiutl at a potlatch, they put their rivals to shame by outspending them: a million spent on a coming-out party for a daughter, thousands on a fur coat for a dog, culminating in the proverbial lighting of a cigar with a five-dollar bill. Worse, the mores of the millionaires and captains of industry infected the middle class. No house big enough, wives and children turned into possessions for display, the husband who boasts that his wife does not have to work, the wife accepting that role, the devaluation of work thanks to the ideal of being a member of an affluent leisure class, the worker hiding his blue collar from his family, the millions longing only for retirement and idleness.

Tawney (1920) sums up the soul of what he calls the "acquisitive society": to gain much without giving respected, to give without gaining despised. As the economy evolved, the captains of industry gave the middle class new marching orders: impulse buying, self-indulgence, and life on a mountain of debt. None of this is very close to the Calvinist virtues Sumner so admired. Veblen and Tawney describe only some features of the social landscape, of course, but they were social realities that Sumner's balance sheet omitted. They are still with us today.

Who were the losers? The late nineteenth century was a time when the lives of millions were blighted by a cycle of boom and bust. The recession of 1892 was particularly severe: Eugene Victor Debs was appalled watching mothers searching garbage pails for food in his hometown of Terre Haute, Indiana. The 1930s saw the Great Depression plus the Dust Bowl, the great drought that struck the American prairie states. These sent people to the wall who had been industrious and thrifty all their lives, many of them impeccably middle class. In 1931, 70 percent of the farmers of Oklahoma were unable to pay the interest on their mortgages; in 1933, unemployment reached a peak of 15 million (Shannon, 1960).

Since 1945, America has enjoyed a time largely free of the cycle of boom and bust, although climate and peak oil and exhausted reserves of ground water may have some unpleasant developments in store for our children. However, social change in the form of the erosion of marriage has created a new poverty trap, namely, solo-parenthood. As *The Bell Curve* revealed, even the white middle class is not exempt. In 1991, a white woman of average ability and from an average socioeconomic background, raising children while separated, divorced, or never married, had a 33 percent chance of living in poverty. The rate for all single mothers was worse at 36 percent, but note how little protection middle-class women actually derive from their status. The effects on American children are profound: 22 percent of all American children under the age of fifteen are being raised in homes below the poverty line (Herrnstein and Murray, 1994, pp. 137–139). It is true that those in poverty may escape after five or ten years, but this ignores the fact that the years when one raises children are a bad time to be poor.

Black women in America are vulnerable to even minor economic fluctuations. Let us compare 1960 and 1990. During those years, the proportion of black men with steady jobs declined from three quarters to about half, and, thanks to a sexual revolution that has affected all races and classes, men became less likely to marry a pregnant partner. Therefore, the number of black women who had children by men unlikely to be permanent partners doubled from 25 to 50 percent. I will later defend the chain of causality implied.

Debs and the war to make the world safe for democracy

Eugene Victor Debs (1855–1926) outlived Sumner by sixteen years. He also lamented America's acquired taste for fighting wars without any legitimate purpose, but the issues seemed so clear to him that he affords none of the interesting detail we find in Sumner.

He opposed the war with Spain as crude imperialism designed to open up the Orient to American goods. However, he recognized that the public was in the grip of a "war craze" born of national pride and told them they were being made accomplices in what was simply "national murder." The US urged the Filipinos under Aguinaldo to help them fight the Spanish. After victory, Aguinaldo declared independence using the American Declaration of Independence as his model. All concede that the areas under Filipino control were orderly and well governed. It is painful to read of his disbelief when American troops drove his forces away from Manila and the US decided to annex his country. He was subdued in a struggle that cost 200,000 lives. Debs remarked that his only offense was a love of freedom (Ginger, 1962, p. 219).

In March 1917, Debs called for a general strike if America entered into World War I. On April 6 war was declared, and the next day the Socialist Party declared its unalterable opposition, opining that the war would not have occurred had governments focused on redistribution of wealth within their societies rather than imperialism abroad. When rumors emerged that Debs had made his peace with the war effort, he undertook a speaking tour and was arrested on June 30, 1918 under the Espionage Act, which made it punishable to use "abusive language" about the government (Debs had referred to the Supreme Court as a kind of craps game). He was convicted before a judge who had been a law partner of the Secretary of War and a jury all of whom were wealthy and a majority of whom were retired merchants or farmers. When the defense attorney asked that Debs be judged by his deeds and works, there was applause in the court. Those who could be identified were fined and the case was adjourned for the day (see Box 2).

In 1920, while in the Federal Penitentiary at Atlanta, Debs ran for President on the Socialist Party ticket (many of its members were also in jail). He was allowed to issue one bulletin a week to

---

Box 2

The defense was playing on the fact that literally no one could dislike Debs as a person. His selflessness was legendary. People noticed that when he traveled he carried the heaviest luggage, slept in the upper berth, and never hurried a waitress. He simply could not help "loaning" money to anyone who came to him in need. When a fireman on the railway told him that lack of a good watch was blocking his promotion, Debs gave him his watch. When his union tried to vote him funds to take a trip to Europe, he refused. He would not accept a salary of over $1,000 per year (they begged him to accept three times that). After receiving a speaker's fee of $100, he had to borrow $5 to get to his next stop (he had run into the widow of a railway worker on the platform). When found not wearing an overcoat on a bitterly cold day in New York, he finally admitted that he had given his coat to a tramp at the entrance to the Brooklyn Bridge (Ginger, 1962, pp. 96–98, 287–288, 312).

The life styles of those who champion the poor today are different. America is supposed to be a republic. How many Presidents in living memory have both entered and left the Oval Office anything but a multi-millionaire? Jefferson was in debt throughout his life.

United Press and received about a million votes (if all votes were counted: in 1908, Debs received no votes in the precinct in which he had voted). His sentence was commuted to the time served on December 25, 1921 (Ginger, 1962, pp. 301, 358–395, 421–435). Family legend has it that my father drafted the petition submitted on Debs' behalf (he was sympathetic but he was also paid) and my son, like so many others, is named after him.

Today, European nations are ashamed they fought one another in 1914. Until recently, I believed that America was incapable of ever again joining a war so foolish and unnecessary. The Kaiser was, of course, not Hitler. He was a typical blustering king and neither deranged nor a mass murderer. Ever since World War II, Hitler's name has been used to derail reasoned debate about US

Box 3

Kim Jong Il may be less well known than the others. He is President of North Korea. His rule confers on his people the blessings of Juche. Kim clarifies Juche as follows:

> Moran Hill is afire with a red glow,
> The Taedong is arched with a rainbow.
> How beautiful this motherland
> In whose embrace I grew up.
>
> Azaleas smile sweetly in spring,
> Larks warble high up on the wing,
> As warm and tender as the vernal sun
> In the land that has brought me up.
>
> The sun rises on the sea buoyant,
> The land glows under the sun radiant.
> Stars twinkle with nocturnal grace
> In my father the General's embrace.

Full comprehension of Juche entails knowing that Kim and his father bathe Korea with a light and warmth so satisfying that the sun is a mere candle by comparison. His people endure almost continuous famine. It appears that Juche does a worse job than the sun when it comes to encouraging crops to grow.

---

defense policy by equating him with people like Stalin, Mao, Hussein, and Kim Jong Il. These tyrants were or are very wicked but not irrational enough to risk national suicide. Assuming that Communist China was ruled by a dead German did little to clarify US policy towards that nation (see Box 3).

Debs and race

Debs was a product of his time and it was a time in which using dialect, including Negro dialect, was thought to add to humor. But he was totally without race prejudice and was disgusted at its existence in the trade union movement. In 1885, as a member of the legislature, he bolted the Democratic Party to vote for a bill that would have abolished all distinctions of race and color in Indiana law. In 1900, when he was first nominated for President, a large crowd gathered to greet the candidate when he came home to Terre Haute. He waved and then startled the onlookers by vaulting the railing. He dashed across the platform to embrace a black porter he had not seen for years: "Why bless my heart, Bob, it's good to see you."

When Debs organized the American Railway Union, the conference limited membership to whites. Debs wrote that rejecting blacks had contributed to the union's defeat in the great strike of 1894 and added that the key proponents were "sent to the convention, no doubt, at the instigation of the corporations to defeat the unity of the working class." Sadly that was probably untrue. No railway union welcomed blacks for many years. Debs refused to speak to segregated audiences in the South, even at meetings organized by trade unions (or the YMCA). When thirty blacks were killed in a race riot at East St. Louis, Debs said that had the unions not barred blacks and forced them, despite themselves, to become scabs, this "atrocious crime . . . would never have blackened the pages of American history" (Ginger, 1962, pp. 33, 56, 225, 276–277, 363–364).

Debs opposed any special actions to help blacks, arguing that a party of the whole working class should not make special appeals to various races. He was mistaken, but blinded by ideology rather than bias. He simply believed that after the emancipation of the working man, all else would follow.

Debs and class

Even after converting to Socialism, Debs had a certain naivety. In 1897, he wrote John D. Rockefeller inviting him to fund a socialist colony that would prove the viability of a cooperative common-wealth, where there would be no "millionaires and beggars" and where "the strong will help the weak, and the weak will love the strong." Rockefeller did not reply.

Debs always kept the scraping knife he used when he first went on the railways at age 14 as a token to remind him of what it was to stagger home exhausted, hands bleeding, from work that paid a pittance. His mature view of class was that the US government was a swindle machine used to exploit the working class. He ridiculed those who thought that public regulation and public ownership was Socialism: "There can be no Socialism . . . so long as the capitalist class is in control of the national government. Government owner-ship of utilities means nothing for labor under capitalist ownership of government." It is difficult to fault Debs here: American history is full of "regulatory commissions" which became captives of the industry they were supposed to regulate.

Capitalist society consisted of a "mass of warring units, in which millions of individual workers have to fight one another for jobs, and millions of business and professional men have to fight one another for trade and for practice." Its principle is that "each is to care for himself alone, without reference to his fellow men." Corporations did not scruple to use force at home or abroad to main-tain their profitability (Ginger, 1962, pp. 26, 247, 389).

His analysis fit the time. At the turn of the century, 300 large corporations controlled over 40 percent of America's industrial capital. Business dominated the Federal government. All major appointees were drawn from the business community. A handful of corporations controlled many state legislatures (members of the Colorado legislature looked up to the balcony to see if an observer from Anaconda Copper was holding up his hand before they cast their vote). When miners were locked out at Coeur d'Alene, Colorado, they fought a pitched battle to beat off armed strikebreakers. President Harrison sent in troops. All union men were arrested and several hundred imprisoned for months inside a barbed wire bullpen where they were starved and mistreated. The Army smashed the union and prohibited the mine from hiring union members. This scene was replayed throughout the West with militia, private armies, court orders, and starvation on one side, and with miners armed with rifles and dynamite on the other (Ginger, 1964, pp. 101–103, 230, 247, 389).

Very well, but that was a century ago and surely class means little today. I will argue that anyone who today views America without class spectacles of some sort is blind to what is most important. The tension between the market and full humanity, the tension between the market and how we would prefer to treat one another, the tension between personal insecurity and civic virtue, the tension between corporate power and minimal tenets of morality, all themes Debs struck, have never lost relevance.

There is speculation as to what Debs would have thought of the USSR, that is, whether he would have seen it for what it was, a bureaucratic elite exploiting ordinary people. Within five years of the Revolution, he began to have misgivings. On July 26, 1922, he wired Lenin to protest "with all civilized people" against the execution of any of the Social Revolutionaries or the unjust denial of their liberties." (See Box 4.)

Box 4

There is a legend on the left, one that I have never been able to track down, that Lenin did not mean the Social Revolutionaries to be executed. When presiding at a boring meeting, he asked the head of what was to become the secret police for the names of all the political prisoners being held in Moscow. When the list came, he marked it with an "X", handed it back, and those on the list were promptly shot. When Lenin heard what had occurred, he said "but I put an X on things merely to show that I have read them." The modern science of management is correct: every organization needs clear lines of communication.

Kefauver and eternal vigilance

During the last sixty years, Carey Estes Kefauver (1903–63) stood as the only serious aspirant to the Presidency that a lover of liberty could support without serious reservation. He never secured the Democratic nomination for President, although he was a popular contender, beaten out by Stevenson in 1952 and 1956 and steam-rollered by the Kennedy bandwagon in 1960. Freedom is always at risk unless its friends have the courage to take a stand in a time of popular hysteria. Despite the "Patriot Act" and the hysteria about the Muslims in our midst, I do not intend to develop this theme. Therefore, it is worth lingering a bit over someone who set a proper example.

Kefauver's idealism and courage were such that his record would seem implausible if it were presented as fiction. He came from a Southern state that was a mix of moderation and reaction with scarcely a prominent liberal other than himself. Despite this, as the biography by Gorman (1971) makes clear, he risked his political career time after time.

In 1950, as Senator McCarthy began to terrorize American politicians with charges of being soft on communism, prominent liberals like Hubert Humphrey and the Kennedys ran for cover or worse. Jack Kennedy was the first to speak in the Senate about how Secretary of State Dean Acheson had "lost" China to communism and Robert Kennedy served as a volunteer attorney for the House Un-American Activities Committee (HUAC).

Perhaps the most pernicious piece of legislation was the McCarran Act (Internal Security Act). It was to be a crime to commit any act "which might contribute to totalitarian government"; and to conspire to establish a totalitarian government, even if the conspiracy was not accompanied by any act of force or violence. Its definition of Communism was based on the assumption that anyone who supported something that the Communist Party had endorsed was suspect. It prescribed deportation of "any alien . . . who prints, circulates, or has anything to do with the sale or circulation of any book which teaches totalitarian dictatorship." This to deal with a Communist Party in disarray and so heavily infiltrated by FBI agents that they sometimes dictated party policy, at least on the state level (they had orders to always vote for the most revolutionary agenda). It passed the Senate with a vote of fifty-three for and with Kefauver as one of the seven against.

In 1954, the Democratic Party panicked. In a shameful effort to save Hubert Humphrey's Senate seat, it actually bettered the Republicans by introducing legislation to make membership in the Communist Party a crime. The vote in the Senate was eighty-one for and Kefauver against. He could easily have absented himself during the roll call. Members of his staff sitting in the gallery burst into tears assuming his political career was over. Needless to say Humphrey and Jack Kennedy both voted for the bill.

In 1955, Kefauver led the fight against the "offshore islands resolution," which gave Eisenhower and John Foster Dulles a virtually blank check to deal with the threat to the islands of Quemoy and Matsu, small islands just off the coast of China but garrisoned by Chiang Kai-shek's army from its base in Formosa. Dulles was preaching his doctrine of depending on "massive retaliation" (nuclear bombing) to deter any communist expansion, however minor. Kefauver feared that Dulles was seeking a pretext for all-out war with China: "That the United States should be plunged into war over Matsu and Quemoy ought to be unthinkable. Yet there are those in high places who are plotting to bring such a war about, whatever the risk" (Gorman, 1971, p. 195). The vote on the Mutual Security Treaty that embodied America's commitment was sixty-four for and six against and the latter included Kefauver's vote. McCarthy attacked Kefauver personally as proof that the Democrats were the party of appeasement.

Kefauver and class

As usual, Kefauver was principled. He fought against the encroachments of the private power lobby on the Tennessee Valley Authority, but the TVA had done so much for Tennessee that this was a popular stand in his home state. He exposed the inflated prices of the steel and automotive industries, and the outrageous overcharges and price-fixing of the big drug companies. He was largely responsible for the Kefauver-Celler Act of 1950, which plugged a loophole in anti-trust legislation, and the Kefauver-Harris Bill of 1962, which improved the pure food and drug laws. But his concern was primarily with protection of the consumer against corporate manipulation of the market. He never went on to confront the need to tame the corporate sector collectively (Flynn, 1967, pp. 27–28).

Kefauver and race

I do not wish to diminish Kefauver in the eyes of anyone. But I want to use him to make a point: how easy it is in America to be a highly principled person, and be without racial bias, and yet not see the state of black America for what it is.

In the late 1940s, when Kefauver was a member of the House of Representatives, at the same time he was voting against loyalty oaths, he opposed anti-lynching legislation. He thought that usurping the police powers of a county in which a lynching occurred "punished" the whole county for the actions of a few and embraced "the Nazi-like theory of collective guilt." He stressed that lynching had declined since 1900 from seventy-five per year to only three per year and added that "it is best to let the humane and enlightened sentiment in the South continue its progress toward eradicating lynchings entirely." He pointed out "that lynching is murder under every state law" and feared that Federal jurisdiction would diminish the incentive of local people to take responsibility in crime prevention (Gorman, 1971, pp. 31–32, 57–58).

There is no reason to doubt that Kefauver believed every word he said, which is to say that he was in a state of denial concerning what everyone who lived in the South at that time knew. Outright lynching by masked riders was becoming rare but police (and others) could kill blacks without fear of conviction in state courts. Police amused themselves by beating up blacks arrested on weekends for drunkenness. A black who did not respond affably to being called "boy" and to the other humiliations of Southern "etiquette" was always in danger. If a black bought a new car that irritated local whites by casting their vehicles in the shade, he was in danger. These things were true even when I was in the South in the late 1950s. Everybody knew it. Kefauver knew it but with only half of his mind.

Kefauver's sincerity is attested by the fact that as civil rights legislation came before Congress with increasing frequency, he often broke ranks with other Southern Congressmen. In 1956, he was the only Southern Senator who refused on principle to sign the "Southern Manifesto," which announced that the signers would use every legal means of blocking the racial integration of schools as foreshadowed in the Supreme Court decision of 1954 (Lyndon Johnson did not sign on the grounds that, as party leader in the Senate, he should not take sides). Both before and after, he championed the right of blacks to vote.

But sadly, he never quite lost his ability to filter out what he did not want to see. In 1959, blacks in Haywood and Fayette counties attempted to register to vote. Most were tenant farmers and they were evicted from their homes to spend the winter in tents. Despite the fact that they lived in his own state of Tennessee, Kefauver did not lament their plight. He was upset that it had been reported inaccurately that blacks were not allowed to dance or drink beer (Gorman, 1971, pp. 236, 314–331).

Once again, Kefauver pleaded for local solutions to these problems. The sympathy of local officials to black attempts to register to vote can be judged by their behavior. In 1963, the State Police reacted to the demonstrations at Birmingham, Alabama by: beatings, prodding with bayonets, and firing into homes; letting dogs loose on the crowd (the youngest bitten was a three-year-old); girls arrested were given eleven to eighteen vaginal examinations using the same glove in an effort to spread venereal disease; when girls fainted they were doused with ice water, when they asked for aspirin they were given laxatives and put into cells without toilets; the black Baptist church was bombed, killing four young girls. The day's prayer was: Dear God, we are sorry for the times we were unkind (Flynn, 1967, pp. 138–143).

Jefferson and growing up

The last of Jefferson, Sumner, Debs, and Kefauver died many years ago. We live in such a different time. Was not Sumner merely preaching isolationism at a time when the Atlantic and the Pacific really were barriers behind which Americans could shelter in safety? Debs spoke about class at a time when capitalism really did use violence to subdue workers and keep them in misery. Blacks are no longer lynched and denied the vote (unless they are convicted felons). Surely, we can today look at black America without soothing myths, see it for what it is, and see something hopeful and improving. So what do all of these people have to do with us?

In addition, we know so much more than they did. If, despite all that has been done, race is still a problem, it may well be due to black genetic inferiority and therefore intractable. *The Bell Curve* tells us that the fact that IQ is heritable plus a proper understanding of social dynamics doom any hope of blunting the edges of class. As for foreign policy, why should America be different from any other great power defending its global interests? We know that God is dead and nature has no purposes. Is it really unfortunate that we are too sophisticated to take our own distinctive ideals too seriously? What the world needs is tolerance of everyone's ideals without reference to whether they are mine or thine.

One of the truly great American novels, our own equivalent to *Don Quixote*, is about a man whose hopes required that he be oblivious to what time and change render possible. Jay Gatsby demands that Daisy deny the reality of her past and her years of marriage to another man and come to him like a young girl in love

35

for the first time. As Fitzgerald (1925) says on the last page of his book:

> When he first picked out the green light at the end of
> Daisy's dock . . . his dream must have seemed so close that
> he could hardly fail to grasp it. He did not know that it was
> already behind him, somewhere back in the vast obscurity
> beyond the city, where the dark fields of the republic rolled
> on under the night.

Gatsby is a child living out a fairy tale about a knight-errant pursuing a quest to win his maid. He is also the only one of Fitzgerald's characters who still believes in anything. Scripture tells us to grow up and put away childish things. Today, many intellectuals believe that the quest for Jefferson's America is simply too quixotic for a mature mind. They had better be sure that they are correct. It is far, far harder to fan cold ashes into flame than to start a fire from scratch. If we lose faith in our ideals, it may be impossible to rekindle the fervor that has kept them alive for over two centuries. Something beautiful may vanish never to come again.

PART II

Blacks and the pursuit of happiness

2 The lost boys

The sole evidence that it is possible to produce that anything is
desirable is that people do actually desire it.
(John Stuart Mill, *Utilitarianism*)

There's a great text in Galatians
Once you trip on it entails
Twenty-nine distinct damnations
One sure if another fails.
(Rudyard Kipling, *Stalky & Co.*)

We must distinguish between endorsing the market and using the
concept of a market as a powerful tool of analysis, one that lays bare
the likely behavior of human beings subject to market constraints. I
think that market behavior explains why black women either find or
do not find a suitable partner with whom to raise children. The fact
that there is a shortage of suitable partners in that market leads us
to a description of the life histories of black men. How black men and
women interact sexually is the best starting point to comprehend
the state of black America. This is to say that black families are the
central problem of black America and the state of black families is
this: 63 percent of black children are being raised in solo-parent
homes and those homes are often poverty homes.

The data herein are recent in the sense of being based on
surveys conducted between 2003 and 2005. Unlike most of the literature, they take into account all black men: not only those who are
resident in households but also those in the military population (not
too important) and the prison population (very important). But the

major weakness of the literature is that it is dismissive of causes that are potent.

For example, it is now received opinion among social scientists that we cannot explain the fact that so many black women are raising children alone simply by citing the shortage of black males who would make suitable husbands. That is quite true: a complex problem of this sort is rarely due to a single cause. But it is quite another thing to dismiss the man shortage as trivial. Blacks themselves are more in touch with reality. Roland Martin (2007), the distinguished black journalist, reports a death-bed scene in which a friend begs him to tell people what is happening in black America, so that his daughter might have a chance to marry a respectable black man one day. Martin adds that his friend would welcome a white son-in-law but knows how slight the chances of that are. And he does not endorse a single cause. He adds that black women should be told not to lie down with any fool.

Martin has described the job I will try to do, albeit with sympathy for those black women who render themselves unpromising wives by having children out of wedlock as teenagers. Which comes first, the chicken or the egg? There is not much point in remaining a suitable wife if you have very little chance of finding a suitable man.

Any analysis is broken-backed if it does not probe into the minds of both black men and women. Therefore, I will not use the usual technique of multiple regression analysis (see Box 5). Rather my method will be: to state a series of predictions based on comparative data; to show that these predictions work; and in the process, to illuminate the psychology of women and men of various races.

Psychological propositions and the marriage market

It seems best to make my key psychological propositions explicit from the start. As foreshadowed, they have to do with how people react to marriage markets:

Box 5 Multiple regression analysis

This is a mathematical technique that allows you to add in the impact of a series of causal factors one by one, so that each counts only as much as what remains after the previous factors have weighed in. For example, if you have counted the effects of poverty, you cannot give full weight to the effect of poor nutrition on its own because poverty has already anticipated most of its effects. Multiple regression analysis allows you to consider all of the factors together and to fairly estimate how much their total impact would explain whatever you are trying to explain, say the extra health problems of families of low socioeconomic status.

Like all mathematical techniques, it has the limitation of not revealing the human condition that lies behind the numbers. I prefer a market analysis because it makes continual reference to people's motives. The predictive validity of the factors it reveals will be tested by simple arithmetic.

---

1 Marriage markets are like a service industry in which women provide a demand for children and men are the suppliers. A secondary demand is for a long-term and productive partner with whom to raise children, a demand that affects both sexes.

2 Women's demand for children is primary in that it will override the desire for a permanent partner when no one who promises to play that role is available.

3 The number of promising male spouses sets limits on the percentage of long-term partnerships. Long-term partnerships should be our focus because they set limits on how many children are likely to be living in one-parent or two-parent homes. It is best measured by a snapshot of how many women are raising children with or without a partner at a given time. Marriage and divorce rates are not central. A woman may be married to an unpromising spouse who is

absent because in prison, or unfaithful, or itinerant, and therefore she functions as a solo-mother.

The first two assumptions can be combined into one proposition: over 80 percent of women of any race will have children even if they must raise them as solo-mothers (true at least up to the present). If this is so, the number of black males who qualify as permanent and productive (worth having around) partners will do much to dictate the percentage of black solo-mothers. The latter will tend to be the mirror image of the former (only fifty-seven promising males for every hundred females will create a tendency toward 43 percent solo-mothers).

Once again, it is not quite this simple: women can make themselves unattractive as wives by becoming solo-mothers before the usual age of marriage and more black women do this. If there is a race difference in psychology, it is here. But one must not equate a difference *between the races* with a difference *due to race*. White women are less inclined to become unmarried teenage mothers than black women; but how would white women react if they faced a marriage market as unfavorable as that available to black women? To put this in familiar language, erosion of positive prospects for marriage may create a "tipping point." At a certain point, you get a radical swing toward negativity in women's attitudes about marriage. This may be race neutral: a really bad market might affect the women of all races much the same.

Honesty requires that a sensitive question be addressed: why are so few black women (with children) living with partners of another race? That fact is so important it cannot be omitted. And there are two possibilities: either it tells us something peculiar about the psychology of black women; or it tells us something perfectly ordinary about the psychology of white men.

Evidence that women do desire children

The proposition that most women will have children even if they cannot find a viable spouse is at the core of my analysis. It refers to collective behavior in response to a marriage market and not to individual behavior. No one knows the number of individual women who passionately want a baby but refrain from having one because they never find a promising partner. What we do know is the general response of women to markets in which there is a dearth of promising male spouses. For women near the end of their child-bearing years (ages 40 to 44), the facts are these: 81.5 percent of non-Hispanic whites have had a child; 80.8 percent of non-Hispanic blacks have had a child; 86.9 of Hispanics have had a child (Downs, 2003).

That the values for white and black hardly differ tells us much. About 59 percent of black women are raising a child on their own as compared to 22 percent of white women (US Census, 2004). Black women are aware of this but it has not killed their desire for babies. About 30 percent of Hispanic women are raising a child on their own, well above whites, and yet fewer of them are childless than white women. It appears that 90 percent of women want children irrespective of the market, given that some who want them cannot have them or put off having a child until too late.

Can we assume that women who belong to our three racial groups are roughly equal in terms of the priority they give to having children, despite an unfavorable supply of promising spouses? All we can say is that the tolerance of white and Hispanic women for solo-motherhood keeps rising to the level that black women tolerated a few decades ago. We cannot know whether one group will hit a ceiling before another. However, history provides us with the tragic equivalent of an experiment that shows that the demand of women for children persists even under the worst of market conditions. At the end of World War II, there were only seventy Russian men of marriageable age left alive for every hundred women. The first reliable census data collected thirteen years later showed Russian women having children at the pre-war levels and 30 percent of them raising a family alone (Brainerd, 2006).

Nonetheless, can we ignore the atypical women who opt out of the market simply because they do not want children? Each one that does this increases the supply of promising male spouses per hundred women remaining.

But this assumes that no males opt out as suppliers. As long as an equivalent number of men are unwilling to father children and they are randomly distributed among men in general, the marriage market would be unaffected. In fact, voluntary withdrawal from reproduction undoubtedly renders the marriage market grimmer than stated herein. More men than women opt out among both whites and blacks. South (1993) found that fewer young men than women want to marry someday (read have children someday). When Houston (1981) surveyed students at an elite university, he got the same results. Worse, when it comes to following through on the intent not to have children, promising males who are brighter and more self-disciplined will be far more effective. They are the ones more likely to use contraceptives consistently.

The marriage market of black women

Box 6 sets out the plight of non-Hispanic black women in contemporary America. For every hundred black women in the peak ages of marriage (25 to 40), there are only fifty-seven men who promise to be permanent and supportive partners. The criterion for this status is that a male is black and worked more than twenty-six weeks in the previous year or was in the armed forces; those few non-blacks who have a black wife are also assumed to qualify. Those who do not qualify are black males in prison, those who worked twenty-six weeks or less, and those who have a non-black wife.

The rationale for focusing on black males is, of course, that non-black males in America do not marry or at least do not stay married to black women. Only 2.19 percent of black women today are living with a non-black husband. Indeed, black women are net losers from what interracial marriage exists: five black men leave the pool of potential spouses to partner non-black women, while only two black women find a long-term spouse outside their race. Recall that

Box 6 Marriage prospects of women (ages 25–40)

For every 100 non-Hispanic white women, there are

86 promising spouses (shortfall = 14)
80 in adequate civilian employment
2 in military
4 men who have married in from another race

20.5 unpromising spouses
15.6 not in adequate civilian employment
1.5 in prison or jail
3.4 white men married someone of another race.

For every 100 non-Hispanic black women, there are

57 promising spouses (shortfall = 43)
53 in adequate civilian employment
2 in military
2 men who have married in from another race

39 unpromising spouses
24 not in adequate civilian employment
10 in prison or jail
5 black men married someone of another race.

For every 100 Hispanic women, there are

99 promising spouses (really 96) (shortfall = 4)
89 in adequate civilian employment
1 in military
9 have married in from another race

30 unpromising spouses
18 not in adequate civilian employment
3 in prison or jails
9 Hispanic men married someone of another race.

Adequate work means worked more than twenty-six weeks in the previous year. Notice that promising + unpromising spouses do not add up to 100. White males and females are about equal in number but the total of males is inflated by counting men from other races who marry white women. Despite inflation, there are far fewer black males than females because many are dead or missing. The Hispanic surplus of males is huge because there are so many male immigrants. I have adjusted the number of promising Hispanic males downward to allow for immigrants who have wives abroad. All will become clear as we proceed. For exact data, see Table 1 in the Appendix.

there is no presumption that black males who are in prison or in intermittent work never marry. I am attempting to estimate the size of the pool of *promising* marriage partners, that is, estimate the extent to which black women can get a reasonable *deal* from their marriage market. A partner who (even if willing to marry) is in and out of jail, rarely employed, or itinerant is a bad bargain. Black women are better at attaining credentials than men and see a dysfunctional husband as little more than an extra child to care for (Jones, 2006).

I am assuming that the *quality* of the marriage market women face is the social reality that does most to dictate whether women will raise their child with a male or do so alone. Box 6 makes it immediately apparent that women from America's other large racial/ethnic populations negotiate on far better terms. There are eighty-six promising males for every hundred non-Hispanic white women (aged 25–40) and ninety-six promising males for every hundred Hispanic women. Moreover, a larger number of white than black women have a genuine option of marrying someone of another race.

The Hispanic population has several unique features. Combining the appropriate categories shows that for every hundred Hispanic women, there are 120 Hispanic men, of whom ninety-nine are promising spouses. However, there are 227,000 male Hispanics (aged 25 to 40) who both are foreign born and have a spouse absent (usually living abroad), while there are only 64,000 females. Box 6 adjusts for this by deducting the males from the pool of promising spouses and deducting the females from the population seeking a reliable spouse. This reduces the number of men to 117, of whom ninety-six are promising spouses. Nonetheless, Hispanic women benefit greatly from a large immigrant population dominated by males willing to work, even under unfavorable conditions, because those conditions are superior to what they knew in Mexico.

As for blacks, my survey shows that about ninety-four black men exist for every hundred women aged 25 to 40. Actually, I did better than most in locating black men. The closest thing you get to a full count from the census is the "standard population," which covers everyone in America plus its territories but misses US military overseas. When that group is added to the standard population (aged 25 to 40), the number of black males for every hundred females rises from ninety-one to ninety-two. So where are the missing men? Something both baffling and tragic is bubbling just beneath the surface of America's consciousness.

The lost boys

Box 7 uses birth and death certificates to estimate the ratios of males to females that actually exist at various ages. These are compared to the ratios that the census found in its standard population (which I have adjusted by adding in the overseas military). Two black males (about 2 percent) are missing from the census at age 15. This rises to six at age 25, reaches almost ten by age 45, and then rises to twelve or more thereafter. For whites, census counts match the predicted gender ratios until age 25 when a very few (less than 1 percent) males disappear. The missing men reappear at age 55. Missing males is almost entirely a black phenomenon.

Very few of the missing black males are dead (it is not easy to die without the event being recorded on a death certificate). The

Box 7

Male/female gender ratios: those estimated by using birth and death certificates compared to those found in the census. For exact values, see Table 2 in Appendix.

Age	Black			White		
	Estimated	Census	E–C	Estimated	Census	E–C
0	104	104	—	105	105	—
1	104	104	—	105	105	—
5	104	104	—	105	105	—
15	104	102	2	105	105	—
25	102	96	6	103	103	—
35	99	90	9	102	101	1
45	98	88	10	101	100	1
55	95	83	12	97	97	—
65	92	76	16	90	90	—

press tends not to distinguish between missing males and dead males and thus exaggerates the effects of violence on the survival of young blacks. But even accurate data show an alarming picture: at 35, there are 6 percent more black males than white males who are dead: and at 45, the extra death toll is 9 percent (see Table 3 in the Appendix). Even black women who find a promising spouse are far more likely to see their partner die, and therefore become solo-mothers while their children are still young. How to put this into perspective? I will treat the white death rate as normal and the extra black death rate as the "casualty rate" incurred by males growing up black in America.

Box 8 compares the peculiar death rate of black males with the battle-related deaths of various branches of the US armed forces during World War II. It is higher than that of any branch, including the most-at-risk infantry. Data from the Western Front (Europe) allow us to distinguish the fate of troops that had the optimum number of tanks in support (281) from those with only the usual number (66). To find a group that exceeds the black death rate, we

Box 8

Black males: extra risk of death (by age 45) compared to deaths from combat in World War II. The "combat zone" to which black males embarked was simply that of being born to grow up black in America. For more data, see Table 4 in Appendix.

Unit	Embarked to a combat zone		
	Number	Deaths	Percentage
Black males	315,241	28,403	9.01
Infantry	1,779,658	142,962	8.03
Air Corps	952,974	51,021	5.35
Field Artillery	437,066	9,585	2.19

The Western Front: Members of units who fought from the time their unit was committed to battle until the war's end (or were killed or invalided)

Troops with 66 tanks	14,400	1,665	11.56
Black males (no tanks)	—	—	9.01
Troops with 281 tanks	11,500	733	6.37

must select out troops that had the lesser number of tanks and were original members of their unit, that is, fought from the time their unit was committed to combat until the end. They suffered between 11 and 12 percent battle-related deaths compared to the black rate of 9 percent. Among the 110,000 marines committed to the Battle of Iwo Jima, battle-related deaths were 5 percent (Iwo Jima, Inc., 2006; US Navy, 1950).

But where are the black males who are not dead but show up missing in the census? No doubt, a few of them sleep on the street or in shelters or are so itinerant that they have no fixed address. But no one knows where most of them are (Wachter and Freedman, 1999). A hypothesis: they are largely men in and out of prison who do not want their existence reported to the US government. If you take the percentage of blacks who will be in prison at some time in their lives and deduct the percentage actually in prison at any given time, this leaves 23 percent of males as "prisoners at large." Assume that 1 percent of black males have no fixed abode. If about a third of black males who are prisoners at large evade detection, you get the right percentage of those unaccounted for (for example, you get 7.57 percent for age 35).

Even if this hypothesis is correct, there is one unsolved mystery. The missing white males reappear at 55. Like Peter Pan's lost boys, America's missing black men go to never-never land and never come back, except as names on death certificates. If I am correct, some of them surface from time to time when they take their turn in prison. I will put them in the category of unpromising spouses.

We can now describe the overall state of black males in America. Take the total cohort born in 1957 whose survivors would be aged 45 in 2002: 19 percent are dead, 8 percent are missing, and 5 percent are currently in prison, for a total of 32 percent. For the same cohort of white males, the total is about 11.5 percent. Which is to say that, when growing up in America, black males pay the price of an extra 20.5 percent of their number either dead or marginalized in a way that does not even approach normal participation in US society (see Table 5 in Appendix).

Candidates for causes

The fact that 43 percent of black women are unlikely to find a promising spouse contributes to the percentage of black women who are solo-mothers. The shortfall of black men who are neither in jail nor without steady work does not, of course, literally dictate the rate of solo-motherhood. If 43 percent of black women were rational actors willing to forgo having children, if blacks practiced polygamy, if all black males became law-abiding upon impregnating a woman, if black women married out freely, the shortfall would be drained of potency. As things are, it plays some role.

Thus far, we have analyzed the marriage market only from the point of view of women seeking a reasonable deal. Focusing on those men not in prison and in steady work, they too would have an image of what they would regard as a reasonable deal, particularly given the large number of women who would find them promising spouses. Almost 90 percent of women who have a child before the age of 20 have it outside wedlock (Downs, 2003). I will assume that they would be unpromising spouses from a male point of view, that is, someone who comes to them encumbered with extra and costly responsibilities. As of 2003, the percentage of white women estimated to give birth before age 20 stands at 11, the percentage of blacks at 26, and the percentage of Hispanics at 34 (Hewlett, 2006).

So here we have a difference between the races. Fewer black women than white women modify their behavior so as to make marriage a likely outcome. I have argued that this difference may have to do with black women's perception of their marriage market prospects. If you are a black girl who has dropped out of school and has eyes to see, you may feel you have very little chance of a promising spouse in any event. There is not much to be lost by taking yourself out of a market in which you have little hope of a good deal.

Promising black men can profitably exploit the fact that they are scarce commodities. They can ignore teenage mothers (except for sex) and still find plenty of black women who have "waited for marriage" from which to choose. There will, of course, never be a perfect match between the promising husbands and the promising wives. Some men who never go to prison and become good earners father illegitimate children by teenage girls and become marriage-shy. Others, given how much the market is in their favor, will feel that they can get steady sex without ever having to offer marriage in exchange.

Let us assume that the fifty-seven black males in steady work are good deals from a woman's point of view; and that the seventy-four black females who do not have a child before the age of 20 are good deals from a man's point of view; and that they encounter one another randomly. These assumptions are, of course, simply an admission that I cannot capture the multiple and

---

Box 9

Our assumptions allow us to multiply the percentage of women's good deals times the percentage of men's good deals (as a decimal) to get the number of good partnerships likely to result. Take that from 100 and you have the percentage of black women likely to be solo-mothers – because they want children and have them despite not finding a good partner. Then you see how well that predicts the actual number of solo-parents.

Therefore, for every race, let us do the arithmetic (PH = promising husbands; PW = promising wives; GP = good partnerships; PS = predicted solo-parents). For detail, see Table 6 in Appendix.

Whites: 86 (PH) × .89 (PW) = 76.5 (GP) = **23.5** (PS). Actual percentage is **22**.

Blacks: 57 (PH) × .74 (PW) = 42.2 (GP) = **58** (PS). Actual percentage is **59**.

Hispanics: 96 (PH) × .66 (PW) = 63.4 (GP) = **37** (PS). Actual percentage is **30**.

---

complex interactions that produce stable black couples with children. I appeal to the time-honored methodology of let's try it and see what happens.

Look at Box 9. We see that our assumptions yield accurate predictions across America's three major racial groups. The combination of promising wives and promising husbands predicts 76.5 good partnerships for whites, which in turn predicts 23.5 solo-mothers, and the actual figure is twenty-two. The prediction for blacks is forty-two good partnerships, which predicts fifty-eight solo-mothers, and the actual figure is fifty-nine. Lest Pythagorean ecstasy reach too high a pitch, the prediction for Hispanics is not so close to perfection. Good partnerships at sixty-three should give thirty-seven solo-mothers and the actual figure is thirty. The Catholicism of most Hispanic males may mean that males are more inclined to marry someone they have impregnated.

More cynically, they are in the worst position to bargain for sex without marriage. I revert to the accusation thrown in the face of black women: that they create their own problem of solo-motherhood by irresponsible early child-bearing. Black women are certainly less "remiss" than Hispanic women. Far more Hispanic women do this very thing, and yet far fewer reap solo-motherhood as a consequence. With so many men available, Hispanic women simply enjoy a much better market.

The percentage of a group's children raised in solo-parent homes is always larger than the percentage of solo-mothers: solo-mothers tend to be poor and the poor have larger families. Circa 2003, although only 59 percent of black households were headed by a solo-parent, 63 percent of black children were living in solo-parent households: the corresponding figures for whites were 22 and 23 percent.

Are black women too choosey?

Data from the NLYS (National Longitudinal Youth Survey) provided by Charles Murray show that there is only a five-point IQ gap between black women raising children with a partner and those who are solo-mothers. If most high-IQ black women secured a partner, we would expect the gap to be greater. Perhaps a lot of high-IQ black women are passing up promising males, that is, perhaps the higher the IQ of black women, the more they raise the bar for what they perceive as a promising spouse. However, that is the wrong way to think. It is black men who have the whip hand in the black marriage market. There are so many surplus women that a black man not in prison and in steady work may not find marriage attractive compared to remaining single and exploiting his advantage. And if promising black men decide to accept the burden of supporting a family, it is they who can afford to be choosey. If high intelligence is not their dominant concern in selecting a spouse, it is they who will dictate a small IQ gap between partnered black women and solo-mothers.

Herrnstein and Murray (1994) rightly emphasize that solo-parent homes have contributed to poverty in America. Unlike most, they have taken the trouble to disentangle the real contribution of solo-parent homes from the confounding variable of lower IQ. They control for IQ by comparing matched samples of white and black women (aged 29) each with a mean IQ of 100. The prospects for white women were that 10 percent would bear a child out of wedlock, 12 percent would at some time be on welfare, and 6 percent would raise a child for the first three years while living in poverty. The prospects for black women were 51 percent, 30 percent, and 14 percent respectively.

Here we see the plight of black women laid bare. Those with an IQ above 100 are in the top 15 percent of blacks. That does not prevent the black marriage market from rendering their pursuit of happiness difficult. This assumes, of course, that you accept that their attitudes and behavior are primarily a response to the state of the market.

Ultimate causes

An important feature of the various marriage markets is the number of promising male spouses for every hundred women of marriageable age. If there are only fifty-seven such, that leaves a shortfall of forty-three and a lot of women who will go begging. However, we can dig deeper to try to lay bare what determines the shortfall of promising males.

Box 10 suggests that this crucial difference between whites and blacks can be predicted. Two factors are sufficient: the net effect of racial intermarriage; and the percentage of males who will become prison (or jail) inmates at some time in their lives. When the combination of these two is taken into account, the remaining shortfall of promising male spouses is 8.7 for every hundred white women and 7.1 for black. The remainders are roughly equal and not very large. Once again, Hispanics are different. With 117 males for every

---

Box 10

If more men marry out of their race than other men marry in, there is a net loss in the pool of available partners. So a net loss from intermarriage is made a minus, a net gain a plus. I do not hesitate to count someone who at some time serves a prison term as unpromising, so they flatly count as a minus. We know the shortfall of promising males for each hundred women (from Box 6), so all we have to do is adjust for the two factors and see what is left as unexplained. For sources, see Table 7 in Appendix.

White: 14 (shortfall) + 0.7 (intermarriage) − 6 (prison) = 8.7 shortfall remaining

Black: 43 (shortfall) − 2.9 (intermarriage) − 33 (prison) = 7.1 shortfall remaining

Hispanic: 4 (shortfall) + 0.3 (intermarriage) − 17 (prison) = −12.7 (see text)

---

hundred females of marriageable age, the loss of seventeen potential spouses to prison hardly registers.

Most of the 33 percent of black males who will be incarcerated at some time in their life history will be convicted felons. Aside from the fact that convicted felons are not eligible for such things as family assistance, a prison record does not enhance the content of a vita. It is probably not accidental that life-time incarceration rates are an almost perfect predictor of the percentage of men lacking steady work; at least this is true for blacks and Hispanics. Black males show an incarceration rate of 33 percent, and 37 percent of them are not in steady work (see Table 8 in Appendix). Hispanics show 17 and 19 percent. With an incarceration rate of 6 percent, white males show a considerably higher figure as not in steady work, namely, 17 percent. Perhaps one in six out of work is the best that can be expected now that so many jobs do not guarantee permanence.

As for marrying out of one's race, this harms black women because the number of other-race women who "rob" them of black husbands is greater than the number of them who get a non-black husband. The net loss is almost three promising husbands for every hundred black women. This of course begs the question as to whether the black men marrying out really are promising spouses. They might be just a random selection of black men no more likely to be in steady work than black men in general. Many black women make bitter comments about women of other races who cream off good black men but this may be dismissed as anecdotal.

The data show that the black women are correct (see Table 8 in Appendix). Among black men who marry out (just over half of them are married to white women), 83 percent are in steady work. This percentage is an almost perfect match for the black men who marry black women. It is far above black men in general, of whom only 63 percent are in steady work.

Why more black men do not marry

Black men are often chastised for the large number of black women they impregnate and leave unmarried. Let us break this down into two questions. Why do the percentages of those who are married differ between the races? Why do those not in a position to marry father children?

It looks as if fewer black men marry because they have lower incomes than white men. The ratio between black/white male median incomes is very close to the ratio of the black/white male percentages that marry. Taking ages 25 to 40 years, the income ratio is .68/1 and the marriage ratio is .62/1 (see Table 9 in Appendix). However, remember that who marries is not central, that is, the important thing is who stays together so that two people raise children. Our key data refer not to how many black males have tried to make a go of a household but to how many males are actually married and functioning in a household at present.

Money problems are perhaps the greatest stress on a couple and the net worth of black households is pathetic. In 2002, the median net worth of black families was $6,000, and for those who owned their homes two-thirds of their money was tied up in their house. Clearly almost nothing was surplus to meet emergencies. White net worth at $89,000 was fifteen times as great. It is easy to misconstrue the true state of the capital resources of black America by focusing on the minority that is securely anchored in the middle class. Black America's wealth is even more highly concentrated in the hands of a few than the wealth of white America. The top 25 percent of black households have 93 percent of the group's total wealth, while the top 25 percent of white households control only 79 percent (see Table 9 in Appendix).

Other factors that would impede black men from committing to marriage (or being wanted as a marriage partner) would be drug addiction, HIV or AIDS, and criminal associations (after all, one-third of them are headed for prison). It may be said that black men should not be as they are, but, taking them as they are, many of them will not see marriage as an option.

But if they are not in a position to marry, do they have to impregnate black women? When we judge individuals, the situation is clear: every man, black or white, is blameworthy if he fathers a child and does not offer whatever financial and nurturing contribution he can. However, when asking why blameworthy decisions are more prevalent in one large group than another, we must, as social scientists, look for possible explanations. After World War II, if most Russian women wanted to have children, and if they were not to be impregnated by married men, they had to be impregnated by single men. The state was so anxious for this to happen that they exonerated men from the usual responsibilities attached to paternity and gave generous family allowances (Brainerd, 2006).

In the current generation, about 43 percent of black women who want babies are unlikely to get them from a permanent spouse. If unmarried black men do not satisfy this demand, married black men will have to do so. The consequences for the stability of the black marriages that do exist may be negative. What would white

57

American sexual behavior be like under similar circumstances? I doubt that any human group that has survived thousands of years of evolution is programmed to allow some 40 percent of its women to go childless. Every man unable or unwilling to help should feel guilt about fathering children. However, I suspect that collective behavior would differ little from group to group.

Causes and barometers

Have we really found the cause of anything? If taken for judgment before Pontius Pilate and asked not "what is truth" but rather "what is a cause," I would be circumspect. At least, our comparative analysis of white, black, and Hispanic marriage markets has revealed an interesting series of barometers:

1 The life-time incarceration rate of males predicts the percentage of males who lack steady work (except for whites and this is probably because some minimum level of unemployment is inevitable).
2 The males in steady work plus the net effect of racial intermarriage predict the shortfall of promising spouses for every hundred women (except for Hispanics thanks to thousands of male immigrants).
3 That shortfall, taken in conjunction with the percentage of females who become mothers before the age of 20, predicts the percentage of solo-parent homes and of children living in those homes.
4 That shortfall also predicts bad things about the life histories of black mothers and their children even when they are matched with white women for IQ.

The few cases in which the predictions do not work relate mainly to Hispanics and market analysis shows that these are exceptions that prove the rule.

Starvation and other remedies

Possible remedies for the effects of the black marriage market include the following: leaving women who have children out of wedlock without income; leaving men out of work without income; affirmative action programs; more aid to solo-parents; and alternatives to the war on drugs.

In *The Bell Curve*, Herrnstein and Murray (1994, pp. 544–549) advocate two steps: that unmarried mothers have no legal basis to demand that the father provide child support; and an end to government programs for all women who have babies, whether married or not. Are these steps really likely to diminish the number of solo-parent homes? Almost certainly, they would be counterproductive. Black men would have even more reason to remain single than at present: not only would they enjoy a favorable market for getting sex without marriage but they would be free of the sort of legal responsibilities single men face if paternity can be established. Would the prospect of dire poverty prevent black women from having children out of wedlock? Not when almost half of them are faced with the prospect of doing so or going childless. Historically, poverty has never prevented the poor from breeding – quite the contrary.

The contrast between the employment rates of Hispanic and black males has attracted attention and engendered a kindred solution. Unlike blacks, many Hispanics are illegal immigrants and not eligible for welfare and therefore "uncorrupted" by the welfare state. The implication is that if there were no unemployment benefits and black males had to work or face penury most of them would find work. I suspect this would have a marginal effect, though outweighed by hardship for those who genuinely need assistance between jobs to hold their families together. But let us ignore that last. This comparison between the economic progress of Hispanics and blacks omits two important considerations.

First, at present, black males are much more involved in the huge illegal drug economy. Unless that tie can be broken, greater penury might merely mean a greater influx into that economy and a higher incarceration rate. Second, the Hispanic marriage market is favorable to women and the black marriage market is favorable to men. As a consequence, the advantage Hispanics enjoy in terms of two-parent homes, family stability, favorable adult to child ratios in the home, male role models, and educational efficiency is immense. These assets accrue from something black America cannot hope to emulate: Mexico as a source of surplus males selected out for resolve by the risks of a dangerous border crossing in addition to the usual positive selection that emigration entails. If the West Indies was as populous as Mexico, and shared a common border with the US, and boosted the total number of men of marriageable age (per hundred women) to something like 117, black America would be transformed.

Government can play a positive role. It should certainly provide information about contraception and make it more readily available to young people. As to affirmative action as a means of aiding blacks, I have no principled objection; quite the contrary, as chapter 4 will make clear. The status quo of affirmative action programs should be defended (for the most part). But those programs are unlikely to be expanded, partly if only because they are difficult to sell politically. The way forward is color-blind support for solo-parent homes in poor areas. This will benefit blacks most because they have the most such homes.

American society will benefit greatly if the environment of solo-parent homes, including the cognitive environment, is enhanced and solo-parents are less isolated and demoralized. At a minimum, I would establish attractive drop-in centers as a special service for solo-parents in disadvantaged areas, centers where parents stay with their children rather than leave them. These would be designed to both increase the range of adults to which the child is exposed and consolidate the services these people need in one place. The play area would be filled with toys and children's books and sub-professionals to interact with parents and children. The annex would have a library, tapes, and professionals to advise on family planning (and to dispense contraceptives) and budgeting and health and problems in general.

I call this a minimal step because it leaves unaddressed how the neighborhoods in which these centers are located can be upgraded in terms of housing, employment, schooling, and so forth. Since this is a class problem affecting all disadvantaged Americans, it will be addressed in Part III.

As for the participation of black men in the illegal drugs industry, which affects their viability as spouses so profoundly, I have had my say on this elsewhere (Flynn, 1991). Take the profit out of selling drugs by providing cheap and legal sources of supply. Except for significant support from the police, not much enthusiasm has been engendered, although it is dawning that the "war on drugs" has been a major factor in escalating black incarceration rates.

Women Irish, black, and Native American

At the start, we remarked on one factor that renders their marriage market so disastrous for black women. They are unique in American history: women of every other group have escaped from unfavorable marriage markets simply by marrying out. For example, at the turn of the century, when alcoholism, unemployment, and household violence were prevalent among Irish men, Irish women married out in huge numbers (Flynn, 1991, pp. 130, 135). The grim joke that an Irish beauty was a woman with two black eyes became a thing of the past. Irish men had competition and had to get their act together. So long as only 2.19 percent of black woman find a non-black and permanent spouse, they are trapped. So long as more black males than women marry out, more interracial marriage just exacerbates their plight, unless the availability of non-black males reaches the point where the supply of black males becomes irrelevant.

Richard Lynn (2002) concludes that more black women than white women have psychopathic personalities. This engenders the

61

hypothesis (not one formulated by Lynn) that many black women would strike white men as unpromising. In fact, Lynn's data falsify this hypothesis in one stroke. He compares American ethnic groups on criteria designed to measure eleven psychopathic traits. Native Americans (American Indians) score no better on these measures than blacks. Indeed, on the Minnesota Multiphasic Personality Inventory (MMPI), Native Americans average far worse than blacks (and all other groups). Yet, white men marry their women far more often than those of any other minority group. Native American women marry out at the extraordinary level of 50 percent (Farley, 1995).

Setting psychopathology aside, group and gender differences in attitudes toward sex and marriage are illuminating. Houston (1981) asked 1,131 students at Brown University about how often they thought about marriage and whether they thought love and sexual intercourse should be related. These data are now more than twenty-five years out-of-date and the blacks in particular would have been a small elite, which would probably level differences between the races. South (1993) reports responses from 926 subjects aged 19 to 25 from a large and representative sample interviewed in 1987–88. They were asked whether they would like to marry someday. This sample (unlike Houston's) included Hispanics. South's data are twenty years out-of-date, but the relative marriage markets have not much altered over that time. Since the question was addressed only to those not married or cohabiting, I have recalculated the percentages to include those already married as positive responses (see Table 10 in Appendix).

Let us see what a market analysis suggests. Almost 18 percent of black females have a negative attitude toward marriage (do not say they would like to marry some day) as compared to 11 percent of white women. This is simply realistic: their chances of finding a promising partner for marriage are far worse than those of white women. If any character disorder is involved, it is rampant romanticism: far more of them should be pessimistic. However, note that they are only expressing an attraction toward marriage. It may be that many are aware that they are expressing a vain hope.

We have seen that the marriage market deteriorates for males (and improves for females) as we go from black to white to Hispanic. There is a huge contrast between black and white males as to whether sex and love should be separate. Black males enjoy a far better market for sex without commitment than white males do. Despite the fact that most black women (like white women) think that sex and love should be linked, if they are to have as much sex as white women, they will far more often have sex where there is no such pretence. Unless black men are unaware of this, their experience will reinforce the attitude that sex is primarily for pleasure.

The white marriage market is much more balanced between the sexes, with only a small shortfall of promising males. We would predict a much smaller gap in attitudes between the sexes. And indeed white males are virtually identical to females in anticipating marriage and a clear majority believes that sex and love should be linked. The marriage market is so bad for Hispanic males that the usual gender pattern is reversed: males want marriage more than Hispanic females. Indeed, almost all of Hispanic men want marriage (93 percent). Far fewer black men do so (79 percent). In sum, the better the marriage market for men and the worse for women, the more men see no reason to marry and the more women become pessimistic.

Imprinting and profiles

Two new hypotheses: during infancy, white males are imprinted with their mother's face as a model mate and therefore find black females unattractive; during infancy, black females are imprinted with their father's face and therefore find white males unattractive. The difficulty of falsifying these by direct evidence is patent, so I will appeal to indirect evidence.

Infant imprinting of white males did not prevent millions of white men from having sex with black slaves at a time when that sex carried no obligation to marry. Both Irish mothers and black fathers must have very different faces in New York and Liverpool. One cannot sit in any waiting room in Toxteth (a mixed black/Irish neighborhood) without being surrounded by interracial children; the same is not true in New York. Infant imprinting must be much biased (read "skewed" if you prefer) toward color rather then facial configuration (particularly of the eyes and the mouth) in that Asian American women have little difficulty in marrying white males (Farley, 1995).

Let us perform a thought experiment (it is unlikely to get through an ethics committee). Imagine that we exterminated all black and Asian American males and, following *The Bell Curve*, selected out samples matched for IQ (at a mean of 100) from the women left behind. What percentage of those black and Asian women would find white husbands? I believe that the Asian women would find many more white spouses. No doubt, color preference would play a part, color preferences internalized long after infancy, but white males (without such a preference) would also eschew black wives purely as rational actors.

Group membership handicaps blacks in America because Americans use negative racial profiles. Sometimes these reflect racial bias, but often they reflect social reality. Therefore, a white male will not want the consequences of marrying a black wife, namely, that his children will bear the handicap of being socially classified as black. The overwhelming evidence for the use of racial profiles in America will be presented in chapter 4. For now, we will merely say that they apply to all aspects of life. They affect the price of cars, rental housing, the availability of capital to finance a business, whether you get a job, whether you are seen as criminal, whether you are likely to be shot by police on the street, and whether a jury is more likely to think you worthy of the death penalty.

Why would a white man want to saddle his children with all of this when he has so much choice? For a white male to want her as a spouse, a black woman must have an appeal well beyond that of a Hispanic or Asian woman. White women will have similar fears about having the children of a black man. As we have seen, they select the best of black men as spouses. However, rational calculation about future prospects may be a bit weaker among white women than white men. At the risk of inheriting the whirlwind, I suggest that they are more influenced by romantic love.

Perpetual war

Every cohort of one hundred black women faces this: an extra twenty-one men dead, missing, or in jail; a similar number who are poorly adapted to civilian life and/or go to jail at some time or cannot hold a steady job; which leaves only fifty-seven men as promising spouses. White women had an unfavorable marriage market during World War II. But the absence of men was so fleeting that it meant little more than a four-year separation from your present or future partner. Black women face it all the time, decade after decade. Theirs is the marriage market of a nation perpetually at war.

Can things get better? Let us set aside the possibility of a more robust welfare state that would aid solo-mothers in the innumerable ways in which it could. That leaves the regeneration of black men as an absolute prerequisite for curing the ills of black women and children. America is unlikely to adopt a more rational policy on drugs. However, police may get bored, or be put to work on tasks such as catching illegal Mexican immigrants, and therefore jail fewer black men. Black IQ has been gaining on white IQ. If that continues, it may translate into more boys doing well at school and seeing education rather than crime as a path to a good income.

Therefore, the number of promising male spouses may increase, and, if black profiles improve, more men of other races will enter the pool of promising spouses available to black women. If low-achieving black men have more competition for black women, they will be pressured toward self-improvement. If black women see more examples of marital success, fewer may take themselves out of the marriage market by way of early child-bearing. The real objective, of course, is not to salvage "marriage" but for children to be reared by good partners or a self-sufficient single parent.

Just as the interrelatedness of these factors locks black America into a cycle of deprivation, so that same interrelatedness could create an upward spiral if a key factor improves. Whether pessimism or optimism is in order, one thing is certain: the terms of the black marriage market must alter. Otherwise, future generations of black women and children will continue to be broken on that systemic wheel.

After completing this analysis, I found a similar one that focuses on the city of Syracuse in New York State. It reports what black women in that city actually say about what their marriage market does to them. Its conclusions are worth quoting:

> In contrast to the policy makers' assumptions that single motherhood is an individual preference, the African American women interviewed in Syracuse wanted to be in stable, nurturing, intimate relationships. They indicate that the dearth of African American men has led them and other women to accept male behavior that they otherwise would not accept if they had other options. According to these women, this struggle to maintain relationships appears to have led some women to adopt a strategy of having a baby to "tie" the man, resulting in single motherhood when the strategy failed. Perhaps most stigmatizing and demoralizing for the women is that, in some cases, an individual man fathers babies of two women concurrently, without the women's knowledge. Clearly, a low male sex ratio robs women of their so-called bargaining power in relationships.
> (Lane *et al.*, 2004, p. 424)

Well, what else would one expect?

Limitations of a snapshot

Since I have speculated about the future, I should make clear the limitations of what I have offered. I have offered one snapshot of the state of different marriage markets at a particular time (c. 2004). This is no substitute for analysis of what is happening over time. For example, it may well be that American women in general are raising their criteria of what counts as an acceptable partner over time. If so, a factor quite outside my analysis would be necessary to explain a rise in the number of solo-mothers between say 1974 and 2004.

An analysis akin to my own cannot explain such trends, but that does not mean that snapshots are useless. Imagine that a series of snapshots from 1974, 1984, and 2004 all showed that marriage market factors were the primary reality differentiating solo-parent rates between black and white women at every given time. That would tell us that, no matter what the peculiar causes working over time might be, they were color-blind. At this moment, there is no doubt in my mind that the market is operating in its usual way, blind to everything but the law of supply and demand. It is a pity that the effects of the market are not color-blind. They have a peculiar and devastating effect on black America and pose a question. Will we be like William Graham Sumner or like Estes Kefauver? Do we have the courage to face what is really going on?

3   What Germany did that America has not

The most tenable hypothesis, in my judgment, is that genetic, as well as environmental differences, are involved in the average disparity between American Negroes and whites in intelligence and educability.

(Arthur Jensen, 1973)

Arthur Jensen threatens to dominate this debate by the range of his learning, his skill as a controversialist, and the sheer volume of his contribution. In much the same way, St. Augustine overwhelmed his opponents concerning whether Christianity played an important role in the fall of Rome.

(James Flynn, 1980)

Thanks to reluctance to confront the possibility of a genetic component in racial differences, Americans have a false impression of the state of expert opinion on this question. As the prefatory quotes make evident, a competent scholar, untainted by racial bias, has led a group of psychologists who, for more than thirty years, have believed that genes play a larger role than environment in causing the historic IQ gap between black and white (of about 15 points). For almost thirty years, I have disputed their position, without vilification and while conceding that the evidence is indecisive. I think they are probably mistaken, but anyone who tells you that they are certain is, in my opinion, either ignorant or unwilling to squarely face the evidence.

There are plenty who do not want to confront the evidence. They generally give four reasons for not doing so:

1 that we cannot define intelligence (false: Flynn, 2007, pp. 49–54);

2 that what IQ tests measure does not approximate intelligence (false: Flynn, 2007, p. 55);

3 that IQ tests are not culture free (true; but no one lives in a culture-free society – it may be that blacks do not have the same chance to access what US society has to offer, but once you say that you have entered into the debate);

4 that race is not a scientifically respectable concept (irrelevant).

The last is irrelevant because American blacks are not defined by race but are a social construct and social constructs can have different genetic potentials. If Irish are divided into those that live on the right side of the tracks (lace curtain Irish) and the wrong side (shanty Irish), they are not divided by race but may have differing genes for IQ for all of that.

The consequences of making it taboo to debate this issue are the usual disastrous consequences of restrictions on freedom of debate and inquiry. I recently completed a tour of fifteen American universities and asked why so few of them had courses on intelligence. The answer was that they were afraid. A student would be bound to ask about racial differences and they were terrified to give a sensible answer. Even if they said it was a matter of environment, they would have had to discuss all of the things I will presently discuss, for example whether black middle-class parents provide as rich a cognitive atmosphere for their children as white middle-class parents do. They would then be crucified for stereotyping, blaming the victim, covert racism.

But the most ironic consequence of this reign of intimidation is not that social scientists fail to teach what they believe a social scientist should know. Young people are not stupid. If one side in a debate (those who think genes are involved) is willing to discuss the evidence and the other side is not, they draw their own conclusions. A recent email from a sociology major:

> I heard all of the screeds about Jensen, Murray, et al., being racists, or worse. Once I began to read the literature, I realized this was absurd. I began to think that the hereditarian crowd must be right, since they were willing to honestly address the issue. Then I read some of your articles and was delighted that a scholar of integrity and erudition was willing to confront the facts head on. I am not yet technically competent to have a firm position but now I have an open mind.

In other words, those who veto and boycott debate forfeit a chance to persuade. They have put their money on indoctrination and intimidation. A good bet in the short run but over the long course that horse never wins.

Americans in general will probably also be surprised at how psychologists debate this question. But learning about the concepts they use will be fun in the sense in which all learning about interesting ideas is fun. The topic will also give me an opportunity to instruct. There are some who believe that they can go to sleep because of the "Flynn effect." This is the phenomenon of massive IQ gains over time, to which Herrnstein and Murray attached my name because of my role in documenting the effect as something that has occurred throughout the world (see James R. Flynn, *What Is Intelligence?*). After all, massive IQ gains from one generation to another show just how potent environmental influences on IQ can be. They do, and they have some relevance to the race and IQ debate. But the role they play has little to do with the kind of evidence that will tip the scales one way or the other.

Scoring today's whites against the original WISC

We will set blacks aside for the moment and discuss IQ gains over time by white Americans. We can measure these because the

Psychological Corporation updates its test for school children ages 6 to 16, called the WISC (Wechsler Intelligence Scale for Children), every so often. It does so primarily to discard obsolete items, but each time it alters the test (the alterations are not radical) it has to administer it to a representative sample of American children. This is because how well the average child (at each age) does on the test is by definition an IQ of 100. The sample used for each version of the test is called the standardization sample and using its various levels of performance (average, below average, above average) to determine IQ scores is called norming the test. The WISC was originally normed in 1947–48 and later editions were normed in 1972 (the WISC-R), 1989 (the WISC-III), and mainly in 2002 (the WISC-IV).

Assuming the various samples were well selected (they were), they allow us to trace the IQ gains of representative American school children over almost fifty-five years. To measure IQ gains from one test to the next, both tests are given to the same group of subjects. If they average higher when scored against the older test than when scored against the more recent test, the older test must set a standard that is easier to meet. Which means that representative samples of children were doing less well as you go back into the past! For example, imagine that subjects scored 108 on the old WISC: that means they were 8 points above the average performance of a representative sample of Americans selected in 1947–48. Now imagine that the same subjects score only 100 on the newer WISC-R: that means they were unable to beat the average performance of a representative sample of Americans selected in 1972. The implication is that Americans gained 8 IQ points between 1947–48 and 1972.

The fact that the WISC was normed on whites only in 1947–48 provides a foundation on which we can build. If we keep adding on to their performance the IQ gains whites made from one test to another, we will have a record of how later American whites would have scored on the old WISC. Box 11 details the gains whites made on the ten subtests of the WISC all of the way from 1947 to 2002. They range from small gains on Information to huge gains on Similarities. The gain for

Box 11

White gains on WISC subtests and Full Scale IQ from 1947–48 to 2002

Information	10 to 10.43	equals **2.15 IQ points**
Arithmetic	10 to 10.46	equals **2.30 IQ points**
Vocabulary	10 to 10.88	equals **4.40 IQ points**
Comprehension	10 to 12.20	equals **11.00 IQ points**
Picture Completion	10 to 12.34	equals **11.70 IQ points**
Block Design	10 to 13.18	equals **15.90 IQ points**
Object Assembly	10 to 13.37	equals **16.85 IQ points**
Coding	10 to 13.60	equals **18.00 IQ points**
Picture Arrangement	10 to 14.30	equals **21.50 IQ points**
Similarities	10 to 14.77	equals **23.85 IQ points**
Full Scale IQ	100 to 125.63	equals **17.63 IQ points**

As the reader can see, the average score on each subtest is put at 10. Since there are ten subtests, it might seem that you would just add them up and get a Full Scale IQ score, that is, your IQ for the test taken as a whole. That would give a gain of 25.63 points. But actually, you have to use a table to convert this sum (called the Standard Score total) into an IQ. Converting each subtest gain into an IQ gain merely means taking it times 5. For example, Information gives a Standard Score gain of 0.43, and times 5 that equals 2.15 IQ points. For specialists, that makes sense because the standard deviation of each subtest is 3 and the SD of Full Scale IQ is 15. See Table 11 in the Appendix for full data and discussion.

Full Scale IQ, that is, your summary IQ for the test as a whole, shows that the average American school child in 2002 had an IQ of almost 118 when compared to the average child of 1947–48 set at 100.

Scoring today's blacks against the WISC

Having scored today's whites against the whites of 1947–48, it is easy to compare today's blacks to the whites of 1947–48. Box 12 shows how this is done and estimates that the blacks of 2002 had a Full Scale IQ of 104.31 scored against the whites of 1947–48 put at 100. Rather than having to depend on a series of comparisons, it would be better to select a representative sample of today's blacks and give them the old WISC. Frantic appeals have not located anyone interested.

Box 12 tells us something interesting about the employability of today's black Americans. As I have often argued, IQs should not be boosted by scoring the test performance of individuals against the norms of the past. But the Vocabulary and Arithmetic subtests are unusual in that, even over time, they seem to shed light on school skills, that is, on how well someone can read or do sums. If that is so, blacks today are about 0.4 standard deviations below the whites of 1947–48 on both, which would equal an average "schooling IQ" of 94. And if we assume that the top 95 percent of whites in 1947–48 had an education such that they could find something on the job market of today, then 90 percent of today's blacks should be able to do so.

It may be said that the literacy and mathematics requirements of the job market have risen over the last fifty years. However, at the level of service work, they are often less demanding. At McDonald's today, you punch a picture of a hamburger on the till and need not be numerate at all. Even jobs higher up the scale are easier, such as being a photographer or flying an airplane. If black men could stay out of jail, there is reason to believe that most of them could do independent work and enjoy a decent life. At least, they could do so with the help of a robust welfare state to provide good medicine, education, and housing, a theme that will recur throughout this book.

Are blacks genetically superior?

The brute fact that we have a representative group of American blacks that outscored a representative group of American whites is more important than the precise number of years it took blacks to accomplish this. In other words, whether our groups are a bit ahead

Box 12

To compare the blacks of 2002 against the whites of 1947–48, we will subtract the black IQ deficit of 2002 (BD) from the white gain between 1947–48 and 2002 (WG). That of course gives us what we want, namely, the IQ of blacks in 2002 scored against the whites of 1947–48 (BvsW47/48). We find that they had a Full Scale IQ of 104.31. The WISC also gives a breakdown into overall performance on subtests administered verbally and subtests where the subject performs tasks. See Table 12 in the Appendix for full data.

Information	0.43 (WG) minus 1.98 (BD) =	**− 1.55** (BvsW47/48)
Vocabulary	0.88 (WG) minus 2.12 (BD) =	**− 1.24** (BvsW47/48)
Arithmetic	0.46 (WG) minus 1.62 (BD) =	**− 1.16** (BvsW47/48)
Picture Completion	2.34 (WG) minus 2.52 (BD) =	**− 0.18** (BvsW47/48)
Comprehension	2.20 (WG) minus 1.62 (BD) =	**+ 0.58** (BvsW47/48)
Block Design	3.18 (WG) minus 2.57 (BD) =	**+ 0.61** (BvsW47/48)
Object Assembly	3.47 (WG) minus 1.96 (BD) =	**+ 1.51** (BvsW47/48)
Picture Arrangement	4.30 (WG) minus 1.96 (BD) =	**+ 2.34** (BvsW47/48)
Similarities	4.77 (WG) minus 2.19 (BD) =	**+ 2.58** (BvW47/48)
Coding	3.60 (WG) minus 0.78 (BD) =	**+ 2.82** (BvsW47/48)

Black (2002) versus whites (1947–48)

106.31 (Standard Score total)	equals	**104.31 Full Scale IQ**
49.21 (Verbal Standard Score total)	equals	**99.21 Verbal IQ**
57.10 (Performance Standard Score total)	equals	**110.10 Performance IQ**

of or behind their time is not too important. The same implications would hold even if the WISC white sample of 1947–48 was a bit substandard and represented where whites were in 1945; or if the black WISC-IV sample of 2002 was a bit elite and represented where blacks are in 2005. Certainly, whether our samples were roughly representative of their time is of interest, but it is of secondary interest. The core issue is this: were the blacks who outscored whites superior or inferior to those whites in terms of environment?

There are excellent data on the occupational status of the homes from which the white children of the WISC standardization sample came. These data are a very good match for the censuses of 1940 and 1950 (Seashore, Wesman, and Doppelt, 1950; Flynn, 1984). The occupational data for the parents of black children from the WISC-IV are useless. Rather than using the whole standardization sample, they selected a group numbering only one hundred. Worse, only forty-six of these returned information and these were clearly atypical of the sample as a whole. Therefore, as a second best, I have taken the black occupational profile from the 2000 census. Data about adults present in the homes of the WISC-IV black children are excellent, with an 87 percent return rate. These indicate that the WISC-IV black sample was representative – about 60 percent of them were living in solo-parent homes. No such data exist for the WISC whites. However, the Moynihan Report shows that only 10 percent of white children lived in solo-parent homes c. 1950, so we will not go far wrong if we accept that as an estimate.

With these data, we can make rough comparisons that reveal two environmental differences. The first difference is that the black children of 2002 came from homes whose occupational status was somewhat better than those of the white children of 1947–48. For example, fewer of them were the children of laborers and farmers. Therefore, the mean IQ of the white children should be raised by 1.77 points. The basis of this adjustment, and the adjustment for solo-parent homes below, can be found in Table 13 in the Appendix.

The adjustment may be a bit generous in that it is based on the extent to which IQ rises with SES (socioeconomic status) in the white community. Frier and Levitt (2006) show that SES differences within the black community are less potent. When children enter Kindergarten, each jump in SES shows white children enjoy 1.6 times the boost in reading and math scores that black children register. This reinforces a hypothesis we will soon evidence: that when we equate middle-class blacks and middle-class whites, using the usual criteria of household income, parental years of schooling, and parental occupation, the equation is false. The black middle-class child does not really get as many advantages in terms of a tradition of educational achievement, cognitive pressures, and so forth.

The second difference between the two samples is that far more of the black children of 2002 (60 percent) came from solo-parent homes than the white children of 1947–48 (10 percent). Therefore, the mean IQ of the black children should be raised by 4.97 points. This too may be generous. It is based on the difference between black children in one- and two-parent homes within the WISC-IV sample, which was 9.93 points. The white difference was less at 6.22 points and using it to adjust the white sample gives a drop in their mean IQ of 2.35 points. Adjusting the blacks of 2002 in terms of 2002 data on solo-parent homes is clearly more sensible than adjusting the whites of 1947–48 in terms of 2002 data on those homes. But in any event, the bonus whites enjoyed from fewer solo-parents homes, whether 2.35 points or 4.97 points, is a reasonable match for the 1.77 points blacks enjoyed from the fact that their parents had somewhat higher occupational status. I will leave the value for black mean IQ unchanged and be content with this: the blacks of 2002 had an IQ of 104.42 scored against the whites of 1947–48 despite no obvious environmental advantage.

Actually, our method of adjusting is an oversimplification. When you select out a superior group for an environmental variable, they are also to some degree a genetic elite. But since one adjustment favors blacks and the other adjustment counts against them, and the two are about equal, this should balance out. It seems that we are driven to the conclusion that blacks are genetically superior for IQ.

Taking something unmeasurable out of the scales

It is a pity not to let this conclusion stand. The revolution on both the political left and the political right as to who would champion and who would castigate IQ tests would be exciting to observe. However, it rests on an unstated and untenable assumption: that we can ignore the fact that much social change separates the environments of 1947–48 and 2002.

After all, the above conclusion assumes that blacks between 1947–48 and 2002 did not enjoy some environmental advantage that operates over time and cannot be captured by weighing factors frozen in time. If so, they were getting an environmental bonus in 2002 that the whites of 1947–48 did not enjoy. I will show that the causes of an IQ difference at any given time do not capture the causes of IQ trends over time; and that since we do not know how to measure the latter we cannot compare their potency to the former. If I can establish this, comparing the black environment of 2002 with the white environment of 1947–48 becomes merely an example of a general rule. Never assume an over-time environmental difference can be balanced in the same scales as an at-the-same-time environmental difference.

I used to make this kind of mistake. For example, I would find that the impact of differences in SES on IQ at a given time was modest. And I would conclude that something like rising affluence over time could not possibly explain huge IQ gains. Let us look at what economic progress over time actually entails.

The industrial revolution hit America in earnest after the Civil War. By 1900, the need for an industrial rather than an agricultural workforce meant a new and powerful demand for school-taught cognitive skills. Each student became surrounded by fellow students who were more motivated and competent; better students became better teachers for the next cohort of students; parents became more serious about schooling and homework; the lengths of the school day and school year tended to increase. Measuring the fact that the number of years of schooling increased between 1900 and 1950 captures only a fragment of this. Even if there had been no increase in years of schooling, the benefit of each year spent in school would have escalated greatly over time.

The post-World War II economic boom did much to weaken the "depression psychology" of the 1930s. Preoccupation with practical concerns like earning a living diminished, so that abstract problems were no longer seen as a trivial distraction from the real business of life. Leisure no longer exhausted by recuperation from the demands of work was a factor that pushed leisure activities toward hobbies (like chess and bridge) and conversation and video games that exercise the mind. The number of jobs emphasizing manipulation of symbols or abstractions and on-the-spot problem solving increased. Middle-class mores and aspirations reduced family size and gave each child a better ratio of adults to children in the home.

The same point can be made about other trends, for example urbanization. Measuring how many people shifted from rural to urban areas from one time to another misses what is going on in both rural and urban areas. Greater industrialization and growing affluence meant greater cognitive sophistication not only within cities but also within rural areas that were no longer isolated thanks to travel and the media. Years of schooling, and SES, and even being a solo-mother are not personal traits that are relatively fixed like fingerprints. They are social creations that may change as dramatically over time as the motorcar you drive.

No one knows how to quantify the impact of environmental factors over time on IQ using the same metric that quantifies the impact of environmental differences at a given time. Therefore, the two are non-comparable. Therefore, we do not know whether the environmental advantages blacks accrued between 1947–48 and 2002 compensate, or overcompensate, or undercompensate them for their usual environmental disadvantages at a given time. Jensen (1998) has complained that the "Flynn effect" is repeatedly thrown at him as a kind of mantra: a chant that is supposed to terminate the race and IQ debate. He now has a ready reply: "Flynn himself does not make (and has never made) such a claim. He believes that IQ gains show that blacks can match whites for IQ; but he does not believe that they can show that blacks can do this when environments are equal."

Enter the g factor

Having weakened the case for an environmental explanation of black–white intelligence differences, we will now attempt to strengthen the case for a genetic explanation. We will introduce the concept of g, often called the general intelligence factor. Remember the ten subtests of the WISC ranging from Vocabulary, Information and Arithmetic to Similarities and Picture Completion. There is a strong tendency for performance on these ten subtests to be intercorrelated. This means that people who are above average on one of them tend to excel on them all, that is, those who are good at seeing what concepts have in common and good at identifying the missing piece of a picture tend to be the same people who accumulate large vocabularies, large funds of general information, and arithmetical skills. That is why we speak of a general intelligence factor or g.

There is nothing mysterious about the notion of g. In every-day life, all of us talk about general abilities that "lie behind" being exceptional at a wide range of tasks. We have all said of someone that they have athletic ability and meant that they seem to excel at all sports not just at one, so they have athletic g. If someone is good at playing a wide variety of musical instruments, we tend to say that they are "musical," which is to say they have musical g. Similarly if someone is good at a wide range of cognitively demanding tasks, we say that they have g in the sense of general intelligence.

A mathematical technique called factor analysis measures this tendency of performance on a wide variety of cognitive tasks to be intercorrelated, and technically g is the quantified result. The g factor explains a surprising amount of individual differences in performance on the WISC subtests, but it is better at predicting performance on some rather than others. This is because good performers consistently open up a larger gap on the average person at some cognitive tasks than others. These tasks tend to be the more cognitively complex tasks, which reinforces the claim of g to be a measure of general intelligence. For example, a high-IQ person excels less on Digit Span forward, which is just remembering numbers in the order in which they were read out, and excels more on Digit Span backward, which is repeating numbers aloud in reverse of the order in which they were read out.

The ten WISC subtests can be ranked in terms of their g loadings. That simply means you rank them from the subtest on which high-IQ people beat the average person the most down to the subtest on which they excel the least. Musical people tend to be farther above average on the piano than the drums, and therefore the piano has a higher musical g loading. A talented cook is likely to exceed me more in making a soufflé than scrambled eggs because the former is more complex than the latter. Therefore, it has a higher culinary g loading and is a better test of excellence in cooking. One can now appreciate the case that g actually captures the essence of intelligence and IQ is merely a vehicle for measuring g.

Jensen and others have stressed the fact the score gap between blacks and whites tends to increase as we go from WISC subtests with lower g loadings to subtests with higher g loadings. For example, Vocabulary has a slightly higher g loading than Information and the black–white score gap on the former is also slightly higher (see Table 14 in Appendix). On one level, this is not very important in the race and IQ debate.

It shows that the black–white score gap relates more to the cognitive complexity of an item rather than to other factors that IQ tests measure such as spatial ability and memory. This means that it is hard to evade the conclusion that the gap signals a difference in something we would identify with intelligence. But I have always believed that the better IQ tests were reasonable measures of intelligence, at least on the level of individual differences and defining intelligence as the kind of intelligence you need to make your way in American society. The fact that there is a real intelligence difference between black and white does no more to decide the debate than say a real height difference. Real differences can be the result of either genes or environment. If the difference is environmental, it means that blacks equal whites in their capacity for intelligence at conception but that their environment impedes the full development of their potential.

People do not like such plain language but that is silly. No one gets upset if we say that two people were born with the same potential as runners, but that one runs better than the other because he has the advantage of a better coach. The notion that you suffer from a worse environment but that it does you no real harm is odd.

It is true that the black–white gap for g is a bit larger than the black–white IQ gap. But I will show that it is not much larger, and that when blacks gain ground on whites they close both gaps to almost the same degree. If the day comes when blacks match whites for IQ, it would be a bit disturbing if they still have a small g deficit because again, g looks a bit closer to the problem-solving ability we call intelligence. But I will show that such an outcome is unlikely. Studies of identical twins raised apart may be a bit closer together for g than for IQ, thus showing that g is more heavily influenced by genes. There is some evidence that this would be so (correlations between g loading and the negative effects of inbreeding). But the tendency of separated twins to be atypically alike for IQ is already robust; and slightly higher values would make no difference to the debate.

Imagine that American society is such that the spectrum of environments that blacks can access is worse than the spectrum of environments whites have available. That might well account for the average cognitive difference between the groups. Now assume that within the white population, genetic similarities or differences between individuals have a heavy weight as to where you end up on the white spectrum. That would mean that white twins separated at birth would be very likely to be similar for IQ. And assume that within the black population, genetic similarities or differences between individuals largely determine where you end up on the black spectrum. That would mean that black twins separated at birth would be very likely to be similar for IQ. But none of this would shake the fact that the average cognitive difference between the groups is environmental. Therefore, the twin data are not relevant to the debate on between-race IQ differences (see Box 13).

Box 13

The Dickens/Flynn model shows that for values beyond those anyone has found, the twin studies are not relevant to between-group differences (Dickens and Flynn, 2001a; 2001b). Take basketball. **Within** any age cohort, height and quickness (much influenced by genes) are likely to determine whether you make the school team, get professional coaching, and so forth. So even if identical twins were separated into different homes at birth, their genetic identity would cause very similar basketball skills as they grew up. **Between** my generation and the next, TV came along and glamorized basketball. The wider participation that resulted triggered a steady gain in the average skill level. First, you only had to shoot and pass well to be average, then you had to shoot and pass with either hand, then you had to do fade away jump shots. When my team came back to play against the varsity basketball team of five years later they killed us. They could do things we never dreamed of doing. But an environmental difference separated the two groups, not superior genes.

IQ gains and g gains

I have promised to show that when blacks gain on whites for IQ over time, they also cut the g difference between black and white to almost the same degree. It may seem that this would follow as a matter of course because the leading IQ tests measure mainly g. But when blacks cut their gap with whites over time, the gains are eccentric in the sense that the ground made up on each subtest does not correspond to the g loading of the subtest. From this it has been falsely inferred that while the black gains may be IQ gains they are not g gains. Let us look at what actually happens when blacks gain on whites.

Dickens and Flynn (2006) showed that blacks had gained 5.5 IQ points on whites since World War II. We think that the gains took place after 1972. Nisbett (in press) adds credibility by showing that blacks made similar gains after 1972 on academic achievements tests (The Nation's Report Card). Others have raised objections and placed the gains earlier. In either event, whether they occurred later or earlier, the gains happened. Upon analysis, we found that the g gap between blacks and whites had narrowed almost to the same degree, that is, by 5.13 points. How is that possible?

The simplest answer is that if one group really could not make g gains on another, they would be incapable of making gains on cognitive tasks that have heavy g loadings. All of the WISC subtests are heavily g loaded (except Coding). Therefore, if blacks make gains on whites on them all, they are making g gains. We should keep in mind why g has a claim to be something close to the concept of intelligence. The greater the g loading, the greater the cognitive complexity of the task: making a soufflé has a higher g loading than scrambling eggs. If it were the reverse, if g rose to the extent a task was simple and automatic, we would dismiss it as an index of regurgitation of memorized material or habitual skills.

Now imagine that black gains on all of the WISC subtests were three times as great as they have been and amounted to over

15 points. They might still have the same pattern, that is, they might not match the g loadings of the various subtests. But could we dismiss a huge enhancement of performance on so many cognitively complex tasks? Here I want to make use of an analogy.

Imagine there were two groups genetically equal in their potential for hearing:

1 Group A has a less favorable environment than Group B because far more of them work in factories where the noise level damages hearing. It damages it more as you go from low- to high-pitched sounds.

2 We have a hearing test with four subtests: traffic noise, conversation, alarm clocks, and music. Each has a different pitch loading running from lower to higher in the order listed. Even sirens have a slightly lower pitch than high C.

3 The hearing aid is invented. Group A benefits disproportionately because, of course, more of them suffer from hearing loss and try to get one. However, the hearing aids are not quite as good at allowing you to pick up high-pitched sounds.

4 Weighting the four subtests equally gives HQ (hearing quotient). Thanks to hearing aids, Group A has made up 5.5 points of its hearing deficit on Group B. However, subtest by subtest, its gains are very slightly in reverse order in terms of pitch loadings. Therefore, they do not match the pitch hierarchy.

5 We weight the various subtests in terms of their pitch loadings (music gets more weight than traffic noise) and derive a PQ (pitch quotient).

6 This shows that Group A has made up 5.13 points on Group B in terms of PQ, almost as much as it did in terms of HQ.

Well, there is nothing mysterious about this. Group A made big gains on Group B on all four subtests. The gains run counter to the pitch loadings but this is mitigated by two factors: the pitch differentials between the subtests are small; the discrimination against high pitch by the hearing aids is also small. Therefore, when the gains are converted from Hearing Quotient to Pitch Quotient by weighting the subtests, the fact that the gains did not match pitch loadings makes little difference. "Anti-pitch" gains convert into pitch gains that are almost as large as hearing gains.

This scenario implies that to reach Pitch Quotient parity, Group A would have to attain a small Hearing Quotient advantage. It is unlikely that hearing aids would ever do this because they would have to somehow favor Group A: they would have to allow Group A to hear high-pitched sounds as well as Group B and low-pitched sounds better. But here is something interesting: why have hearing aids not given group A pitch parity with Group B? It is because hearing aids have not addressed the root cause of the hearing gap. Group A is still disproportionately in factory work, something that damages hearing differentially in terms of pitch. The only way to address the root cause would be to close the occupational gap between the groups, so that they both had the same percentage in white-collar and blue-collar jobs.

Even though hearing aids in themselves cannot address the root cause, they might serve as a means by which Group A can do so eventually. Thanks to better hearing, they start to learn more at school and get more white-collar jobs. At last, the root cause would be addressed and the pitch gap would disappear without the need for hearing superiority.

I hope it is clear how this applies to the races. There are two messages. The first is familiar. You cannot dismiss black IQ gains on whites just because they do not tally with the g loadings of subtests. But the second is new and unexpected. The brute fact that black gains on whites do not tally with g loadings tells us something about causes. The causes of the black gains are like hearing aids. They do cut the cognitive gap but they are not eliminating the root causes. And conversely, if the root causes are somehow eliminated, we can be confident that the IQ gap and the g gap will both disappear. So although g does nothing to tip the scales in favor of a genetic hypothesis about the racial IQ gap, it has given us a wonderful bonus: a powerful instrument to diagnose the nature of causes. We can use it to see whether root causes are being addressed over time or whether something is happening that merely addresses the effects of those causes.

Persistence of the g pattern

I will call the tendency for the black–white score gap on subtests to increase as g loading rises, the "g pattern." It is measured by the correlation between the WISC subtests ranked in terms of the size of their black–white score gaps and the same subtests ranked by the size of their g loadings. For example, if the biggest black–white gap was on the subtest with the biggest g loading and so on right down the line, the match would be perfect and the correlation would be 1.00. If the size of the black–white gap and the size of the g loadings were randomly distributed, as if by chance, the correlation would be zero.

There was a big gain by blacks on whites between the WISC-R of 1972 and the WISC-IV of 2002. And yet the crucial correlation fell only from 0.636 to 0.488 (see Table 14 in Appendix). Even more significant, let us compare the blacks of 2002 with the whites of 1947–48. Even though the black–white IQ gap disappears (indeed blacks are 4 points higher), the correlation stands at 0.491. This confirms the thesis I have argued: that the causes of the black IQ gains over time are too different from the cause of the black–white IQ gap at any given time to be comparable. It also illustrates that this kind of closing of the racial IQ gap does not address the root causes.

While the g pattern does create a g gap between black and white larger than the IQ gap, it is not much larger. A correlation of almost 0.500 (0.491) sounds impressive, but how much difference does it make in terms of the magnitude of the black–white cognitive gap? To measure this, we will calculate both IQs and GQs for blacks normed on whites at 100. IQ just treats the ten WISC subtests as equal. GQ is the result of weighting them to give those with the higher g loadings more influence and those with lower g loadings

Box 14

Showing that black GQ is only about one point lower than black IQ. Take the Standard Score gaps (SG) between the blacks of 2002 and the whites of 1947–48; multiply by the g loadings (GL) of each subtest; and adjust that by dividing by the average g loading (.648). This gives a new score gap (NG) for each subtest. These reduce the Standard Score total by 1.27 points, which equals a loss of about 0.90 IQ points. See Table 15 in Appendix for full data.

Information	−**1.55** (SG) × .727 (GL) =	−1.12685: adjusts to	− **1.74** (NG)
Vocabulary	−**1.24** (SG) × .777 (GL) =	−0.96348: adjusts to	− **1.49** (NG)
Arithmetic	−**1.16** (SG) × .650 (GL) =	−0.75400: adjusts to	− **1.16** (NG)
Picture Completion	−**0.18** (SG) × .581 (GL) =	−0.10458: adjusts to	− **0.16** (NG)
Comprehension	+**0.58** (SG) × .684 (GL) =	+0.39672: adjusts to	+**0.61** (NG)
Block Design	+**0.61** (SG) × .705 (GL) =	+0.43005: adjusts to	+**0.66** (NG)
Object Assembly	+**1.51** (SG) × .597 (GL) =	+0.90147: adjusts to	+**1.39** (NG)
Picture Arrangement	+**2.34** (SG) × .574 (GL) =	+1.34316: adjusts to	+**2.07** (NG)
Similarities	+**2.58** (SG) × .744 (GL) =	+1.91952: adjusts to	+**2.96** (NG)
Coding	+**2.82** (SG) × .436 (GL).=	+1.22952: adjusts to	+**1.90** (NG)

Total (+100):   **106.31**   Total (+100): **105.04**
                    IQ: **104.42**   GQ: **103.53**

less influence. For example, Vocabulary has almost twice the g loading of Coding. Therefore, when we multiply the black–white gaps on the two subtests by their g loadings, the Vocabulary gap gets twice the influence on GQ as the Coding gap.

Box 14 does the necessary arithmetic and reveals that black GQ (2002 blacks normed on whites of 1947–48) is 103.53 as compared to an IQ of 104.31. So GQ takes only about one point off black IQ, which will hardly affect the race and IQ debate. Note how little difference adjusting for g loadings makes for every subtest but Coding. That is because all of the others have very similar g loadings, ranging only from .574 to .777. But do not forget that the g pattern is very important in terms of whether the causes of the black–white cognitive gap have been eliminated.

What Germany did to the g pattern

One piece of the puzzle is missing: Klaus Eyferth. Eyferth's study has always been an important piece of evidence in favor of genetic equality between black and white Americans. However, my purpose is not so much to review its credentials in that regard, although I will add a bit at the end, as to see what light it sheds on the relationship between environment and the persistence of the g pattern.

Eyferth's results

Just to rehearse the facts (Flynn, 1980, pp. 84–102). After World War II, America maintained an occupying army in Germany. Eyferth selected a representative sample of the children black servicemen fathered with German women and a matching group (matched for the SES of the mothers) of the children of white servicemen. He collected IQ data for 170 of the former and 69 of the latter on the HAWIK or the German version of the WISC. The mean IQs of the two groups were virtually identical, implying that there was no advantage in having a white father rather than a black one. Moreover, he compared the scores of blacks and whites on eleven subtests of the WISC. The eleventh was Digit Span, which I have omitted because it is not used in calculating full-scale IQs. The question arises: when black and white genes are taken completely out of the American context and transplanted into Germany, what happens to g?

Box 15

German occupation children: black and white (almost) equal for both IQ and GQ

	Whites	Blacks		Whites	Blacks
	Standard Scores		(g loading)	g weighted scores	
Arithmetic	8.87	8.63	0.657	7.91	7.70
Similarities	10.36	10.29	0.691	9.72	9.66
Block Design	9.66	9.38	0.716	9.40	9.12
Picture Arrangement	9.89	9.53	0.730	9.81	9.45
Picture Completion	9.57	9.60	0.753	9.79	9.82
Vocabulary	10.08	9.93	0.815	11.16	11.00
Comprehen-sion	9.95	10.22	0.817	11.05	11.34
Object Assembly	10.17	9.58	0.829	11.46	10.79
Information	9.04	9.11	0.908	11.15	11.23
Coding	8.50	8.97	[0.442]	5.11	5.38
Total:	96.08	95.20	(Ave: 0.736)	Total: 96.55	95.48
IQ:	**97.00**	**96.50**		GQ: **97.47**	**96.86**

Correlations between score differences and HAWIK g:
Spearman without Coding: −0.267
Spearman with Coding: +0.079

As Box 15 shows, the white and half-black children are not only virtually the same for IQ but also virtually identical for GQ. The g pattern has disappeared; that is, there is no tendency for the magnitude of black–white score differences on the various subtests to correlate with the g loadings of the subtests. I have given correlations both with and without Coding because strictly, the data for Coding

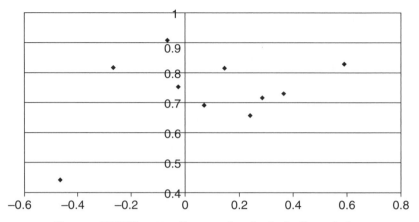

Figure 1 HAWIK scatter diagram: showing lack of correlation
between subtest g loadings and racial standard score differences

does not allow it to be taken into account. However, the data necessary can be approximated (see Table 16 in Appendix).

In fact, Coding should not be included in the WISC battery of
subtests if GQ is our objective. Figure 1 is a scatter diagram that gives
a graphic illustration of how atypical it is. Coding is the "diamond"
at the lower left. First, it has a g loading far below that of any other
subtest (they are at .66 or above and it is at .44). But more important,
it is an "outlier" well removed from the others. The others form a
cluster whose message is the lack of any correlation between subtest
g loadings and black–white score differences. Germany did what
America could not. The g pattern has disappeared, and therefore we
know that the root causes of the black–white cognitive gap have disappeared. In Germany, these black children did not get hearing aids;
they got out of the factory.

When black genes were transplanted into white German
women, the resulting offspring grew up in a nation with no black
subculture. The half-black children became Germans with a darker
skin, no more no less. This is not to say that they suffered from no
color prejudice. However, as the Moor of Venice shows, that is not the
same as being socialized in a wounded subculture. In America, fifty-

five years of history from 1947–48 to 2002 left the root causes of the black environmental disadvantage virtually untouched. They signal their durability by the persistence of the g pattern.

Eyferth's sample

As we shall soon see, the black American soldiers in Europe were a more elite group than the white soldiers. I will argue that this bias is not great enough to undermine Eyferth's results, but assume I am mistaken. Assume that the black soldiers were more elite than I believe. Their elite character would not explain the absence of the g pattern.

First, assume that the g pattern is genetically determined. Men and women provide an example of a genetically determined difference. Girls are very nearly the same height as boys up to about 13 and then boys pull away as both sexes age. The height gap between the two suddenly increases as you go from ages 13 to 14 to 15 to 16. If you selected an elite sample of women at maturity that would certainly cut the gender height gap. But if you had a record of heights from ages 13 on up, you would find that the sudden loss of ground with age would persist even among your elite women. It is genetically programmed.

Now assume that the g pattern is environmental and recall our hearing analogy. If the black men who went to Germany were an elite this would of course cut the hearing gap between the black and white soldiers. And if it just so happened that they were mainly white-collar workers, then the root cause of the pitch pattern would be eliminated. Since they were not in factory work, the peculiar handicap that damages hearing most at high pitch levels would be absent among them. However, the fathers could not pass on their fortuitous environment to their children. They could only pass on their genes. If the pitch pattern were absent among their children, it could only be because it is not genetically transmitted from a parent but arises from the environment in which a child is raised.

Another way to put the point: the main way in which the black soldiers in Germany were elite was that low-IQ blacks were eliminated. If their absence eliminated the special tendency of blacks to do worse the more cognitively complex the item, then that tendency must affect only low-IQ blacks. Intelligence is a polygenic trait (many genes interacting affect it) and it is very unlikely that low-IQ blacks have some special gene that the others lack, or some genetic peculiarity that marks them off from the rest of blacks as if they approached being a separate species.

Let us take stock. IQ and GQ were identical for the black occupation children. The correlation between the magnitude of black/white score differences on subtests and the g loading of the subtests disappeared. And we have shown that this disappearance of the g pattern among the black occupation children owes nothing to whether or not their black fathers were elite. If the fathers were elite for genes, they were probably elite for environment and vice versa. But in any event, the very fact the g pattern disappeared among the children shows it cannot be a product of genes. It has to be a product of the environment in which blacks are normally raised, and somehow the German environment eliminated the root causes of the g pattern.

Therefore, the American black environment must be damaging in some way that the German black environment was not. We can specify the peculiar damage it does: it damages blacks more the greater the cognitive complexity of the problems they must solve. The obvious candidate is the peculiar black subculture that has evolved in America and has no counterpart in Germany. Keep that on file for future reference.

Eyferth and Eysenck

Eysenck (1981) questioned the significance of Eyferth's results on the grounds that the half-black German children might have benefited from hybrid vigor. That is, he suggested that black fathers outbreeding with white mothers had enhanced the genetic quality of the offspring. For many years, I was among those who took this contention seriously. However, I will now attempt to show that it lacks merit.

Outbreeding can benefit a group either as an antidote to the deleterious effects of inbreeding (called inbreeding depression or IBD) or by happy accident. The classic study of IBD and IQ is that of Schull and Neel (1965, table 12.19). Schull and Neel administered the WISC to 1,854 children in Hiroshima: 989 were outbred (their parents had no significant percentage of genes in common); and 865 were inbred, varying from being the issue of first-cousin marriages to second-cousin marriages. They found that the impact of inbreeding on full scale IQ is very small indeed. Blacks would have to be inbred (compared to whites) to the degree that they were all analogous to the offspring of first cousins to explain away 3 points of the racial IQ gap. If they were analogous to the offspring of second cousins that would explain 0.8 IQ points. Both of these assumptions are, of course, absurd. IBD is far too impotent to explain Eyferth's results (see Flynn, 2007, pp. 100–102).

Granted that no major racial group suffers from inbreeding depression to a significant degree, could outbreeding benefit a group by happy accident? For example, some people have sickle-shaped red blood cells, and since these are poor carriers of oxygen they suffer from anemia when under stress. However, their blood cells also make them resistant to malaria (the parasite that causes malaria finds such cells hard to invade). When they mate with a normal person, the offspring tend to have red blood cells sickle-shaped enough to be resistant to malaria but not so sickle-shaped as to make them much more prone to anemia. To get this happy medium between two selective pressures is very rare and there are few known examples among humans.

As for IQ, it is hard to imagine genes both of which have good/bad consequences for intelligence and therefore might combine to foster the good and eliminate the bad. After all, genes unfavorable to intelligence have been weeded out over most of human evolutionary history. Remember that both white and black servicemen in Germany were breeding out. The black Americans were breeding with German women. But the whites were as well: almost none of them would have been German Americans; rather they would have been of English or Irish or Swedish origin. A happy combination that occurs when a black mates with a German, but does not occur when a non-German white mates with a German white, is logically possible. But it should be treated as a remote possibility until evidence is produced in its favor.

Nagoshi and Johnson (1986) compared the test performance of sixty-three offspring of Japanese–European marriages with the performance of the offspring of within-race marriages, either both parents European-American or both Japanese-American. Over a set of fifteen cognitive tests the mixed-race children averaged 2 IQ points better and on a g factor were 3.9 points better. None of the score differences attained statistical significance. The study should be replicated using larger numbers. However, let us assume that Japanese enjoy a fortuitous IQ gain from outbreeding with whites. This does not mean blacks would enjoy a similar fortuitous gain. Particularly since, unlike the Japanese, American blacks have already bred with American whites, when they were slaves, to the extent that they have about 20 percent white ancestry.

Indeed, there is one study that suggests that blacks do not in fact benefit at all. I refer to the Minnesota Trans-racial Adoption Study. Scarr, Weinberg, and Waldman (1993) compared the IQs of white, half-black, and entirely black adopted children. This is an embarrassment to the environmentalist, because at age 17 the black/white IQ gap was unaltered between the white and all-black adoptees – and was only halved between the white and half-black adoptees. Lynn (1994) concludes that there is no advantage in a white home environment; and that the percentage of black versus white genes determines IQ. However, the Minnesota Trans-racial Adoption Study is also an embarrassment to those who think that outbreeding renders Eyferth's results suspect. Where is the advantage the half-black children should have got from hybrid vigor? It is nowhere to be seen. Otherwise, the half-blacks, thanks to that advantage, would have made up well more than half of the white/black IQ gap.

Environmentalists can at least suggest a scenario that fits the results. First, that the all-black children fell behind white adoptees as they approached maturity because their home environment could not insulate them from their black peers as they aged and became autonomous. More on this later. Second, that the half-black children made up half the gap with whites because, while their white home environment did little permanent good, they had two advantages: a greater likelihood of peers of all races; and a white pre-natal environment – although, as we shall see, showing that the latter was important is not easy. Pathetically, all of the half-black children had white mothers. Clearly, in America, the white mother of a biracial child is much more likely to give her child up for adoption than a black mother.

The Trans-racial Adoption Study poses problems for everyone. The IQ pattern from black to half-black to white forces the environmentalist to assume that a white home environment does little to prevent blacks from being socialized by a black subculture. The same pattern suggests that mating between black men and white women pays no dividends in terms of hybrid vigor – and fortifies the credentials of Eyferth's results. There is simply no reason to believe that black American soldiers enjoyed a special hybrid vigor bonus when mating with German women – a bonus denied to Italian-American or Irish-American soldiers when they mated with German women.

Back to Eyferth's sample

The fact that adoption of black children into white homes paid fewer dividends as children aged has caused lamentation that there are no IQ scores for the German occupation children after the age of 13. Eyferth (1961, pp. 229, 231) attempted to determine whether or not there was an IQ trend with age by classifying the occupation children into age groups and comparing the races at 6–8, 8–10, 10–11, and 11–13. There is no consistent trend. Half-black girls start with a large advantage over whites, dip well below them at age 10, and rise well above them as they approach 12. Half-black boys start below white boys, catch them at age 10, and fall well beneath them as they approach 12. These are cross-sectional data with as few as four subjects in the younger age groups, and fluctuations "with age" are probably fluctuations due to small sample size.

Finally, there is the elite nature of the black servicemen in Germany. During this period, the US military used tests to screen recruits and more blacks than whites were rejected on mental grounds. This means blacks in Germany were a bit more of a genetic elite than whites and gave their children an advantage of about 1.5 IQ points (Flynn, 1980, pp. 96–99). Therefore, the environmentalist must argue that black children suffered a small environmental disadvantage even in Germany.

Eyferth (1959) believed that their skin color was a handicap because it advertised their illegitimacy. It certainly was visible evidence that their mothers had consorted with the occupying foreign army. Wolff (1955) says that Germans at that time were prejudiced against black children purely because of their skin color. An associated objection is that German women may have had children with black soldiers who had above-average IQs, and who therefore were a genetic elite. We can only give a partial answer to this objection. Looking at those blacks who contracted venereal disease or went AWOL (absent without leave), we can make a strong case that the blacks who had sex with German women were actually slightly below the average IQ of blacks in Germany (Flynn, 1980, pp. 94–95). However, blacks who had long-term affairs (rather than casual sex) with German women may have been more likely to become fathers and nothing can tell us their mean IQ.

Eyferth and Charles Murray

In both 2006 and 2007, I debated the race and IQ issue with Charles Murray (with courtesy shown on both sides). He made two important points. First, he emphasized that reliance on Eyferth alone for a case that the black–white IQ gap is overwhelmingly environmental was to acknowledge that one's evidence was slender. Second, he emphasized that the traditional explanation of the racial IQ gap argued that the differing home environments of black and white were crucial. And he pointed out that all recent evidence shows that home environment has no permanent effects on IQ; indeed, by maturity, whether you were raised in this home rather than that home accounts for little or no IQ variance. The SES of your parents, how many books they had about, and so forth, might affect IQ during childhood but the effects faded away with age.

Eyferth taught us one thing that endures: look for signs that the black environment in America does not develop the skills needed to solve cognitively complex problems. That said, I put him aside in order to make a fresh case. I believe that recent evidence gives the race and IQ debate a whole new focus. I refer to the following: blacks tend to lose ground on whites in terms of IQ as they age; the causes of this are a series of environments each taking over as its predecessor is exhausted; blacks have cut the size of the IQ gap over time.

Blacks lose ground with age

Dickens and Flynn (2006) found that if we plot black IQ against white IQ (with whites set at 100), black children lose about 0.6 IQ points per year for a total loss of about 12 points from ages 4 to 24. We suspect (Flynn, Dickens, and Breslau, in preparation) that black IQ continues to fall (though at a much slower rate) right up to retirement and then stabilizes with even a hint of ground regained. What causes blacks to lose ground with age may be a clue to the causes of the black/white IQ gap.

I will offer an analysis based on the assumption that the loss with age is environmental in origin. Although that assumption can only be tentative, it is probably true. When a genetic factor causes one group to fall behind another, it rarely causes a smooth loss with age. Rather it kicks in at a certain age, causes a sudden dip, and then levels off. Like male versus female height: males are ahead only by half an inch at 13, then add almost 5 inches to their advantage from 13 to 16, then add very little more. The black on white IQ loss with age is not like that. They do not hit some ceiling on their intelligence at an earlier age than whites. If they did so, beginning at that age, there would be a period in which their losses would be disproportionately large. In fact, the rate of black IQ loss on whites looks constant all of the way from age 4 to 24.

I am wedded to the Dickens/Flynn model which emphasizes the influence of the environment at the time (the intensity of its demands for cognitive complexity) as far more important than preceding environments. This means that I actually endorse Charles Murray's point that pre-school home environment does not imprint some indelible mark on children from various families that continues to differentiate them from one another for IQ at adulthood. Insofar as those who gave an environmental explanation of the black–white IQ gap made such an assumption, they were mistaken. And it means we must describe a succession of environments that hamper blacks all the way from conception to maturity.

But it does not mean we can simply ignore some earlier environment in the series and simply leap to the environments that separate black and white at the age of 21. Each environment has a causal link to the next spectrum of environments available to the group as a whole, despite it impotence to determine the pecking order of the individuals within the group as they exploit that new spectrum.

Some words of explanation are in order. Imagine we did twin studies in rural Nigeria. We find that the influence of family environment on IQ fades away with age in the sense that which family a particular Nigerian comes from does not correlate with his IQ at adulthood. As the influence of parents wanes and Nigerian children are absorbed into their teenage peer groups, they distribute themselves over the spectrum of cognitive environments various peer groups offer. Within that spectrum, their genetic quality tends to match their environment, that is, those with better genes for IQ tend to gravitate to the more cognitively demanding peer groups and this happens irrespective of family. As we know, the same phenomenon of family environment fading away is true for American blacks (and whites for that matter).

But would anyone say that the difference between rural Nigeria and New York City would not afford US blacks a higher mean IQ? The fact that family environment fades in both places as a determinant of individual differences in IQ does not affect the fact that the two groups live in very different cultures; and that Nigerian rural culture offers a less enriched spectrum of cognitive environments all the way from infancy to adulthood. It would not even mean we could ignore the early childhood environment of Nigerians. Their childhoods have a causal affect on the kind of peers they encounter post-childhood. The fact that Nigerian children are not groomed for life in a modern society means that, as they age, they are surrounded with peers none of whom makes the cognitive demands characteristic of that kind of society.

This example structures the environmental explanation I will offer as to why black Americans lose ground on white Americans for IQ as they age. I believe that they tend to live in a distinctive black subculture that offers a less rich spectrum of cognitive environments at every age. And the quality of environments at every stage influences the quality of the environments available at the next stage.

From conception to age 4: nutrition, words, and names

What sets the cognitive level of the social group of which the infant is a part? Its own capacity to respond to stimulation and its parents' performance in offering such.

The pre-natal environment affects the infant's potential at birth. Breslau, Dickens, Flynn, Peterson, and Lucia (2006) have shown that low birth weight (LBW), an indicator of unfavorable pre-natal environment, causes an IQ deficit of 5 points independently of other factors. This deficit persists unaltered until age 17. Nonetheless, I do

---

Box 16

The calculations, for those who enjoy such as much as I do. Comprehensive data show that the birth weight gap between black and white is 0.419 SDs (Martin *et al.*, 2003, table 45). Breslau *et al.* (2006) suggest that when the mothers of LBW children are matched with mothers of similar IQ and levels of education, the correlation between birth weight and IQ is about 0.178. Therefore, the birth weight gap would not account for more than 1.12 points of the racial IQ gap : .419 $\times$ .178 = .0746 SDs; this $\times$ 15 = 1.12 IQ points.

---

not believe that birth weight makes a large contribution to the black/white IQ gap. There is a birth weight gap between black and white, but the correlation between birth weight and IQ is so low that it would make a difference of about one IQ point. That explains something, of course, assuming the handicap persists, thanks to, say, brain physiology damaged by the pre-natal environment (see Box 16).

Turning from the new-born to their mothers, a comparison of black and white suggests one factor that causes a worse black pre-natal environment, namely, nutrition: 4 percent of black mothers suffer from anemia compared to 2 percent of white; about 18 percent of black mothers show a sub-optimal weight gain during pregnancy, about 10 percent of white; 18 percent of black mothers have pre-term infants as compared to 11 percent of white. There may be a causal line running from worse food to less weight gained to pre-maturity. But pre-maturity has already been captured to a considerable degree by low birth weight. Moreover, black mothers when pregnant drink no more and smoke less than white mothers (Martin *et al.*, 2003, tables 25, 28, 31, 43).

If the case that black infants at birth have, on average, less capacity to respond to parental stimulation is lean, the evidence that black parents offer less stimulation is more robust. Black parents themselves are more likely to be in a less cognitively stimulating environment. The black parent is more often than not a solo-mother without the cognitive stimulation of another adult present in the home, more often unemployed or employed in a less cognitively demanding job, and less likely to have the time, energy, or inclination to undertake cognitively demanding leisure pursuits. Solo-parenthood also means a less favorable adult to child ratio in terms of family interaction.

Recall the WISC-IV data showed an IQ gap between children being raised in two-parent homes and one-parent homes, 10 points for blacks and 6 points for whites. Since 63 percent of black children are being raised in one-parent homes and only 23 percent of white children, we have a 40 percent difference between the races. It might seem that this would explain some 2.4 (.40 × 6) to 4 points (.40 × 10) of the racial IQ gap on it own, at least during childhood.

In fact, it is not that simple. Solo-mothers have lower IQs than the mothers in two-parent homes, and since a portion of their own IQ deficit is due to genes, a part of the IQ deficit of their children will be due to genes. Worse still, you cannot just magically transform solo-parent homes into two-parent homes and assume you would be automatically upgrading the home environments. It may be that the kind of person who becomes a solo-mother at present is sometimes someone whose problems have had something to do with that, say alcoholism or neurosis. She might carry those problems over to a two-parent home, so the home created would not have as favorable an environment as the actual two-parent homes we have at present.

Finally, Charles Murray has given me data from the National Longitudinal Survey of Youth (NLSY) that is at variance with the WISC-IV data. After wading through all of this, I conclude that the environmental disadvantage of the greater prevalence of solo-parent homes in the black population could be worth as little as 1.05 IQ points. Anyone who wishes to email me will receive the ten pages of analysis and calculations I have done.

Having assigned a minor role to environmental differences between the races in how home environment affects IQ, I will now suggest that I have probably omitted something significant. It is likely that some kinds of counterproductive child-rearing practices are more common among blacks; and that these have an effect over and above the impact of either pre-natal environment or solo-parenthood. Willerman, Naylor, and Myrianthopoulos (1974) compared two groups: 101 children who had white mothers and black fathers; and 28 children who had black mothers and white fathers. The black-mother children were superior on the Bayley Scales of Infant Development at 8 months, which suggests that they had suffered no disadvantage prior to that age. Fewer of the black mothers were unwed (39.3 percent as compared to 50.5 percent). Yet, at age 4, the mean IQ of the mother-black children on the Stanford-Binet was almost 9 points below that of the mother-white children (Flynn, 1980, pp. 167–171).

Hymowitz (2003) stresses that poor black parents have a quite different image of child-rearing than most white parents. They have not signed up for the "great educational mission" of the middle classes, namely, the constant search, beginning at the day of birth, to find ways of stimulating intellectual growth. Rather they have an image of "natural growth": responsible parents should give their child food and love and all will be well.

In terms of verbal environment, the black child on average is surrounded by less talk. Professional pre-schoolers are exposed to a vocabulary of 2,150 words, working-class children to 1,250, and welfare children to 620. If you ask a black mother on welfare why she does not talk more to her young child, she will say, "Why should I – he can't talk back?" The quality of the talk differs, with the poor black child much more likely to hear commands (dos and don'ts) and reprimands. The mother offers a less effective response to the child's remarks: if a child points out a horse, the mother will say, "yes, that is a horse," but she will not add, "what noise does a horse make?" There is also the factor of modeling: children copy their parents and it is not easy to pretend an interest in ideas and books if you have no interest.

A recent study reveals something so strange that it would cry out to be discounted if the evidence were not so strong. Some black parents are making a mistake in the names they give their children at birth. Figlio (2005) looked at brothers and sisters within the same families and divided them into two groups: those that the parents had given middle-class sounding names like Drew and those that the parents had given lower-class sounding names like Da'Quan. He examined their results on tests of basic skills, not IQ tests but tests that have a high correlation with IQ. The lower-class names were more prevalent among blacks than among whites and accounted for 15 percent of the score gap between the races or the equivalent of 2 IQ points. Figlio speculates that teachers have lower expectation of students with "worse" sounding names. However, lower expectations by any group with whom the children identify could be responsible.

Ages 4 to 12: family versus peers

At about the age of 4, children begin to interact with peers who will eventually swamp the family as the group whose level of cognitive complexity provides primary conditioning.

If black children enter school with a lower IQ than white children, thanks to the poorer cognitive environment of the black home, a factor I call "growing physiological maturity" begins to kick in. In our industrial society, school begins a period in which the pressure on children's cognitive development becomes more and more intense. Equally important, every year brings the brain to a higher level in terms of the cognitive content it has the capacity to handle. If the black peer group enters school manifesting a lower level of cognitive complexity, the escalation of demands on the black child's cognitive development from peers will be less intense than the escalation that envelops the white child. Therefore, black children will not capitalize on their ever-growing cognitive potential as efficiently as white children.

The mind is more like a muscle than we once believed. It is something that must be constantly exercised to attain and maintain peak fitness. Just as an athlete must train harder and harder as he or she matures, so children must think with greater and greater complexity as they pass through school. Blacks tend to fall behind because at each stage their average level of "fitness" is lower. They may want to do as well in school, and even spend as much time on homework, but they are unaccustomed to the kind of mental discipline that is required.

One of the most potent arguments against black genetic equality for IQ has been the relatively poor academic performance of black children from well-to-do black homes. Surely, black teachers and lawyers provide a rich pre-school verbal environment, cultivate their children's cognitive skills, and send them to school ready to identify with achieving peers. And yet, Moore (1986) suggests that they simply do not surround their children with the same kind of cognitive environment that the white middle class establishes.

She compared two groups of black children, twenty-three adopted by white middle-class families and twenty-three adopted by black middle-class families. The white and black adoptive mothers had the same number of years of schooling, that is, sixteen years. As is characteristic of the black middle class, the black fathers did not quite match the white fathers, with 15.6 years of schooling compared to 17.3 years. As a consequence, the income of the black homes was a bit lower, with an SEI (socioeconomic index) of 63.5 compared to 70.3, both quite respectable. When tested at ages 7 to 10, the black-adopted black children had a mean IQ of 103.6, the white-adopted black children a mean of 117.1, a difference of 13.5 IQ points. This is actually somewhat larger than the Dickens/Flynn data would predict at that age (8.5) at that time (1985).

As usual, the numbers are small and bias cannot be ruled out. It is unusual for white parents to adopt a black child and those who do might be unusually focused on making sure the child progresses academically. It is a pity IQs have not been tested as the children matured. I would predict that the 13.5 point advantage the white parents conferred on black children would diminish – recall that this happened in the adoption study conducted by Scarr *et al.* (1993). At 13, all of the black children, whoever their parents, would be ripe for induction into black teenage subculture, whose effects on IQ we will soon explore.

Nonetheless, it is interesting to note what Moore found when she observed (over two 20-minute periods) the mother's interaction with her child while the latter was trying to perform a difficult cognitive task. The mothers were told they could help their children. Although both sets of mothers had the same number of years of education, there was a sharp contrast. White mothers tended to smile, joke, give positive encouragement (that is an interesting idea), and applaud effort. Black mothers tended to frown, scowl, criticize (you know that doesn't look right), and express displeasure (you could do better than this if you really tried). Understandably, children were more likely to ask for help from white than black mothers when confronted with cognitive problems.

Ages 13 to 17: the teenage subculture

Advisors often see students who have not capitalized on their full potential and who now wish to excel. The best advice is not to expect hard work to immediately pay off in terms of good grades. They simply have not acquired the information, sophistication of style, and intuition as to what on the page is most salient that good students have, and some two years of unusual effort are needed to achieve this. But the hardest advice to give goes beyond study time and study habits.

It often becomes clear that a serious student should seek out new companions who are more challenging and more disciplined than those who have been their social circle up to now. Very few teenagers can be expected to introduce such a social revolution in their lives.

Here we must pause to summarize a controversy. Cook and Ludwig (1998) give survey data that suggest that black youths are actually more pro-education than whites. Sowell (1972; 1975; 2000, p. 222) provides anecdotal evidence drawn from his life as a black

student and black educator. He believes that blacks respect education in the abstract but do not appreciate the need for persistence,
uninterrupted work, and an atmosphere conducive to intellectual
interests. Rather, families and peers reinforce achievements with
immediate appeal – athletic triumphs, musical promise – more than
those that require self-denial or long-range planning. He recounts
sadly how often he has sat in a university library and has seen black
students as the last to arrive, the slowest to get down to work, the
most easily distracted, and the first to leave.

The Harvard sociologist Orlando Patterson (2006) may reconcile these two views. He argues that black males do not despise education and are aware of the benefits it brings, but that their youth
culture offers rewards that they cannot resist. Dressing sharply,
hanging out, sexual conquests, party drugs, and hip-hop music and
culture are powerfully attractive, and the admiration they get from
both black and white peers bolsters self-esteem. White teenagers find
imitating the postures of this culture attractive but they do not live
it. Rather it is a hobby, something they set aside every time they think
of the looming presence of the SAT (Scholastic Aptitude Test) that will
determine their fate.

Perhaps survey data can be supplemented with something
that helps us penetrate to the reality of black youth culture (cameras
that record what actually goes on during the hours of homework
reported?). For now, I will add my own impressions for what they are
worth. It seems to me that a subculture that legislates atypical
speech and puts song and dance ahead of cognitively demanding
leisure activity has to be a negative influence

Ages 18 to 24 and after: jail, motherhood, and jobs

After high school, blacks continue to lose IQ ground to whites at a
rapid rate, at least to age 24. Therefore, an environmental hypothesis must posit that the environmental gap between black and white
continues to grow significantly between those ages.

As we have seen, for black males, incarceration is often an imminent after-school experience. For those between the ages 20 and 29, 40 percent find themselves in jail and subsequently on parole or on probation. More black males go to jail than attend college (Drucker, 2003, p. 155). This does not mean they spend four years in jail rather than four years in college. Their time of actual incarceration may be either long or short. But it means that they are more often surrounded with a peer group on the fringe of criminal activity rather than a peer group working hard to get a university degree.

Although the black IQ loss may slow down at about age 24, it still takes a gradual toll. Therefore, current environment must become at least a bit worse (versus white current environment) than it was during school or early adulthood. I suspect that the immersion of both black and white in formal schooling is a leveler that begins to disappear at age 18. It continues in weakened form between ages 18 and 23 because, after all, many blacks do get tertiary education, particularly black women.

After age 23, the school leveling effect is entirely gone. Black women in particular face solo-parenthood and comparative isolation from other adults; blacks in general get less cognitively demanding jobs; blacks are less likely to engage in cognitively demanding leisure pursuits. All of the things are operative that we noted when diagnosing why black parents are less likely to provide a stimulating environment for infants. We have come full circle.

Even the fact that blacks may start to close the IQ gap with whites at age 65, while poorly evidenced, makes sense. Raising children under more difficult conditions no longer afflicts black women; the death of white males has left more white women without constant adult company; people have retired from their jobs. This may be the time of life when the current cognitive environments of black and white are becoming more equal.

Black IQ c. 2002

Figure 2 provides the latest data as to where black IQ stands today. At every age, blacks are normed on whites (not including Hispanics) set at an IQ of 100. It shows the decline with age that I have attempted to explain in terms of a succession of environmental factors. It also shows that the day when the black–white IQ gap could be put at 15 points as a sort of eternal fixture, like using the stars to navigate, is gone forever. Blacks are quite capable of reducing the IQ gap if the environmental gap between the races lessens. It seems incredible that anyone ever believed the contrary. You can now put the racial IQ gap at anything from 4.6 to 16.6 points depending on the age you select between 4 and 24. As a consequence of the ground gained over time, blacks aged 4 have an IQ of 95.4.

In Figure 2, the 0 represents birth. The solid vertical line just before 0 represents conception and the broken vertical line just after 0 represents 10 months old. I have hypothesized that blacks are at 100 at conception (equal to whites) and have fallen to 99 by 10 months old, which allows for a one point loss due to inferior pre-natal environment. Our analysis showed this loss to be a reasonable assumption. But is there any evidence that blacks really are this high at 10 months? This brings us to an interesting recent study.

Frier and Levitt (2006) report results from the Early Childhood Longitudinal Survey Birth Cohort (ECLS-B). Representative samples of black and white infants (aged 8 to 12 months) were given the BSF-R, a shortened version of the Bayley Scale of Infant Development. This test has a higher correlation with later IQ than any other infant intelligence test, but the correlation is still modest (it stabilizes at 0.30 at about 5 years of age). It "tests" for babbling, reaching for and holding objects, using another object to get a toy that is out of reach, using words, and trying to discover what makes the ringing sound in a bell (see Box 17). The difference between black and white children was too small to be statistically significant but black children were slightly below at an "IQ" of 99.04.

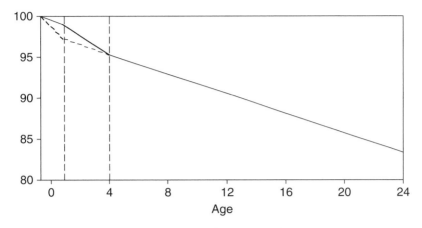

Figure 2 Estimates of black IQ from conception to age 24

Box 17

Scholars at Columbia have pointed out that offering a description of an infant intelligence test is dangerous. After the last reference to one in print, 872 parents in New York City drove their
infants insane by constantly ringing bells at them. No racial
breakdown was provided because it was considered politically
sensitive.

The solid line in Figure 2 takes this study seriously and
shows an interesting pattern. From conception to 10 months, blacks
lose ground on whites at exactly the same rate (.60 points per year)
as they do from ages 4 to 24. But from 10 months to 4 years, their
environment deteriorates at almost twice the rate, which suggests
that Willerman and Hymowitz were right in directing our attention
to parent–child interaction in early childhood. The broken line in
Figure 2 discounts the study and suggests that pre-natal and early
post-natal environment is the period of greatest deterioration.
Clearly both periods are worthy of intense scrutiny.

Hoping for a reprieve

What do we know? First, we know that the black–white IQ gap disappeared in Germany. But the numbers are scant, there are unknowns that could have biased the results, and one study should not convince anyone. Second, that the g pattern disappeared in Germany. This shows that the German environment at least addressed the root causes of the IQ gap insofar as it is environmental, something America does not seem to have done to date. The contrast focuses attention on the peculiar black subculture that exists in America. Third, what causes the g pattern is a special inability to deal with cognitive problems the more complex they become. Therefore, we would do well to look at anything in the American black subculture that signals a less cognitively complex environment.

Fourth, about a third of the traditional black–white IQ gap has disappeared. This is encouraging, but we do not know whether it is due to hearing aids or addressing root causes. Fifth, there is reason to believe that the black loss of ground on whites with age is environmental. I believe this is plausible because of the steady trend to lose 0.6 IQ points per year after infancy. But more to the point, at each age, there seem to be environmental factors that would engender a less complex cognitive environment. Sixth, if that is so, and if hints that black and white are equal in terms of their genotype for IQ at conception are not deceptive, then the entire black–white IQ gap is environmental. The number of "ifs" tells the reader why I believe all conclusions are tentative. And why I said at the start that anyone who claims to know that black and white are genetically equal for IQ is too bold.

The race and IQ debate has raged for almost forty years. I have been entangled in it for thirty years. It has been a constant and unwelcome companion, rather like living with an uncongenial spouse from an arranged marriage. It has occupied the time of legions of scholars and laid waste acres of trees. Will we ever see the end of it? At least the debate is entering a new and more sophisticated stage. Given the relatively high values for black IQ in infancy and age 4, the focus should now be on whatever causes the decline of black IQ (compared to white) with age. If that can be settled, the main event will be over.

The significance of the debate should not be exaggerated. Everything I say in this book about what afflicts American blacks, the injustices they suffer because of their group membership, and what could be done to give them access to a good life is untouched by the outcome. If there is a genetic component in the racial IQ gap, blacks as a group will always have less favorable statistics compared to whites for academic achievement, occupation, income, and mortality. However, the intense feelings that surround this question are largely a product of human misery. If America afforded access to a good life to all of its citizens, blacks would have about as much interest in why there are fewer black than Irish doctors as Irish have about why there are fewer Irish than Chinese accountants.

4 Do we want affirmative action for whites only?

> From a black perspective . . . the notion that a black [who passes
> for white] might reclaim his ethnic identity to take advantage
> of preferential admissions can only trigger an almost
> inexpressible sense of outrage.
>
> > (J. C. Livingston, 1979)

We return to market analysis. Costs are important in making decisions, not only market decisions but also decisions by public officials
about how to allocate scarce resources. The cost of information is
often central to a decision and there is a trade-off between cost and
quality. Even rough information may be preferred if the cost is virtually nil and the price of better information is great. I will argue that
black skin provides information at a bargain price and that blacks
suffer as a consequence purely because of their group membership.

    The reason black skin provides information is that it can
allow rational actors to predict behavior, or at least make statistical
predictions. Once again, it makes sense to act on statistics if more
accurate information relevant to an individual's behavior would be
costly. Social scientists are often naïve on this point. They say, "It
makes no difference if we show that blacks on average are less
prudent and self-disciplined than whites and tend more often to be
criminal. Only a biased person will discriminate against people
according to their group membership rather than judging them by
their individual traits."

    Sophisticated social scientists know that this last asser-
tion is demonstrably false. They know that honesty about the facts

sometimes means less social justice and therefore are tempted to suppress their data. This is wrong because it is too crippling of the long-term human quest to understand the world. But even in the short run, accurate data are usually less damaging to a disadvantaged group than allowing popular stereotypes to go uncorrected. I want to stress that rational actors who disadvantage blacks may well not internalize any bias against blacks as such. Herrnstein and Murray (1994, p. 506) believe that, while undeniably some bigotry still exists, the majority of Americans are fair-minded and free of racial prejudice. Rather than challenging that conclusion, I will treat it as a window of opportunity. If I can show that even in the absence of bias, individual blacks are gravely disadvantaged simply because of their group membership, we would have the strongest possible case for affirmative action.

Race as an information-bearing trait: the police

Levin (1991) points out that race can be an information-bearing trait. He cites facts we have already shown to be true: for example, that one black male in three is incarcerated at some time for the commission of a felony, while the rate for white males is only about 3 percent. Therefore, a random black male is ten times more likely than his white counterpart to be a criminal.

He endorses the practice of the police of stopping young black males in expensive new cars for random drug searches. After all, police resources are stretched, and their ability to control the drug traffic is maximized by information that enhances the probability of finding illegal drugs. The dividends of targeting extend to other areas of crime prevention. As police officer Mark Furhman of O. J. Simpson fame put it, if a black man is driving a Porsche and wearing a suit that costs less than $100, you stop him on the assumption that the car may be stolen. Anyone who listens to a police radio will discover that blacks who walk through a white neighborhood are labeled suspicious, while whites in a black neighborhood go without remark (except as to their lack of prudence).

It is rational for police to use race as a low-cost information bearer to enhance their efficiency. Is it rational for blacks to resent this and take steps to make the information more expensive? A few examples may help.

Irish Americans have a rate of alcoholism well above that of most ethnic groups. When resources are stretched, as always, and the highway patrol is conducting random checks for drunken drivers, they would do well to stop only Irish male drivers, particularly where Irish are heavily concentrated. The problem is that they cannot be identified by appearance, and stopping all drivers to verify whether or not they were Irish would be self-defeating. Irish could be forced, and everyone else forbidden, to drive green cars, but that law might be evaded. The rational solution would be shamrocks indelibly tattooed on the foreheads of all Irish males, perhaps luminescent at night. There would be a cost in this, but it could be shifted to the Irish themselves. Levin also notes that people associate insider trading with Jewish Americans. This association may not be based on evidence, and the resources of the Securities and Exchange Commission may not be stretched. But if those conditions hold, the utility of Stars of David becomes obvious.

Every black knows that Irish and Jewish Americans would raise the cost of collecting this sort of information to a prohibitive level by political action of the most impassioned sort. Black efforts to ban the use of racial profiles have had mainly a cosmetic effect: police omit race from the criteria of criminal profiles but continue to use it in practice. Therefore, added to whatever humiliation blacks feel at random searches, there is a sense of overwhelming political impotence. Since blacks cannot use politics to raise the cost of profiling, it is almost inevitable that they will pursue other means both individually and collectively.

On the individual level, those stopped for random searches will tend toward non-cooperation, verbal abuse, attempts at escape with attendant low-level violence. The police, being rational agents, are likely to anticipate this and resort to preventive measures, that is, they are more likely to handle and search black suspects roughly, even to perpetrate the occasional beating, hoping to intimidate and achieve control. The black community can collectively increase costs to the police by making it clear that if black suspects are abused, there is an ever-present chance of riot.

You now have a significant level of random violence between police and black males, but there need be no animosity or real bias on either side. Black males may not dislike police simply because they are police nor police blacks simply because they are black. Both sides may recognize that the other's behavior is simply a rational response to objective group differences. David Stove (1995, p. 95) provides an observation that takes us back to reality: even rational behavior, just so long as it inflicts injury, can engender strong negative feelings between groups. It can indeed.

Police use race as an information bearer to justify giving blacks atypical attention. There is considerable debate about whether they use it as a rationale for atypical neglect. The incentives are complex. On the one hand, solving violent crimes in the black ghetto might require a disproportionate investment of time and energy and be given low priority. Livingston (1979, pp. 44–45) reports a homicide detective who gave what he called a "niggericide," the killing of one ghetto black by another, a much lower priority than other homicides. The term is obnoxious, of course, and it is unlikely that it was used playfully.

On the other hand, if promotion depends on a high rate of arrests and convictions, police would be motivated to pursue blacks with vigor. In 1996, the National Black Police Association gave me data that indicate that blacks suffer from too proactive law enforcement. Between 1941 and 1994, twenty-three black police were shot by their white colleagues in New York City alone (Charles and Coleman, 1995). In the 1994 incident, the officer was shot five times, leaving him with a permanent disability. The Review Board set up at that time interviewed more than eighty police officers of all races. Chief Bracey said: "Just like white officers, black officers indicated that they were more apprehensive if there was a black male with a gun. Whether you want to face it or not, blacks are committing a lot of crimes. But a black cop has never shot another officer while on duty or in civilian clothes or killed him."

Corvet Curley, a black officer of thirteen years' experience, found that being in uniform is not necessarily a protection (Hanley, 1997). His right thigh was shattered by the blast from a white trooper's shotgun at a toll plaza on the George Washington Bridge as he stood, in uniform with his gun drawn, near the wrecked getaway car of an ex-convict. Surgeons at the Columbia-Presbyterian Medical Center in Manhattan saved Curley's leg during an eight-hour operation.

Race as an information-bearing trait: loans, rooms, prices, jobs

Thomas Sowell shares little of the author's political program. However, he has done much to illuminate how the cost of information affects banks, landlords, employers, and retail outlets in their treatment of blacks. There are two relevant costs: the cost of classifying blacks as members of their group, which, thanks to their appearance, is nil; the cost of determining whether a black is an exemplary individual, which can be significant.

For example, take a bank that has an excess of apparently sound white applicants for loans over the amount of funds it has to lend. The bank knows that blacks on average have less managerial experience, that their businesses tend to be undercapitalized, that their failure rate is higher, that their collateral is less salable. All in all, the bank knows that the risk of non-payment is greater. It can conduct a thorough investigation of a particular black applicant to determine whether he or she is an exception to the group. But unless its competitors also do so, it has incurred an extra cost to its

116

disadvantage. Therefore, the bank will tend to assess the black applicant as a member of his or her group and refuse the loan.

Landlords also use race as an information-bearing trait. Take a widow with a room to let. A Korean American female and a black American male knock on her door. The cost of hiring a private detective to check them out as individuals is prohibitive. She will use a group profile and make a statistical decision. Asian female affords a good chance of a tenant who is docile, will please neighbors thanks to sobriety and reticence, will be prompt and reliable in paying rent. Black male means a significant chance of someone who is criminal, destructive, noisy, and insolvent. In every such case, the cost of investigating individuals is high and the cost of identifying race nil.

It is easy to show that minimizing costs is a rational factor not tied to racial bias. Sowell (1994, pp. 11, 114) cites the evidence of Light and Williams that successful black banks tend to invest outside the black community even more than white banks do. He cites Tucker, who found that black landlords as well as white landlords prefer white tenants.

Clearly, similar considerations extend to other areas. Retailers who provide goods and services in the ghetto bear higher costs, not only losses from theft and vandalism but from installing iron grates and hiring security guards. These higher costs are passed on to ghetto residents in the form of higher prices. New car dealers assume blacks will be less knowledgeable and less confident in bargaining, and therefore name and get higher prices (Ayers and Siegelman, 1995).

The fact that employers see race as a cheap signal of an applicant's skills, motivation, and attitudes toward authority has been amply documented (Kirschenman *et al.*, 1996). A recent study was particularly revealing. Bertrand and Mullainathan (2003) sent 5,000 résumés randomly assigned to either white or black sounding names (Emily and Greg or Lakisha and Jamal) to 1,250 employers who had placed help-wanted ads. The white names received 50 percent more callbacks. Indeed, average white applicants got many more callbacks than highly skilled black applicants; and high-quality black résumés got no more calls than average black résumés. Which is to say that black applicants were treated as if their qualifications did not matter.

Human resources managers consulted beforehand were stunned. They believed that the results would reflect employers hungry for qualified minority applicants and aggressively seeking diversity. As Sowell (1994, p. 89) says, "It is bitter medicine to the fully qualified individual to be denied employment because of the racial, ethnic, or other group to which he belongs."

The price of just being black

Hersch (2008) found that just being black is a magnet that attracts ill fortune even for those who are not African Americans. Using data from the New Immigrant Survey 2003, she showed that skin color affected wages among new legal immigrants after controlling for education, English language proficiency, occupation before arrival, family background, country of birth, ethnicity, and race. Immigrants with the lightest skin color earn on average 17 percent more than comparable immigrants with the darkest skin color. It turns out that being short is also bad. Each extra inch of height above the US average was associated with a 2 percent increase in wages.

As for survival, looking black holds dangers for African American males beyond being shot by the police. A very black male looks more deathworthy than one less black. Eberhardt *et al.* (2006) divided black males convicted of murder into forty-four whose victims had been white and 308 whose victims had been black. Although 41 percent of the former received death sentences, this was true for only 27 percent of the latter.

When the photos of the defendants were ranked from most to least stereotypically black in appearance, records showed that appearance made no difference in cases where the victim was black. But when the victim was white, it made a big difference. Even after factors like mitigating or aggravating circumstances, severity of the murder, and defendant's SES were matched, the half of the distribution classed as most "black" received a death sentence 57.5 percent of the time. The half classed as less so, only 24.4 percent of the time. The latter is almost identical with death sentence percentage for black males whose victims were black. Thus, black males are 2.4 times as likely to get the death sentence if they look very black and happen to murder a white. The authors speculate that juries look upon the black–white cases as interracial conflict and the black–black cases as merely interpersonal conflict.

A phrase I have consistently used must not pass unnoticed: that the cost of classifying an individual as black is negligible. This puts blacks at a disadvantage compared to white ethnic groups because the cost of classifying the members of those groups can be expensive. When Mr. Bell comes to your door, it may be almost impossible to determine that his father is Mr. Bellini and that he has strong ties with suspect elements in the Italian community.

Imagine an omnipresent mutation that left blacks exactly as they are except their appearances became a random sample of white America. Overnight the cost of classifying blacks as such, of identifying the people who had once been black, would be far too great for anyone to pay, whether police, bank manager, landlord, retailer, or employer. Certainly, the phenomenon of being more likely to be shot by the police and being more likely to get the death penalty would disappear overnight. Disadvantage among the no-longer blacks because of group membership would fade into the lesser disadvantages of class or neighborhood. Blackness really does make a difference.

White awareness of the price of being black

In chapter 2, we saw how the reluctance of white men to marry black women helped to produce a marriage market devastating for black family structure. This may seem puzzling. After all, a white man in a long-term relationship with a black woman gets to know her as an individual without extra cost and need not react to her as a member of her group. What deters white men from having and raising children with black women is their knowledge of the disadvantages of being born black in America. White women do not welcome disadvantaging their children either. But in our society, a woman's self-esteem is much more tied to the achievements of her spouse. Therefore, the prize of an outstanding black man can be a heavy counterweight. Within all minority groups, even those for whom interracial marriage is far more frequent than it is for blacks, men marry out more often than women.

So on one level whites are aware of the significance of being black. But on another level they do not want to know. My purpose has been to raise knowledge to the level of awareness and to note that the role of crude racial bias is limited. Most of the black experience in America is dictated purely by a rational response to objective group differences. On the other hand, there may still be one or two racists left in American society, and, if so, racial prejudice will encumber blacks with additional negative experiences.

Needless to say, I, like Thomas Sowell, lament the consequences. Two-thirds of black males are never convicted of a felony, and most blacks are good workers, tenants, and neighbors. That is the whole point: they suffer because of bad luck in terms of group membership. A few white Americans will have such a strong sense of fair play that it will override self-interested decision making. Given what Adam is like and given what Eve is like, there will not be many. Blacks will suffer disadvantage until group differences alter. No one expects police to search white matrons in suburban neighborhoods for drugs as often as they do young black males.

Affirmative action for blacks

What are the available remedies? Legislation to force banks, landlords, employers, and retailers to treat blacks as individuals or as typical consumers is clumsy and often counterproductive.

Sowell (1994, pp. 206–207) details how laws have been evaded when rational responses to group differences dictated non-compliance. The best historical example benefited blacks. Prior to the abolition of slavery, Southern cities passed law after law against teaching slaves to read or write, forbidding them access to bars and prostitutes, forbidding paying them wages, all to no avail, because employers could hire skilled blacks more cheaply than they could their white counterparts. Legislation will never circumvent human ingenuity, or abolish discretion, or close off private networks, unless you recruit an army of secret police. It will not even touch the extra risks to the lives of black males or the marriage market of black females.

Since we cannot address adequately the specific evils blacks suffer, compensation must come in other areas. The public service is not subject to market pressures, and preferential entry into jobs can compensate for disadvantage in the private sector. Public housing can compensate for disadvantage in the private housing market. Efforts must be made to upgrade the ghetto, but for many the only solution is escape, and preferential access to education provides a means. The consequences of affirmative action programs must be carefully assessed because good intentions are not enough. They are meant, after all, to benefit blacks, not harm them. Blacks who have attended elite universities (and few would do so without affirmative action) have benefited in terms of both graduation rates and income (Kane, 1998). However, some were so unprepared that their courses became a bizarre non-learning experience (Sowell, 1972). It is no service to anyone to go to a university or have a job whose demands they cannot meet and to spend their time feeling humiliated and defeated.

A case for compensation must answer the question of how much. America already compensates blacks in a variety of ways. Perhaps compensation has already gone too far and should be diminished. The empirical task of assessing whether benefits conferred counterbalance disadvantages suffered because of group membership may be beyond the wisdom of a Solomon. Therefore, I

Box 18

This question will remind some philosophers of Rawls. He imagines people ignorant of what they need to know to calculate their interests and asks them to tell him what kind of society they would want in the light of their interests. I will comment on the oddity of this later. My question is quite different. It is addressed to real people, namely, contemporary white Americans whom I assume to be quite knowledgeable of where their interests lie in an ongoing society.

---

will suggest a criterion for an easier task, namely, determining how many American whites *really believe* that compensation has gone too far.

It consists of a question: How many whites would choose to become black, assuming continuity of those personal traits like intelligence and motivation most relevant to achievement? (See Box 18.) If white Americans really believe blacks are advantaged beyond their competence in American society, then any rational white should find the black experience attractive. What is being chosen, of course, is a black life history, to have had a black past, have a black present, and face a black future. It may be objected that a different socialization would have produced a different human being. Very well, we will guarantee not only continuity of personal traits but of core personality, so as to solve the problem of personal identity.

Ethnic identity or group pride can also act as a distracter. Many whites take considerable pride in being an Irish American or an Italian American. Many blacks know that it would be advantageous to be white but would not choose to join a group toward whom they have developed a certain degree of ambivalence. For whites with a significant degree of ethnic identity, the best way to honestly confront our question is this: assume you are being forced to give up your present ethnic identity; choose between being black and a white identity that awakens no special sense of belonging, perhaps being an Icelandic American.

Some of these complications can be avoided by reformulating the question: Were you and your partner to die soon after the birth of a child, would you prefer that child to be raised by black adoptive parents or white adoptive parents? Assume that the two couples were matched for personal traits and that the child would magically absorb the skin color of the parents, so as to eliminate any alienation arising out of different appearance. Most people care as much for the welfare of their children as they do for themselves, and if few whites would choose the black option, there is a prima facie case that few of them believe that the black experience has become a privileged one.

The principle that blacks merit compensation because of bad luck in their group membership may be accepted as a prima facie one, and yet objections may be posed as candidates to override it. A frequent objection is that blacks will sometimes be compensated at the expense of whites even more disadvantaged. That is true, and the ideal would be to collect information about individual differences that would allow us to isolate such cases and make exceptions. But if the price of this information is prohibitive, then we must choose between accepting affirmative action without it and abandoning affirmative action. The argument against abandoning affirmative action is clear: failure to compensate blacks because that would injure disadvantaged white individuals will leave an even greater number of black individuals injured without compensation. So is the price of the information prohibitive?

Affirmative action for veterans

I believe it can be shown to be so by analyzing the case of veterans' compensation (Ezorsky, 1991, pp. 79, 91). This program was by no means negligible. After World War II, America decided to compensate over 10 million people who had served in the armed forces, a group that inclusive of their immediate families outnumbered blacks. Veterans received preferential entry into civil service jobs and targeted benefits, ranging from subsidized education and health care to pensions, special hospitals, and retirement homes. Veterans often benefited at the expense of non-veterans who were more disadvantaged. Ideally, there would have existed some sort of ambulatory philosopher king, a source of walking wisdom, who would say, "This Boston Brahman had a cushy job in army supply, while this Polish American spent the war in Gary, Indiana, working in a dangerous mill." Therefore, no preference.

That was not a realistic alternative. The only real-world alternative imaginable is a semi-judicial inquiry with the brief of assessing the advantages and disadvantages of life histories. The cost of that sort of information about individual differences would include unacceptable invasions of privacy, enormous difficulties in securing testimony and assessing its reliability and relevance, huge expenditures in time and money.

Affirmative action for blacks does indeed use the crude device of group membership as an information-bearing trait. It is odd that this is castigated as so morally objectionable, when innumerable Americans commit exactly the same sin: the police, the banks, the landlords, the employers, and the juries. They use race to make statistical judgments about personal traits. Affirmative action uses race to make a judgment that is beyond dispute: some people on average have suffered much more because of their group membership than others.

To burden affirmative action with collecting information about individual differences would sink it, because the relevant information carries the highest cost imaginable. Thanks to the market, banks, landlords, and employers are not willing to abandon their present practices even though the information needed to be fair is considerably less costly. American after American finds the cost of information about individual differences too high when disadvantaging blacks. To use such costs to forbid benefiting blacks makes an interesting exception to the rule.

Affirmative action for whites

The real difference between veterans' preference and affirmative action is that America really did want to confer a group benefit on veterans, and America is ambivalent about conferring a group benefit on blacks. This ambivalence is striking when we reflect on why blacks need compensation. The very essence of racial profiles is to confer a group benefit on whites while ignoring individual differences among blacks. They amount to nothing less than a systemic affirmative action program that gives whites special access to loans, housing, jobs, an advantageous marriage market, driving and walking the streets without harassment, getting a fair jury trial. Whites do not think of this as special access, of course, because it is only special compared to what blacks get.

When affirmative action for whites causes a problem, why is affirmative action for blacks objectionable as a remedy? The question that faces America is not whether it shall have affirmative action: it has had it for almost four centuries. Affirmative action for whites began the day the first black was brought to America as a slave and has persisted right up to the present. The only question is whether affirmative action for whites is to be balanced by a measure of affirmative action for blacks.

It may be said that the case for veterans' preference was based on the fact that they were better than others, suffered because they defended their country, while the case for affirmative action is based on the fact that blacks are worse than others. They suffer many of their ills because their group is the most criminal and dysfunctional. This reaction shows, more than anything else, how thoroughly judging people in terms of group membership permeates our thinking. In reply: individuals are not responsible for the behavior of their group; if innocent blacks suffer because of group profiles, no matter what the social reality behind those profiles, they deserve compensation.

The champions of lower-class blacks

Another objection pushed as a candidate to override the principle of compensating blacks is that benefits go disproportionately to the black middle class. If this were a constructive criticism, it would engender proposals to target programs to ensure that lower-class blacks benefit. Public housing is likely to attract a largely working-class clientele; special bonuses for teachers and administrators can be used to upgrade ghetto schools; clinics and other amenities can be located in working-class areas; educational programs for basic job skills, budgeting, knowledge of welfare rights, and fertility control can be directed toward those areas. These proposals by the champions of the black poor are rarely forthcoming.

A good test of the sincerity of those who claim sympathy with lower-class blacks is whether they have no objection to preferential entry into the lower, as distinct from the upper, levels of the civil service. It is always hardest to benefit the most demoralized members of any group. But it is not sensible to benefit no blacks at all because benefits cannot be class-neutral within the black community. Would it make sense to exclude middle-class blacks from benefits? Only if it could be done without excessive costs, which is highly unlikely, and only if it is contended that they have prospered to the point that they suffer no significant disadvantage because of their group membership.

That contention suggests a variant of the original question we put to white Americans: How many whites who are clearly middle class would choose a black life history, assuming continuity of personal traits and core personality?

This last reminds us that our original question has gone unanswered. I prefer the adoption formulation of the question: How many whites would be indifferent as to whether their newborn child got white or black adoptive parents, assuming a match for traits and color? It would be difficult to conduct an honest opinion survey. But, as Plato in *The Republic* said of justice, has not the answer to this question been lying unnoticed at our feet all the time? The reader will know by now what I mean: the pathetically low rate of black and white Americans raising children together. White after white, despite powerful sexual attraction, has chosen not to make their children black because they know, they know very well, that to do so would be to give their children bad luck in terms of group membership. Even the violent and drunken Irish, the hyperemotional and clannish Italians, the stolid and Pinochle-playing Poles found it easy to marry out. But does anyone want to marry blacks? They do not.

And yet, during slavery, when they did not have to care about their children's prospects, white men fathered numerous black children. I am not stating a general thesis, something like, whenever there is little intermarriage between white Americans and an ethnic group, whites must be skeptical about the life prospects of the members of that group. Orthodox Jews and the Amish have built a fortress around themselves to preserve an atypical way of life. Obviously, their low rates of intermarriage do not signal whether they are regarded as disadvantaged or advantaged in terms of opportunity. Surely no one believes that such cases are relevant. Neither whites nor blacks have voluntarily turned their back on the mainstream of American society, and their failure to intermarry has its own peculiar significance.

The notion that whites believe blacks of any class are privileged is suspect. A society that acknowledges that the members of a group suffer much because of their group membership and yet gives high-minded reasons for refusing to compensate them as such forfeits a measure of respect.

From race to class

This analysis does not assume that justice requires equal outcomes for black and white. It merely aims at a situation where whites believe there is an equal chance of equal outcomes, assuming traits relevant to competence are held constant. If such traits are unequally distributed between the races, outcomes will not be equal. It also makes no assumptions about the origin of group differences, about whether they are caused by genetic or environmental differences or a combination of the two.

The case for affirmative action has a value that transcends its effectiveness in producing tangible results. It is priceless as a pedagogical exercise. Even if one rejects all programs to put affirmative action into practice, nothing can substitute for the education the case itself offers about the realities of race. It forces us to acknowledge the privileges the market confers on whites, the disadvantages suffered by blacks. The programs that institutionalize affirmative action will always be on the fringes of public tolerance. Privilege dies hard when it can defend itself with moral indignation and talk about injustice. The most important instrument to remedy the state of black America will always be a color-blind but robust welfare state. That brings us to the significance of class.

PART III

Yours for a better world

5 Saving equality from the dustbin of history

If we take for granted as common knowledge that a just and well-ordered society is impossible, then the quality and tone of those discussions will reflect that knowledge.

(John Rawls, speaking to Joshua Cohen, 1995)

Turning an elephant loose in a crowd offers everyone, except the beast and his rider, equal opportunities of being trampled.

(R. H. Tawney, 1931)

The old friend to whom this book is dedicated always signed his letters, "yours for a better world." He was a Jeffersonian of Democratic Socialist persuasion whose idealism never faltered, although the stonewall of indifference he battered himself against had something to do with his alcoholism and early death. He was sustained by the fact that, however negative the reception, his egalitarian ideals would have benevolent consequences if they prevailed. It is hard to see how anyone could persist without this kind of expectation. He also had a vision of a better America that would promote peace rather than conflict on the international scene.

Part III consists of three chapters that argue that such hopes and expectations have substance. Our first task is to defend the viability of egalitarian ideals. This brings us back to *The Bell Curve*. What with the sound and fury of race, both its fans and its critics ignored its main challenge, perhaps because it was too hope-destructive to face. I refer to the meritocracy thesis.

Abandon all hope

The meritocracy thesis is simply stated: (1) assume we make progress toward the equalization of environments – to the degree that occurs, all remaining talent differences between people will be due to differences in genes for talent; (2) assume we make progress toward abolition of privilege – to the degree that occurs, there will be a social mobility that brings all of the good genes to the top and allows all bad genes to sink to the bottom; (3) therefore, the upper classes will become a genetic elite whose children inherit their status because of superior merit, while the lower classes become a self-perpetuating genetic dump, too stupid to be of use in the modern word, an underclass that is underemployed, criminal, and prone to drugs and illegitimacy.

Such a thesis does nothing less than imply that humane-egalitarian ideals self-destruct in practice. Somehow it is perceived as a challenge for the left. I would have thought that it posed a challenge for both left and right in that, whatever their differences about the sanctity of the market, both the democratic left and the democratic right share Jefferson's dream (the American dream) of a people none of whom is crippled by circumstance or inheritance from pursuing an individual quest for self-perfection.

Whatever ideal the thousands that laid down their lives for social reform or the defense of the Republic may have had, it was not this: a class system frozen into a caste system by a genetic inequality enhanced by every step toward social justice. Although I will analyze the meritocracy thesis from the perspective of a Social Democrat, most of my critique has to do with social dynamics and is apolitical.

The degeneration of the school race

The meritocracy thesis is a classic case of a model that is underidentified, that is, a model whose applicability is not grounded in a real-world scenario. To rank everyone by genes for talent, a competition must be such that all actors are motivated to the maximum degree

---

Box 19

Tawney's image of an elephant loose in a crowd (above) is brilliant. When something that lacks respect for humanity, in all of its diversity, dictates our fate, equal opportunity is not much compensation. The market economy of the boarding school is worse than the one we have, but there is no reason why both should not be tamed so as to trample on fewer people's aspirations.

---

and compete on an equal footing. Let us try to make good its omissions by way of a real-world example of a meritocracy.

Imagine a boarding school at which all cash must be earned by how well you do in the annual cross-country race. Everyone gets an equal chance; all are provided with the same excellent coaching, health care, diet, and so forth. But the stakes are high: if you win, you get cash enough to meet all your needs with ample pocket money left over. If you are last, you starve unless your classmates are willing to sustain you by private charity.

I have little doubt that all would train and try for the annual race to their utmost and that the results would rank everyone pretty well for their genes for distance running ability. But note why its draconian sanctions are necessary. The system creates enormous tension between what society forces you to do and what you ideally want to do. Those who prefer chess, or the literary magazine, or even other sports, will have to sacrifice these to hours and hours of training for something many of them loathe. When told it is a meritocracy, they will label it a bastard meritocracy because of all the human excellences it sacrifices on the altar of its competitive ideal (see Box 19).

Let us chip away at the system a bit. The stakes of the race are altered so that everyone gets the quality of environment from year to year needed to maximize performance. After all, should the bad performance of a single year doom you to failure the following year? So now we have a welfare state that gives everyone the coaching, food, lodging, medical care, they need to compete on an equal footing. All that is now at stake is whether you get ample or no pocket money. Even this might be enough to sustain near maximum training and effort. But now assume you can get some, though much less, pocket money by excelling in other activities more to the taste of many: chess, algebra, the school paper, the poetry society, shop, other sports. Few will now do the full Lydiard schedule of running 100 miles per week. Most will settle for the 15 miles per week sufficient to race at 10 seconds per mile slower than your optimum pace.

Moreover, every individual who does this lowers the quality of performance needed to run an average time in the race. And when that happens, some will find they can do pretty well by training 10 miles a week, which will further lower the average performance, which will further lower the training you need to do to be average, in a downward spiral. This concept of a social "multiplier effect" is borrowed from the Dickens/Flynn model of intelligence: it means simply that a rising or falling average performance becomes a potent causal factor in its own right. In any event, the school race has degenerated in the sense that it no longer ranks people very well even for genes for running ability.

We have learned three lessons: (1) A competition for money must include a robust welfare state or it is not fair. (2) Money rewards tend to create a tension between what society wants and what I want to do to realize my own chosen excellence. (3) Unless the penalties for not acceding to what society wants are draconian (and they cannot be if the competition is to be fair), it will fall short of even a bastard meritocracy. It will not achieve a perfect ranking of genes even for the talents it rewards. And the less draconian the penalties, the more that sane people will be inclined to pursue other talents and build a true meritocracy.

Keeping the competition fair

I cannot stress too strongly that a robust welfare state is not a gratuitous boon but the very soul of a meritocracy. If environments are to be even roughly equal, the sins of the parent must not blight the lives of the children, which means that the lack of merit of the former must be ignored to the degree that is necessary to provide every child with a non-demoralized home, good diet, good health, good education. The notion that a meritocracy of any sort could lead to an underclass is absurd, unless the "meritocracy" is to be a shooting star that persists for one generation.

The existential tension

How a people deals with the tension created by the mismatch between what others are willing to pay you to do and what would realize your own unique potential is the measure of the worth of that society. Aristotle compared Athens and Carthage, partially no doubt as ideal types. Athens was a true polis with a cherished way of life, rich in its variety of amusements, ceremony, sport, philosophy, art, theater, and truth seeking, united by the kind of fellow feeling so that any citizen's inability to participate in that way of life was an affront to all. Many tried to walk their own path despite a mismatch between that and what the market rewarded (Socrates for one).

Carthage was a commercial society (Kipling called it a sort of God-forsaken African Manchester) where the mismatch was minimized by money love. People were socialized not to want to do anything that the market did not reward. They enjoyed the art, theater, and so forth that they did not produce by being mere spectators, or consumers who bought it as a product. Their social glue was so weak that their navy once went on strike for higher wages when faced by an enemy fleet bent on invasion. Like all money and status obsessed peoples, the successful were not much interested in having money taken out of their pockets so the children of the less successful could enjoy justice as fairness or equalized environments. When an underclass threatened to develop, they sent them off as a colonizing expedition.

One of the oddest features of the meritocracy of *The Bell Curve* is this: it assumes people so dedicated to the school race (maximization of market rewards) that the race ranks them by genes for talent. Yet they are so non-materialistic that they are willing to see huge transfer payment to the disadvantaged so as to equalize environments. And the payments would have to be huge. Even upgrading housing in America's depressed urban areas, as a first step toward rejuvenating them by making them attractive to the middle class, would cost billions (Dickens, 1999). A people both money drunk and justice drunk is rare.

The degree to which people will settle for Carthage rather than Athens will fluctuate with their psychology and the economy. If most people live in poverty, they will readily compromise what they really want to do. They will have little use for justice as fairness. In a third world country, you treasure any privileged position that you can get, say in the civil service, and maximize its benefits for your family by way of "corruption." Even after a society has its first taste of affluence (practically no pocket money up to now), for a generation or two, most may well seek to maximize their spending power.

The true meritocracy

After a while people become accustomed to affluence. Then, unless you are a sick society infected by materialism, the money intoxication will wear off and the school race will be modified in the direction of a better society. Most people will be happy with a decent income, and allocate time to pursue those interests, whether philosophy or history, or doing arts and craft, or playing sport, whatever they feel brings out the best in them. They will want a welfare state that gives all a decent life irrespective of "merit." They will prefer a job that maximizes overlap with what you want to do rather than a job that maximizes income. Not so bad from a humane-egalitarian point of view!

> **Box 20**
>
> Those who seek great wealth can, of course, have high ideals and see money only as an instrument. When Bobby Fischer won the world chess championship at Reykjavik in 1972 and was asked what he would do next, he replied: "get me a Cadillac and a blonde."

If the intoxication with money never wears off, this does not show that humane ideals are counterproductive in practice. It means that something at their very core has been omitted: you do not sell your soul for money (see Box 20). In other words, if Carthaginians get a bastard meritocracy, they deserve nothing less. And remember, even to get that, they must be justice drunk as well as money drunk. Otherwise the school race would deviate so far from fairness that it would degenerate as a measure of genes for "talent" to the vanishing point. Athenians will get something far better: the boarding school after obsession with the school race has waned and a welfare state been introduced.

A dialectical analysis

Imitating my master Plato, I use dialectic to isolate the logic of the discussion: EITHER people are drunk on materialism OR they are not. The fate of a money-drunk population is hardly a reflection on humane ideals in practice. Therefore, we focus on the latter. Among a people who have rejected materialism, EITHER the market is benevolent OR it is not. Either it creates no tension with what people want to do, or it creates a tension.

First, we will assume a benevolent market. There is a perfect match between what other people want to pay you for doing and what you want to do in order to follow your own star. Admittedly, the money you get from the market will tend to be a function of how well you do it, and that will reflect your talent. But there will be a thousand different hierarchies of talent; and all will be valued for their human qualities; and there will be a general willingness to see wealth redistributed to compensate those who are less talented; and therefore, all will have a decent life irrespective of talent.

After all, everyone is trying and no one deserves credit for a superior genetic endowment. It is clearly unfair that I get both the wonderful reward of exercising an outstanding talent and lots of money as well. So even if you are an average violinist, but that is your passion, I will want to see transfer payments that give you more than the minimum guaranteed by the welfare state. This true meritocracy sounds like a utopia of humanism.

Second, we will assume a "wicked" market. Even though there is a tension between market rewards and cultivation of individual excellences, as affluence grows, the members of an uncorrupted polis will compromise less and less in favor of market rewards. Since this is possible without want, the tension is no longer very important. The main problem is that it will probably create even greater disparities of income because society is divided into who can maximize their income without any sacrifice of their peculiar excellences and those who cannot.

So larger transfers of wealth by progressive taxation and so forth will be necessary. But willingness to do so should be no less. The rich are aware that their wealth is a product of good fortune and that others who have perfected less rewarded talents deserve redress.

Despite their corruption, it is worth analyzing a people drunk on materialism. EITHER they will be drunk on justice as fairness as well OR they will not.

It is unlikely that they will care much for justice, but if they do, at least their bastard meritocracy will be a better society for the absence of an underclass. On the other hand, assume that they have only the dedication to justice that people in America have today. Then greater and greater demands for efficiency will make their polis worse than a bastard meritocracy because there will be an underclass. More and more people will be unrewarded and poor. But the answer is to try to make more of the population humanists, not invent arguments that humane ideals somehow self-destruct.

The IQ prognosis

It may be objected that the above does not address the specific prediction of *The Bell Curve*, namely, that as environments tend to equalize and privilege to recede, the offspring of the upper and lower classes will tend to diverge further and further in terms of their mean IQs. So we need a supplementary analysis.

Assume that environmental differences that affect IQ tend to diminish over time. Keep in mind that if such a trend is to be very significant, America will have to do what it has never done: institute a robust welfare state. If environments really do become radically more equal, the first result will be that the environmental portion of IQ variance would diminish. So the total spectrum that separates the top and bottom performance on IQ tests would diminish as well.

However, this could be offset by a tendency toward assortive mating. Segregation of young Americans by education may be producing a heightened tendency for like to mate with like. If children were the offspring of either high-IQ/high-IQ parents or low-IQ/low-IQ parents, with few high-IQ/low-IQ offspring as a moderator, this would enlarge the total IQ test performance spectrum.

Assume that privilege gives way to social mobility. That plus the trend to greater environmental equality would increase the correlation between the income and IQ of parents (and the IQ of their offspring). But would this really mean greater income differences? Steve Ceci has pointed out that if America really attained a state of affairs where only IQ affected income differences, it would be the most egalitarian nation on earth. Other sources of income variance greatly expand the spectrum of incomes. However, much of the non-IQ-caused variance may be due to chance factors difficult to eliminate. If these remain in existence, and IQ increases its potency to differentiate income, then the income spectrum must expand.

Moreover, as we evolve to a more complex society, IQ-related skills might be more and more at a premium, and therefore each point of IQ might be worth more and more money.

So what?

Assuming that these trends actually occur, what is their human significance? If we find a huge income spectrum obnoxious, we should not be hypnotized by the fact that IQ has become somewhat more important as a causal factor. We still have all of the usual techniques for redistribution of wealth at our disposal; that is, progressive taxation, progressive inheritance taxes, and the equalizing platform of the welfare state. All of these were on the humane agenda as far back as Marx, that curious thinker whose spectacles have never quite fit Americans, if only because the lenses were ground in a Europe they had left behind.

How much IQ is a true index of merit is irrelevant in human terms. Even if every hierarchy of talent was perfectly correlated with IQ, even if there was a high correlation between artistic creativity, musical talent, athletic ability, good handicrafts, sociability, good character (none of which is true by the way), the only thing Athenians care about is how much the market rewards their personal path to excellence. IQ is no more than the middle term of the match. EITHER the market rewards IQ and IQ correlates highly with all excellences, so the market rewards all excellences. OR the market rewards IQ and IQ correlates badly with certain excellences, so there is a mismatch between what the market rewards and the excellences most people want to cultivate. We have already analyzed those two possibilities.

The point is that the tension or lack of tension is the significant thing. Imagine we had never invented IQ tests and did not know about its causal role. Would that make any difference as to how much we resent these tensions or how we ought to deal with them?

Incentives

It may be objected that measures to redistribute wealth deprive the winners of market competition of some of their toys, and give the losers more toys than they would otherwise get, and that this would fatally compromise incentives. If so, the problem is that we are not Athenians but Carthaginians and that is hardly the fault of humane-egalitarian ideals. As Tawney once said, if people have the opportunity to perfect their talents and enough money to allow them to do that properly, they have all of the happiness that is good for any of the children of Adam.

But what if work is often awful? What if what one must do for the economy bears almost no relation to what any sane person would want to do – then surely huge money incentives must be left intact. They must indeed, but then you have a problem money cannot really solve: an almost complete dissonance between economic and psychic well-being. That problem should obsess us, not pseudo-problems based on underidentified models. The chances of even a bastard meritocracy fall to near zero. People will be unwilling to cultivate market-relevant skills to the utmost (won't try in the school race). And to the extent their income compensates them for work they really dislike, they may be unwilling to be taxed to finance the welfare state.

Past, present, and future

However, IQ is important in another way: it is a rough measure of intelligence. *The Bell Curve* predicts a depressing future in which the IQ gap between the children of the upper and lower classes becomes very large indeed. It would not be very nice if the most successful in earning money could label the children of the less successful as intellectually dull. I will show that that is not true today and is unlikely to become true.

Let us take stock of the way things actually are. In America, Flynn (2000c) found that the historic value (from 1932 on) for the mean IQ of the children of the lower third of parents (on the occu-pational hierarchy) is 95. I will chance my arm and predict that it will not sink below 93, which leaves the children of the middle third of parents at 100 and the children of the top third at 107.

This implies that middle-SES children will, of course, be split evenly, with 50 percent in the top half of the IQ scale and 50 percent in the bottom half. The low-SES children will have 32 percent of their number in the top half of the IQ scale and 68 percent in the bottom half. The high-SES children will have 68 percent in the top half and 32 percent in the bottom half. And note that this high rate of chil-dren of all classes shuttling about the IQ scale goes on generation after generation. This hardly conveys a picture of an American underclass permanently anchored to their fate by bad genes for IQ.

I should add that this analysis refers only to a homogeneous IQ community like white Americans: adding in a lower-IQ and lower-occupation and expanding immigrant group (Hispanics) compli-cates things in a way that has nothing to do with the meritocracy thesis.

What about income? Zagorsky (2007) uses regression analy-sis to calculate that each point of IQ in America is worth about $400 per year on your income; but that IQ has little correlation with accu-mulated wealth because high-IQ people are more likely to get them-selves into financial difficulties. His raw data show that the 10–point IQ advantage of the children of the top third occupationally over the children of the bottom third does have a pay-off, but that is not very impressive. An IQ of 105 gives you an income of $40,600 per year and an IQ of 95 gives you $36,800, a difference of $3,800. If I am correct about the IQ gap not widening much, the income difference will never go above about $5,500 in today's money. As for net worth, 95 gives you $57,500 and 105 gives $84,000. But going higher still to 110, the average net worth drops to only $71,400.

My conclusion, that there has been no trend for the rela-tionship between economic success and IQ to rise, has support from others. Strenze (2007) summarizes four recent studies. He observes that America seems static and, if anything, the association between IQ and occupational status in England has been declining.

However, my confidence in predicting that future differentials, that both IQ and income differences between the classes will not much increase, is not based on mere precedent. There is a growing literature showing that non-IQ factors are at least as relevant as IQ in terms of academic, social (avoiding jail and illegitimacy), and ultimately market success. The work of Nobel Laureate Jim Heckman is particularly impressive (Heckman and Rubenstein, 2001; Heckman, Stixrud, and Urzua, 2006). And recall, growing affluence should mean that a lot of high-IQ people (if they are Athenians) will feel that they have enough money, and therefore have better things to do with their time than try to get more and more.

But who can predict the long-term effect of technological progress? What if more demanding work roles leave the bottom 25 percent with nothing useful to contribute and the burden of a welfare state becomes too great for the affluent to bear? Well, 25 percent in hopeless poverty would create an underclass. But if this is inevitable, even a bastard meritocracy is not possible. The children of the hopelessly poor will live in a bad environment that cripples their prospects.

I believe that the notion that technological progress will render a large portion of the population useless is false. As long as we all have money in our pockets, we can always hire one another to service our desires for a more convenient and relaxed life style. For every computer programmer, technology creates a McDonald's worker who need not have even basic literacy or numeracy. The cash register shows a picture of a hamburger you strike to ring up the correct amount.

Take the thesis of technological depletion of the job market to its logical conclusion. There is a gigantic machine that churns out every product needed for good living, but the skills required to service it are so difficult that they isolate the top 1 percent. Does anyone really believe that the other 99 percent are going to stand around shivering and starving because they have no technologically relevant skill? Such a notion is close to the Marxist thesis that automation will immiserate the working class into a revolutionary fervor. Have we learned nothing since the simplistic labor theory of value?

You are not good enough

A discussion of the human significance of IQ would be incomplete without some comment on its role in credentialing. Today, many paid jobs require long and expensive academic training and society issues credentials that are a prerequisite for doing them. In one sense nothing has changed: throughout human history, when an individual has gone to others and asked for payment for what he or she wants to do, they have said "we would pay you if you were better at it, but you are simply not good enough." Our time differs in terms of how often the message is delivered, by whom, when, and its content.

Today, there are many more jobs requiring academic training than in the past, and therefore there are more aspirants and people are more often barred from entry. Would we prefer that there were fewer such jobs? The fact that there were only few scientists or doctors barred entry to lots of people far more effectively than the fact that there are many and some fail to qualify. Only the very best actors, musicians, and athletes were ever paid well and those who are outstanding are paid far better today. Moreover, there is far more opportunity to develop unpaid talent outside work. Work is less exhausting, we have far more leisure, and there is a multitude of amateur outlets for those who want to act, play the violin, run marathons, do crafts, or merely be the best raconteur at the local pub.

Today, the message that we are not good enough to be paid much is more likely to be delivered impersonally by an exam, rather than in person by one's parent (you are just not good enough to follow in my footsteps), or mentor (you just do not have a talent for medicine, the piano, carpentry), or a clientele. Which you mind most depends on your temperament.

The timing of the message has shifted from after you start to practice a profession to before you begin: you are more likely not to get into medical school than start butchering patients, more likely to be turned down at Juilliard than be booed off the stage. Set against this is a legitimate cause of rage: irrational credentialing. Sometimes credentials are not really relevant to job performance and therefore are actually a bastion of privilege. They raise the correlation between occupation and IQ, but they do so artificially. And insofar as they are irrelevant, they make no contribution to meritocracy, not even a bastard meritocracy.

Note that our discussion has entirely omitted the fact that getting credentials has a moderate correlation with IQ. That is because that makes no real difference except that the content of the message is more insulting. When we are told, "you are not good enough," there is the subliminal text, "and that is because you are too unintelligent." Well, that is irritating but life deals many insults and if that is the worst one we ever get from institutions, friends, spouses, and so forth, we should be very pleased. If we want solace, we can read a good book that puts the kind of intelligence measured by IQ tests into perspective by contrasting it with other human skills (including other intellectual skills) and the galaxy of human virtues that go beyond academic ability.

What we are worth

I assume that no one will say that transfers of wealth leave them paid less than they are worth. That would be a kind of blasphemy. What people are worth is known only to themselves and their God or, for some of us, only when we confront the self-knowledge vanity hides deep below the level of normal consciousness. Whether Thomas Jefferson's ideals can be realized is in our hands, not at the mercy of some inexorable trend toward "meritocracy." America will become like a meritocratic Carthage only if Americans become like the citizens of Carthage. If they set aside the galaxy of excellences and virtues a diverse and civilized people would cultivate, in favor of maximizing skills only to the degree a market rewards them, they deserve what they get.

Eugenics

The Bell Curve sets out another thesis that puts humane ideals at risk from a historical trend. There is a correlation between education and IQ, and in America today those with less education are having more children than those with more education.

This means negative selection of genes for IQ and would tend to drive the average IQ down by one point per generation. Over the next hundred years, the total loss would amount to about 3.3 IQ points. The genetic trend might be swamped by environmental progress and turned into an overall rise. But the environmental factors that have been raising IQ throughout the twentieth century may be weakening, as has happened in Scandinavia, in which case there would be cause for long-term concern. Moreover, the reproductive trend would slowly erode the quality of genes for intelligence and this in itself might become a drag on environmental progress. If we value the achievements of humanity, it is unwelcome to imagine art, music, literature, and science slowly drained both of creators and of appreciative audiences.

On the other hand, if we survive the next hundred years with civilization intact, other trends may eliminate genetic decline. If we follow the path of nations like Finland and eliminate poverty, everyone would have middle-class aspirations for their children and reproduction might no longer be correlated with education. If we follow her example in creating half-time jobs that offer a promising career path, buttressed by tax-supported quality child-minding facilities, career-oriented women would have children at younger ages.

It is very likely that science will come to the fore. The age of puberty is dropping, and faced with multiplying 10- and 11-year-old fathers and mothers it may become universal for boys and girls to be inoculated against parenthood, just as it is for them to be vaccinated against childhood diseases. Those who have difficulty in seizing control of their lives have far more unplanned children than others. Beset by emotional stress, violence, uncertainty, they have more difficulty planning against pregnancy. Imagine that, having been inoculated, both male and female would have to plan to use a series of antidotes in order to impregnate or get pregnant. Over night the situation would be reversed. With every child a planned child, those in a position to manage the mechanics of planning would have the larger families.

Attempts by government to influence who has children and who does not by some system of rewards or punishments are obnoxious and usually ineffective. I think it is far too early to panic. The future may be bright: no juvenile parents, no victim of rape pregnant, and no reason for concern about the quality of our genes.

6   Jefferson and Social Democracy

The mind of Eugene Debs fashioned a supreme maxim:
happiness is never a solitary search; no man rises far above the
ranks.

(Ray Ginger, 1948 [1962])

Refuting the meritocracy thesis gives us permission to abolish privilege and reduce environmental inequality without trepidation. Greater equality is an indispensable goal of American Socialists like Debs and myself. I have claimed that we too walk in the footsteps of Jefferson. I want to show that this is so and how Social Democracy can help to revive idealism in American politics.

From Aristotle to Social Democracy

A tradition that originated in Aristotle and passed through enlightenment thinkers like Jefferson culminates in the values of Social Democracy. The contribution of Social Democracy is to render these values viable in industrial society by way of an awareness of class and using the modern democratic state to tame the market. There is, by the way, no agenda to abolish the market. That is no more sensible than believing that it has no deleterious effects or that nothing can be done to mitigate them.

We begin with Aristotle's wonderful description of what civil society is all about. It is more than a market because you can do business with foreigners; it is more than a military alliance because you can negotiate mutual defense treaties with foreigners; it is more than marriage ties because you can marry a foreigner; it is more than physical proximity because two groups can occupy the same city and be divided by hate; it is more than abstaining from injury to others because one can be kind to foreigners. The foundation of a true civil society is a shared way of life, a life rich in achievement, sport, amusements, and cultural diversity, whose consummation is a sense of personal loss if anyone else suffers the deprivation of non-participation. It seeks the good life for all of its citizens (Aristotle, *Politics*, III.ix.1280a–1281a).

Aristotle is speaking about access to social life on the part of the citizens of a state. He excludes slaves, partially excludes women, and says nothing about duties obligatory in dealing with peoples outside the state. Enlightenment thinkers became aware that the patterns of behavior that divide human beings into tribes, races, genders, and classes are social conventions. Jefferson had no doubt that all human beings were equal in two senses: as they came from the hand of their creator, all were worthy of moral concern; none within the borders of a civil society should be debarred from access to a decent life, liberty, and the pursuit of happiness.

The ethics of Social Democracy

The ethics of Social Democracy include a definition of the circle of moral concern, a concept of justice, and a concept of civic virtue. These are shared by all humanists. Its concept of rights and the limitations of the market is more distinctive.

Moral concern

That all human beings count in the moral equation and that this imposes certain imperatives on behavior toward other peoples is unlikely to be disputed by most Americans. We need not undermine the viability of our own society, one that provides a home such that some can enjoy the good life, in a futile attempt to redeem all mankind from poverty. But outside our borders, we must refrain from doing harm and must do good in cases of extreme hardship. We must not reduce other peoples to slavery, or conquer or exploit them for profit, and, when possible, famine and the consequences of natural disasters should be alleviated by food and relief. This egalitarian delineation of the circle of moral concern provoked an alternative delineation. Nietzsche argued that every human being must earn a right to moral concern by exhibiting some outstanding excellence. He thereby became the most searching critic of humane-egalitarian ideals and we will confront him in chapter 9.

Justice

Once an egalitarian circle of moral concern is posited, the fundamental principle of justice follows: bad luck should not place great obstacles in the way of the pursuit of happiness. Operationalizing this principle suggests the welfare state as compensation for bad luck of genes or life history, supplemented by affirmative action as compensation for bad luck of group membership.

Affirmative action has already been discussed. But one can also have bad luck concerning the family one is born into. Therefore, there should be free access to good health care and education and nutrition for all, so that the role of luck is limited in access to these fundamentals. Means testing for these things is counterproductive because it is difficult to administer and more political support will be forthcoming if all classes find they benefit. Closely allied to this is bad luck in terms of what neighborhood or even state one is born into, and good public housing (of a new sort) and ample amenities should exist everywhere.

Then there is the bad luck of being born a woman. As Bertrand Russell said, femininity should not constitute some sort of incurable disease contracted at birth and terminated only at death. We have spoken of programs for working women that might soothe those who worry about eugenics, but their real justification is that they are only just. Having primary responsibility for raising children is the major reason women fall behind men in income and advancement. Government should offer huge blocs of jobs at all levels that are half-time and offer the same security and career paths as full-time jobs. Some people would prefer these as a matter of life style but their main function would be to offer women a choice other than full-time work or nothing (or dead-end part-time work). This should be supplemented by quality child-minding facilities for all women in the labor force. Large concerns that wish to be eligible for government contracts would have to set aside similar blocs of jobs.

Women are particularly at risk from bad luck of life history. The new poor in America often live in solo-parent homes and inevitably most of these are solo-mother homes, that is, teenagers who became unwed mothers and mature women who are separated from their husbands. It would be intolerable to set the state up as an arbiter of guilt or innocence, that is, decide who was irresponsible or who was relatively blameless. A large number of black women who become solo-parents are guilty of nothing save wanting to have a child. Do we exonerate them as victims of an unfavorable marriage market and indict Hispanic women because of their favorable market; or proceed on a case-by-case basis assigning responsibility like a gigantic divorce court?

In passing, the older one gets the more likely bad luck. A workman is abstemious, supports his wife and children, and saves. William Graham Sumner would love him. At 60, his wife contracts cancer and becomes convinced that a quack in Mexico can save her. Is he to say no, just lie down and die? Every cent goes and upon her death he is indigent and no longer vigorous enough to ply his trade. Does he really deserve to live in misery over the next twenty years?

We must treat all alike. The choice is between amelioration and deterrence and the choice is stark. *The Bell Curve* chooses deterrence for all solo-mothers. In chapter 2, we saw that Herrnstein and Murray (1994, pp. 544–549) advocate starvation as a disincentive. Unmarried mothers are to have no legal basis to demand that the father provide child support; and there will be no government programs for all women who have babies, whether married or not and whether "rich or poor" (there is a strain of radical egalitarianism in *The Bell Curve* often overlooked). Private charity might alleviate the lot of poor solo-mothers of course, but one must hope that it is not forthcoming. Any systematic private charity that made their lot easy would undermine the incentive system.

Let us focus on the "rich" for a moment. Stable marriages are more common among the middle and upper classes but nonetheless their divorce rate is substantial. A truly hard-headed and egalitarian policy to protect marriage would aim the weapon of starvation at "both rich and poor." Make the penalty for divorce, at least divorce before one's children are 18, no assistance plus the confiscation of all assets. The only result, of course, would be paper compliance and marriages "intact" that were no longer marriages in fact. The notion that the survival of this institution can be much affected by external reward/punishment incentives is a flight from reality.

As an old Socialist, I must here intrude a digression on looking at society through the spectacles of class. I have never found a conservative who even discusses whether penalties designed to preserve marriage should fall primarily on the poor. The fact that the state does not actively discriminate against the poor is all they demand. We need not consider differential consequences for rich and poor as these arise "naturally" out of the operation of the market. The fact that the rich possess property as a shield against hardship and the poor do not is irrelevant because whatever advantages ownership confers is what property rights are all about. Of course I profit from what I own, what else? It appears that class affects what we actually *see* when we look around us; look at Box 21.

America should accept that the solo-parent home is here to stay and that our prime objective should be amelioration. We should begin by trying to ensure that solo-parents are less isolated and demoralized. In chapter 2, I suggested some very limited measures to ease their lot. This chapter will spell out the potential of a robust

---

Box 21

Just to help the reader new to wearing class spectacles. All over the Western World, working-class jobs of every description have been eliminated for the sake of efficiency. Feather bedding on the docks or the railways is a sin. At the same time, feather bedding that provides jobs for the children of the middle and professional classes has grown exponentially. Schools have more staff administering them and servicing them than they have teachers. University and hospital managers grow faster than the number of lecturers and doctors. Private industry, despite market constraints, has motivators, counselors, and administrative assistants everywhere; executives compete in terms of the number of their secretaries. That this waste is justified in the name of efficiency merely underlines what class has the power to protect its interests and what class does not.

---

welfare state. Aside from steps to ease their participation in the workforce and to alleviate their poverty, providing single-payer health and education are the most relevant

Civic virtue

Aristotle has already told us what civic virtue is. It of course includes a willingness to defend your nation against attack. Beyond that, the citizens of a civil society should take pride in their shared way of life; they should feel it offers them a life rich in achievement, sport, amusements, and cultural diversity. But these things are hardly very onerous.

The real test of civic virtue is fellow feeling, that is, a sense of personal loss if anyone else suffers the deprivation of non-participation and a resolve to end that deprivation. The necessary fellow feeling cannot survive once citizens no longer have faith in one another, once they assume that their fellow citizens are primarily creatures of self-interest rather than reliable allies in the pursuit of a common good.

Rights

When Social Democrats use progressive taxation to promote justice and reduce inequality, the question of rights comes to the fore. When discussing taxes with conservatives, I have often asked them why they are so opposed to helping those less fortunate than themselves. Invariably, the answer is that they do help the unfortunate through private charity, but that no one should be coerced into a charitable act. What is virtuous should not be made a duty enforceable by law.

They assert a right of control over their own income and property: may I not do as I like with my own? This is echoed in every radio talk show in which people speak about the government spending *their* money, which is again a claim that control over one's income and property is a right. They do not go so far as to say that the right cannot be overridden in an emergency, such as when taxation is needed to fight a war. But the implication is that taxation is either theft (when no such emergency exists) or confiscation (as when resources are commandeered for emergency purposes).

Here I draw heavily on Tawney's great book, *The Acquisitive Society* (1920). The fundamental level of ethics is not rights but moral judgment because the proper foundation and delineation of rights are moral judgments. A right is a power to do something. Otherwise it would be worthless. It is a power protected by either law or custom. As a power, it must have both moral justification and moral limits. Without justification, a "right" is transformed into a privilege. Without limits, it becomes a tiny tyranny.

The justification of some rights is so persuasive that they are near absolute, such as the right to free speech. It is so fundamental to democracy and the temptation of governments to forbid speech simply because they find it obnoxious is so strong, it should be deeply entrenched in law. Governments who wish to limit free speech should have to go through procedures that give the public plenty of time to be alarmed and call a halt. But even it is subject to limits, such as the classic example of shouting fire in a crowded theatre. The justification of property rights is similar, namely, that up to a certain point their free exercise is in the common good. No one should interfere with the ownership and use of personal possession necessary for convenience and comfort when put to their normal use. When a car is used to drive 100 miles per hour through a city street that is another matter.

However, there are many examples of property rights that once had a justification but became privileges when that justification was undermined by social change. When the feudal lord protected his serfs from brigands, the right of sustenance from their crops had a certain justification. When this function was centralized in the state, his attempt to retain his "rights" was no more than a defense of privilege. When lords were commanders experienced in leading troops into battle, it made sense for them to head companies that collectively constituted the national army. This practice carried over into the nineteenth century, as when Lord Cardigan was allowed to purchase the right to lead the Light Brigade during the Crimean War. By then, lords were often idle aristocrats who merely played at being soldiers. The incompetence displayed by the British officers led society to rethink the matter and property rights over commissions were abolished as no longer functional (see Box 22).

I have said that rights are powers and that power without moral limits is tyranny and I mean this literally. The very definition of tyranny is power that recognizes no moral limits. If a ruler had a royal estate that hedged a city in between his lands and the sea, and blighted the life of those living therein by overcrowding, and put his hunting ahead of their welfare, we would call him a tyrant. We would not be moved if he cited a property right over the estate, but merely reply that the instrument by which he ruled purely in his own interest was not relevant. But what if he were a private owner? If private owners were protected in law from all interference, the law would simply have created a multitude of petty tyrants who could put self-interest ahead of the common good. Thus today we regulate industry in a thousand ways to protect public access to pure air and water, untainted food, and so forth.

Box 22

Woodham-Smith's book *The Reason Why* (1991) gives both a fascinating insight into the times and a probable explanation of the charge of the Light Brigade. Lord Cardigan had his light cavalry drawn up at one end of a valley facing the French and Russian cannon at the other end elevated on hills. He received a message from Lord Lucan, his regimental commander, which he interpreted as a call for a suicidal charge toward the guns.

It might seem reasonable to ask for a clarification but he was a stupid man and, more important, he was not on speaking terms with Lord Lucan. He led his troops forward, most of whom were killed, while he, seething with rage, managed to march his horse to the enemy lines and back unscathed. Courage he had. Later he married a woman who was reputed to thrash him with a switch. His troops did not die entirely in vain. The Crimean War was the first overseas conflict to have on-the-spot press coverage, and public admiration for the common soldier and contempt for the leaders led to reform of the British army.

It may seem that disposal of my income, whether from dividends, interest, or wages, is different. As long as it is not spent wickedly, such as to take out a murder contract on someone, it does no direct harm. Why is it different? Well presumably because it is my own creation. That would be true if I hacked out a farm in an uninhabited wilderness where land had no scarcity value, but it is not true within a civil society for three reasons.

First, beyond civil society there is no property but merely possessions at the mercy of anyone strong enough to seize them. Society creates my right of control over my wages and protects them for my use.

Second, in most of human history there was no such thing as a wage. At a certain point, society created modern capitalism with its market economy. That is a wonderful thing for many purposes, but if it has unanticipated harmful consequences, why should not society alter it? If social forces give rise to a church that practices human sacrifice, the state intervenes. If social forces give rise to an economic system that sacrifices some people to a life of want, illness, and insecurity, why should the state not intervene? Is the economy the one untouchable social institution, a sort of Frankenstein's monster that cannot be improved once created but becomes free to do violence to all and sundry?

Third, my wage is a joint creation of my work and a huge infrastructure of roads, harbors, and services that constitute social capital accumulated over generations. Certainly some fee is due for the rental of these things, sufficient to maintain and improve them and hand them on as an inheritance to our children.

But even if taxation is legitimate for public order and infrastructure, what about forcing me to be charitable to those less fortunate than myself? The answer to this is that you are part of a civic society wherein a democratic government is legitimized by its pursuit of the common good. If a majority deems it unjust that some suffer due to ill fortune, or that civic virtue is undermined by insecurity, or that human capital is deteriorating because of untreated illness and undereducated children, or if it does not want inequality beyond certain limits, you must argue either against these as social goods or against the steps to attain them as counterproductive. If you think private charity can render tax unnecessary, prove it.

Rights do not trump morality but morality trumps rights, albeit a morality that creates no rights is suspect indeed. The word right is abused when people use it as a conversation stopper in moral debate. The assertion that something violates my rights is the beginning of moral debate, not its termination, although the debate may be favorable to the claim.

The market and the five great tensions

We have now liberated the state to collect taxes and control property. This gives the democratic state the right and the power to promote the pursuit of happiness in ways not conceivable in earlier times.

Throughout most of human history, there have been five limitations on virtue and happiness:

1 the tension between *justice* and coerced self-interest;
2 the tension between *personal autonomy* and work;
3 the tension between *equality* and coerced competition;
4 the tension between *civic virtue* and personal insecurity;
5 the tension between *morality* and institutions beyond morality.

All of these existed under feudalism. Most people were rewarded with the necessities of life only by way of constant agricultural labor that made them serfs or peasants and nothing more. The struggle for bare survival limited conduct so that morality was little more than kindness within the family and religious duty. Powerful institutions existed that practiced exploitation with only the weakest of moral limitations. The knight was supposedly bound by a code of respect for the weak but his lawless and violent behavior earned him the label "terrible worm in an iron cocoon" (Tuchman, 1978).

These tensions are still with us, but today market capitalism determines their character or peculiar historical manifestation:

1 Rational behavior molded by market considerations sharpens the conflicts between self-interest and being just to blacks. The expense of information that would allow blacks to be treated as individuals is often too great to be paid.
2 In chapter 5, we emphasized that the market cannot accommodate the full spectrum of human activity that promotes excellence and pleasure. An activity must provide goods or services or spectacles that others are willing to pay for if there is to be a money reward.
3 Humane-egalitarian ethics posits that all should have access to the good life, but the market makes access to basic goods into prizes won in a competition by those who can pay.

4 The moral glue of the social order is civic virtue or fellow feeling and the market undermines the sense of personal security that allows fellow feeling to flourish.

5 The market has created its own powerful institutions that willingly acknowledge no moral limits.

The state must remedy the market's deficiencies. We have said enough about how we can use it to balance the affirmative action the market affords whites with some affirmative actions for blacks. Therefore, it remains to detail how the state can ameliorate the other four tensions and promote the pursuit of happiness.

The individual versus the market

Here the power to tax is the power to create. It can subsidize all of the good things that the market does not reward. The great passions of human beings, outside of sex and religion and these can take care of themselves, are sport, the crafts (including gardening) which shade into the plastic and visual arts, music, dance, learning, and sociability.

Sometimes subsidies can create paid work, as with subsidized local theatre, music, and sport, for those who are competent rather then great and who are willing to forgo maximizing their income. Sometimes they allow people to live their real lives outside of work during their leisure. It is easy for professionals to forget the extent to which work is still soul destroying for so many. The most effective passage in *A Man in Full*, the strange novel by Tom Wolfe (1998) in which the main character becomes an evangelist for Stoic philosophy, is the description of "the Suicidal Freezer Unit."

As Conrad Hensley reports for his night shift, he thinks of the man who had his ankle crushed the previous week and the hours ahead of everyone coughing and sneezing and taking pills. The freezer unit is a warehouse with a vast refrigerated chamber at one end kept at zero degrees Fahrenheit (18 degrees below zero

Centigrade). Despite the freezer suits, the cold is intolerable. The job is to steer a vehicle with a lift to the freezer, go deep into it, go down on your knees, grab a carton of frozen meat weighing 80 pounds, strain every muscle to free it, carry it bent over to the lift with tremendous stress on arms, back, and thighs, put it on the lift, put more cartons on the lift until you have a full load of twelve, shift them to the warehouse loading bay, and keep it up for eight hours. You hurry because too long in the freezer and your face feels like it is burning up. When you emerge from the freezer, the heat seems overwhelming (at 80 degrees Fahrenheit). The warehouse floor is crowded and often slick with spilled produce, a place of danger where driver error can send a vehicle out of control and maim or kill those in its path. The pay is good at 14 dollars an hour and the men are terrified at the periodic layoffs that come without warning.

Anything that can brighten leisure hours is precious. If we trusted to the market, there would be no free museums, art galleries, concerts, or libraries. In fact, most of them are underfunded and therefore not free now. There would be no Central Park in New York City. As Al Smith said, "only God can make a tree but only the city can make a park."

I have listed the "arts" first to anticipate those champions of the working class who argue that all of these should be fee for service because they are upper-class pursuits paid for in part by the tax dollars of workers. To the extent that is so, we again see where power lies. The antidote is subsidized activities with broader appeal: more playgrounds, sports facilities, money to create semi-pro leagues, encourage sporting and craft clubs, build premises where those who like to work with their hands will find space and others who share their interests, and free community college courses of all kinds. Working people who want to build their own boat in their garage or assemble a vintage car could get help. We have barely scratched the surface of ameliorating the tension between following my own star and the market.

Universal access versus the market

How are we to start America on the path to open access to quality health care and education? The best way to begin is free pre-natal care and care for all children aged 5 and under. Existing facilities and doctors would submit the record of patient visits to the state and be paid a fee large enough to make it worth their while, as in the countries that already practice socialized medicine. New clinics would be established to meet the new demand. The first children would continue to receive free care as they aged, thereby extending the coverage. When the teething problems were ironed out, you could either jump a few years ahead to move more quickly or begin to work downward by introducing free care for those over 65.

I will not waste time justifying socialized medicine as preferable to the US health system. Anyone who accesses comparative data will find that the US system delivers less care for more money than would seem possible. Americans might ponder the fact that when the US government really cares about keeping a large group healthy, it gives them all of the advantages of socialized medicine. I refer to US military personnel. At least it gives them to those on duty. It does not seem to care much about the health of those who have been invalided out of the firing line in Iraq and are no longer useful.

The fundamental problem in US education is the huge gap in quality between the best and the worst schools. At present, the market turns this into a competition for access. Parents usually want the best education for their children and this often means buying a home in the best school district they can afford. If 50 percent of parents do this, their children enjoy an additional advantage. If everyone does it, no child gains because all end up in the same school they would have attended had no competition occurred. The price of housing is inflated by demand that is extraneous to the quality of housing as such. Even those who do get better homes than they would have had without entering into this competition may have spent more on housing than they really desired. They might have preferred to save for their children's university education or for their own old age (more parents will now become a burden on their children).

In either event, the overall quality of education is not increased at all. Indeed, it may fall because parents accrue larger debt and are more resistant to taxation. Even if that is not true, the exit of the professional and middle classes from some schools and their concentration in others lowers the quality of the former. The ability of the wealthy to purchase quality education is therefore not neutral, like buying a dress that is expensive but does not render cheaper dresses worse than they are. It is like the purchase of commands in the British army: a power whose exercise is counterproductive in terms of the common good, which is to say that it is a privilege. It is analogous to having the right as a wealthy person to go to the head of a line for something scarce like a theater ticket.

As a benchmark, what would be an ideal Social Democratic solution? Within a large and diverse area, everyone would register their child with the school board for any school they wished (public or private) with a list of preferences for their second, third, fourth choice, etc. Transport services would be afforded to cover reasonable distances. Any school that had a registration list greater than its capacity would have its roll selected for it by random ballot from among those that named it. Private schools would get a reasonable state grant to cover tuition fees and would be allowed to charge nothing extra. Since this gives even the wealthiest a strong chance of their children being randomly assigned, it would have the desirable effect that the entire school system would be upgraded very quickly indeed.

The freedom of choice of less wealthy parents would be enhanced enormously, far more than by the libertarian proposal of vouchers. And the despotic rigging of choices by the present competition for advantageous schooling would be at an end. But politics does not always allow for an ideal solution, so other programs are needed, as both a fall back and a supplement. Every state should train a cadre of outstanding teachers of basic literacy and numeracy that would serve as a flying squad to be called in by any school that needed them, with poor performing schools first in line.

However, the most basic solution for bad schools is to upgrade the neighborhoods that surround them. Problem neighborhoods should be invited to apply and select local representatives to work with planners. Public housing with a focus on law enforcement and education would be the core. Every building would have resident police to keep it crime and violence free and resident teachers to help with homework and tutoring space with access to what children today need, computers included. The focus of a cluster of buildings would be an educational park with recreational facilities, elementary vocational training, and child minding facilities. The last would double as the sort of drop-in center for mothers and their children previously described, with its book and tape library, sub-professionals, free legal and budgeting and contraceptive advice, and so forth (see Box 23).

Where the development is largely black, the question of "honor" must be addressed. Thomas Sowell (2005) argues that the culture of black American males stipulates that personal offenses should be settled by interpersonal violence without recourse to the law. Whether or not his thesis that blacks absorbed this culture from their sojourn in the American South is correct, its prevalence is evident. How far should the development's local gang be allowed to go in defending itself, for example, in terms of access to weapons?

This poses the problem of size. Unless the community is large enough to support a high school, it will not give teenagers the kind of in-group they seem to want as a buffer against the rest of society. It must be large enough to provide its own social "microclimate." Conservationists who want to preserve an endangered species must calculate the size of the reserve needed if it is to be self-sufficient. Social scientists who want a community to survive must make it self-sufficient in the sense that its residents can find personal attachments therein.

Box 23

Another homily on class. What I advocate here has nothing to do with what passes for "city planning" as it exists at present. All too often, such plans merely reorder a city to advantage the affluent with no regard for those they displace. For example, urban renewal usually means exiling the poor so that a center city business district will be more appetizing or a university neighborhood safer. Regulations to preserve the character of a neighborhood or the minimum size of lots simply protect affluent areas from an influx of people who cannot afford large sections, expensive homes, and private architects. Debs said that public ownership leaves unanswered the question of who will benefit from how the public corporation is run. Similarly, city planning leaves open the question of what class will devise and implement the plan. The record thus far is an education in class politics.

I have no illusions about my proposals for upgrading neighborhoods. Class will intrude because the truly demoralized cannot take advantage of them. A neighborhood would have to have the leadership, local pride, hope, and aspirations to take part. This is not to say that nothing can be done for a demoralized neighborhood. Police and teachers should be offered whatever incentives are necessary to get them to reside in every building there as well.

As for university education, the US government should imitate the British Open University, which offers courses and degrees by distance teaching. Its purpose is stated succinctly: "To break the insidious link between exclusivity and excellence." Its costs are low; for example, six years of study toward an MA (BA Hons.) in Psychology costs about US$7,000 altogether. Fees are reduced or forgiven if you are below the average income (dependents are taken into account for those above), unemployed, or on a benefit. There is money for computers, to access the internet, and for childcare. Its quality and standards are high and are recognized as such. Over

50,000 employers have sponsored study by their staff. Indeed, one in five MBA (Master of Business Administration) students in the United Kingdom is studying at the Open University. There is no reason why American Open Universities should not exist in every state and have a tutorial and examination center in every major city.

Health and education do not exhaust what can be done to promote equality, of course, and there should be a government department with that as its goal, a department alert to relevant policy initiatives. For example, although beaten when opposed by moneyed agricultural interests, there is no reason why the Brandon Plan should not be revived and improved.

If there was a bumper crop of corn, or any other crop, it would go to market, thus pushing prices down and cutting the cost of food for the consumer. If there was more than could be absorbed at any price, the surplus would go into bio-fuel or food aid abroad. Farm incomes that fell below their level in normal years would be made good by direct payment up to a certain amount. If it became clear that there were too many in some branch of agriculture, payments would be progressively lowered until enough producers had shifted to other areas. Social Democrats know the value of market forces as well as conservatives do. It is just that, rather than manipulating them purely for private profit, we would use them for more egalitarian goals.

Morality versus the market

Corporate power is the creation of modern capitalism. The first corporate law held that a corporation was a fictional person, which was doubly advantageous: as a person, it had a multitude of rights; but as a fiction, it was not a moral agent that could be held responsible. It had neither "pants to kick nor a soul to damn," the latter point endorsed by Pope Innocent IV (Paine, 2002).

The last decades have seen an erosion of this conception, thanks to corporate sins that exhaust all possibilities and corporate power of a sort (over scarce resources) that threatens the very future of industrial civilization. Nonetheless the old ethos is alive. There are laws on the books that require investment firms to maximize returns to their clients, even if that means advising them to invest in that premium earner tobacco. US arms manufacturers are free to sell on the international market, a practice which simply makes those states who can spend the most more and more powerful than their poor neighbors. No one questions that unethical behavior is sometimes good business: the slave trade was highly profitable to investors.

The first step is to establish a National Business School which does four things:

1 describes what must be done to ensure a viable future – a scenario that takes into account things ranging from peak oil to the exhaustion of ground water in India (where mass starvation seems almost inevitable);

2 describes what the behavior of each major corporation in America would have to be so as to promote (rather than undermine) viability and to obey a moral imperative of "do no serious harm" to the world's peoples;

3 assesses whether that behavior conflicts so clearly with making a profit that the corporation in question cannot be left to the play of market forces;

4 educates a cadre of potential business executives who are not only outstanding in their professional skills but also sworn to a code of business ethics, like the Hippocratic Oath for doctors, which commands moral behavior and transparency.

With that knowledge and that cadre, we can frame effective policies. I should note that Social Democrats are not fixated on nationalization. Tawney (1931) pokes fun at both the dogmatic capitalist, who shudders every time he posts a letter (state run), and the dogmatic socialist, who quakes every time he makes a phone call (privately run). Corporations should be judged in terms of how they function. If they can be profitable without behavior counterproductive in terms of the common good or basic moral principles, all well and good. If they cannot meet this criterion, the next question is whether they perform some essential function. If not, they can be phased out. If so, the function must be preserved despite the absence of a profit and some sort of state ownership is dictated.

Sometimes full nationalization will be appropriate, probably of most transport because of the need to systematically balance service against energy scarcity, and possibly of oil because of the need to favor oil products (plastics) over its use for fuel. In other cases, regulation would be enough: what foreign nations get arms from the US should be a matter of national policy, which means that all domestic arms producers would sell arms that have military significance only to the US government. It will deal with all foreign governments.

The graduates of the business school must develop their own ethos and code of honor. They must think of themselves as guardians of humanity (shades of Plato), with their mutual bonds reinforced by every device known to social science (short of mating festivals). They have a mission. As they accumulate experience, they could be used as receivers to replace the staff of corporations who have behaved irresponsibly. If Harvard wants its graduates to be eligible to play this role, it would have to show that its graduates get a similar education and are bound to the same code. Eventually, it will become a reason for disquiet if any major corporation seems reluctant to hire graduates. Graduates should return a yearly statement affirming that they have lived up to their code and return to "school" to deliver a brief as to how their corporation has met its obligations. Otherwise their credentials will be revoked. This may prevent their capture by the corporation to which they have been assigned.

There is another ethical consideration that cannot go unmentioned. Even if every American corporation, and every American business, and every American consumer were not amoral in their behavior taken one by one, the sum total of economic activity is already such as to endanger the planet's environment. Jared Diamond (2005) estimates that as the third world achieves first world living standards, the total impact on the environment will increase twelvefold; indeed, China alone would double the impact. At some point, there will have to be a stipulated "sustainable standard of living" that Americans drop toward in return for developing nations not rising above it. Soon such an agreement will not be a matter of choice.

America can try to defend its affluence by arms. But if the rest of the world loses sustainability, it will be overwhelmed as Rome was eventually overwhelmed by starving Germanic tribes flooding across the Rhine. As other nations fail, America will face more than a loss of "trading partners." It will face a tide of terrorism, war, disease, and frantic attempts of the desperate to cross international borders. No one can advocate a planned withdrawal to a lower standard of living today and survive politically. But the first step toward something better than chaos would be the National Business College's calculation as to what the sustainable standard of living is. The very effort to discredit the estimate would create a debate about the future that would force every American to admit they were asking their leaders to deliver the impossible. It is hard for most people to live by lies that they know to be such.

The "coerced" enlightenment of the people is a prerequisite of the bottom-up pressures Diamond cites as hopeful, such as the Australian Landscape Trust. In America, when sales fell off, McDonald's accomplished within weeks what the government had been unable to do for five years: force the meat packers to give up practices associated with the spread of mad cow disease. Sometimes industries themselves face the fact that they must plan for sustainability, such as the timber industry in its foundation of the Forest Stewardship Council. But the Council is effective only because wood products with its label attract consumers who care.

Civic virtue versus the market

There are two measures of civic virtue: the willingness of the average citizen to defend the nation against a foreign aggressor; and the sort of fellow feeling that makes another's alienation from social life a concern for all. The two are quite distinct in terms of their roots. A society has to be suffering from terminal illness if the former is not the case and hatred of the alien (and therefore patriotism) has often been strongest among the most deprived members of society. The legend that the most patriotic members of French society during World War II were the prostitutes of Paris has a ring of truth. The fact that Congress dare not institute the draft to raise soldiers to fight in Iraq is not a sign of no patriotism but a sign of no confidence, signaling that the public does not really believe that this is a war of national defense.

Turning to civic virtue as fellow feeling, a robust welfare state is its foundation, at least in modern society where all have high hopes and aspirations. The two are linked by the concept of personal security. When people can no longer depend on the welfare state for a decent life in old age, treatment of illness, and education for their children, they become insecure. They must become self-sufficient and that means accumulating enough wealth to satisfy these needs by paying fee for service. And in fact, no amount of private wealth is enough: anyone may suffer catastrophe, may lose their pension when their employer goes under, have a child that needs endless medical attention, or children whose talents and ambitions merit extensive and expensive education. Therefore, to forfeit any of one's private wealth to pay taxes to help others becomes frightening and resented. The decline of the welfare state erodes civic virtue in favor of an anxious quest for absolute security; and the erosion of civic virtue further undermines the welfare state.

This downward spiral culminates in the greatest loss of all: absence of trust in one another. Even if I am willing to be taxed for the benefit of others, I no longer believe that they have the same fellow feeling toward me. What is the point of being taxed heavily for a social service, if you believe that people will vote in a government the following year that will abolish it? Distrust in one another breeds despair of anything better and a retreat into the private acquisition that is your only safeguard against misfortune. Americans should ask themselves one question: why is virtually every proposition to raise taxes for better schooling doomed to defeat whenever it appears on a local ballot paper?

Where will the money come from?

This question has no doubt been uppermost in the minds of many as program after program has been endorsed. On April 27, 2002, Steve Braye of Greensboro, North Carolina wrote a letter to the Editor of *The News and Record* calling the Department of Defense budget at $420 billion "outrageous." The editor demurred but Mr. Braye was correct. Since the beginning of the war in Iraq, the Department of Defense budget has swollen to $585 billion. That level of spending is creating huge economic problems and cannot be sustained. On the other hand, military spending involving other departments than Defense totals $122 billion, so normal expenditure would be some $550 billion. This does not include the cost of past wars such as veterans' benefits or interest on the national debt.

The diversion of $200 billion from military spending would have an enormous impact. The total Federal spending on human resources (everything from health and education to social security and housing) is $748 billion and some of this could be diverted to the programs described. This kind of cut in military spending would hardly leave America defenseless.

With expenditure converted into purchasing power parity terms, the US spends more than China, India, Russia, the UK, France, and Japan combined, and almost three times as much as China, its nearest rival (Stalenheim, Perdomo, and Skons, 2007). A 36 percent cut would leave America at almost twice China's expenditure. Cutting the

> **Box 24**
>
> In 1984, a New Zealand Labour government began to undermine the welfare state and conservatives were happy to follow its lead. There has been the predictable erosion of fellow feeling that attends personal insecurity. The only transcendent purpose, at least on a domestic issue, that has united society since has been a bipartisan agreement to set aside a huge superannuation fund to help pay pensions in mid-century. Sympathy for the elderly is better than military spending as a concern that rises above party politics. But that only this is viable shows how small the role fellow feeling any longer plays. A whole generation is being cheated of the social capital needed to provide quality health care and education. As if a well-educated and healthy people were not necessary to sustain the social services of the next generation.

boondoggles like the so-called early warning system would initiate the staged reduction of expenditure needed. The number of US professional soldiers would be reduced and military adventures abroad have to be limited to what 50,000 troops can accomplish, unless a citizen army was to be drafted. That limitation would be all to the good in that if 50,000 troops cannot complete a mission abroad within a reasonable time, it is almost certainly a mistake.

Rhetoric is no substitute for showing that these cuts make sense in terms of national security. That task constitutes a promissory note to be redeemed by the end of the next chapter. For now, there is something pathetic about a society that can mobilize social resources only by whipping up hysteria about national security. Not that my other country, New Zealand, has done much better (see Box 24).

The sane society

Since the end of the Cold War c. 1987, the great betrayal of American liberalism has been its unwillingness to take a stand on the diversion of funds from military to civic purposes. This betrayal is the reason for the trivia that occupy the center of American politics. Is it any wonder that what pass for a moral dimension in US politics are issues like teaching creationism, praying at school, and family values? Create a moral vacuum and something will rush in to fill it.

This is not to deny that family values are important, but no one can do much about them except loving parents who care more about their children than their own convenience. And one must concede that Bush has a transcendent moral purpose. Unfortunately, it is founded on a false conception of what American military power can accomplish abroad.

It is all very well to set out a political program, but where is the political muscle to come from? There would have to be a realignment of American political parties that created a coalition between those who have the most to gain from a robust welfare state, those appalled by the excesses of US foreign and military policy, those who see that curbing corporate power is becoming a matter of life and death, and those who would be out of pocket but are secure enough to be motivated by reason and humanity. The shadow of such a movement existed for a moment in 1968 behind Senator Eugene McCarthy, only to be derailed by the unprincipled ambition of Robert Kennedy about whom we will say little. It is wrong to speak ill of the dead.

To those who say that such a movement already exists behind some Democratic aspirant for the Presidency, let any one of them take on the issue of diverting $200 billion from the military budget. Those who dodge this issue are really promising little more than business as usual. So are we to have another third party that will be castigated with causing the election of the greater of two evils?

For once, let us pass through the horns of this dilemma. Run a candidate for President who begs people not to vote for him or her except in the public opinion polls. (This will entail some duplicity in that the polls ask what candidate you would vote for if an election were held today.) This tactic would show the strength of the desire for something better than the status quo without tearing voters apart. The Presidential candidate will "accept" your vote only if you sign a document swearing that you had not intended to vote at all – or that you have paired yourself with someone who supports the other major party, so the casting of your two votes will cancel out. The real appeal for votes would be in those 300 Senatorial or House races in which the winner is a foregone conclusion. People living in these districts should feel free to vote for the Party of Jefferson. Wherever it begins to finish second, the supporters of the newly third placed party will be the ones who have to worry about wasting their vote. On the day that polls show the Party running second for President, votes for that office will be seriously sought.

If another party steals the platform, all the better. The slogan for the good cause might be "the sane society." It lacks the immediate appeal of "the new deal" because it has to be explained, but that is also its strength.

When Tito's police rounded up those who dissented from his totalitarian regime, and sarcastically asked them to identify themselves, knowing full well that they had been systematically denied access to jobs of any kind, an ordinary worker stepped forward and proudly said "Social Democrat." I hope to write other books, but if that does not happen, this stands as the last will and testament of a Social Democrat.

7   The America who would be king

What is at stake is not Iraq but our global role.
    (Zbigniew Brzezinski)

This war . . . shows that the US administration is trying to make the world its own province.
    (Mikhail Gorbachev)

Our history of the last 50, 60 years is quite clear. We have liberated a number of countries, and we do not own one square foot of any of those countries except where we bury our dead.
    (Colin Powell)

America once hoped to show the world a shining example of a nation free of the corruption that attended being a great power in the classical European tradition. One of the most shattering blows to our morale is the general contempt for our international behavior that prevails. How might we revise our thinking to give us a global role that would command respect?

My language is that of moral idealism. I well recall my dismay as a student when my lecturer Hans Morgenthau attacked idealism in general, and Wilsonian idealism in particular, as a possible basis for American foreign policy. Later I understood what he meant: that ideals had to be firmly grounded in political reality. But that term needs clarification. What I will propose is not politically realistic in the sense that there is much chance of American policy makers accepting it in the near future. I am not a candidate for office. What I wish to do is sound an alarm that American foreign policy has lost contact with the real world and that there is no remedy for its failures until that is remedied.

It is important not to seem to profit from hindsight. Therefore, the first half of this chapter begins with a paper delivered in early 2003, before America's excursion into Iraq in March of that year, with only stylistic changes and references added. At that time, to emphasize that my idealism was grounded in realism, I wrote it assuming the role of an acolyte of Thomas Hobbes, the thinker who gave that approach its classic statement in the modern world.

World sovereign versus great power

We stand at a unique moment in history. American power dominates the world scene and she is surrounded by nations ready for leadership against a common enemy – the threat to well-being posed by weapons of mass destruction whether in the hands of nation-states or networks who answer to no nation-state. America has a choice: it can either play the role of a good world sovereign who rules by consensus; or merely behave like a victorious great power who treats the whole world as a sphere of influence.

The emergence of a single great power offers irreducible advantages. A great power looks no further than its national interest and imposing its own chosen moral goals. But better one of these than many. When there were two, the US and USSR, each could point to the other as enemy and justify force to seek advantage and self-defined moral goals within its own sphere of influence. When there were several, the US, Russia, Britain, France, Germany, Italy, and Japan, each did mischief in its immediate vicinity and colonial sphere (Kennedy, 1987). As Hobbes said, better to have power invested in one actor because one appetite demands less than the insatiable appetites of many. Even America's power is limited and fewer need fear arbitrary behavior with so many eliminated from the game of great power.

However, a world sovereign can make the world better still. In particular, it must *not* do whatever it believes to be right if that is destructive of consensus. A world sovereign has a higher moral purpose: to make peace wherever possible and to consolidate and consensualize its rule. This means creating a certain state of mind. A great power can function if it is feared. To be a good world sovereign, you must win respect not because others fear you but because they fear what the world would be like without you. Here are a few propositions about the role of world sovereign in the hope that America will learn to be a gracious king, perhaps not one who rules with our loves but at least one who rules with our grudging regard.

A world sovereign must expect to be hated

Americans often ask why their country is hated. The Bush administration has revived the aim of a Global missile defense system that would make it invulnerable to attack from any other nation. While this is not fully possible, America's enormous capacity to retaliate offers a pretty good substitute. It has a military technology that allows it to kill whoever it wants, at least in the developing world, without serious loss even to its own professional military personnel. This is something new and astonishing in world history.

Imagine that Mexico had invented a force-field that rendered it utterly invulnerable and a death ray it could use anywhere on earth. It might use its power only for things that were unambiguously good, such as taking out American mayors who are incurably corrupt or those Los Angeles police who are undeniably racist (that is, it could do America the favor of enforcing US laws where America itself has failed). It might even give America a miss and take out Saddam Hussein and the North Korean elite. One thing is certain. A wave of fear and loathing would sweep America. Every resource and mind would be mobilized to discover how to break that force-field and neutralize that death ray.

Add to this that America has used its power to take sides in morally ambiguous situations like the Middle East, that it has invaded nations in its sphere of influence when its construction of its interests so dictated, that it has instituted and supported governments (including Hussein's regime in Iraq in the 1980s) whose citizens have suffered much – and it takes a moral blindness quite extraordinary to wonder why it is hated.

However, the point is that a world sovereign that has these powers, and that has come to the throne by conquest (winning the Cold War) rather than by institution (consent), will be hated however circumspect its use of power. It can seek to minimize the world's animosity but it must not sulk if unloved. Assuming office requires some psychological preparation as every politician knows.

A world sovereign should move toward rule by consensus

How can America go from simply being feared toward a world in which most nations are far more afraid of what the world would be like without America's preponderant power? The primary goal must be "to make peace wherever possible," that is, to show that American power is indispensable to protecting nations and peoples from the most horrific forms of violence. Such a goal if pursued sincerely and realistically will maximize consensus for your rule. Its realization involves two tasks: eliminating the weapons of mass destruction that *other* states possess; reducing the threat posed by the privatization of such weapons.

It is sometimes asked how America can justify eliminating the nuclear weapons of others while retaining its own. The answer is that the emergence of one power with overwhelming military might provides the only instrument that can eliminate nuclear weapons. Universal disarmament is not a practical option. Were all the weapons to disappear tomorrow, the knowledge of how to create them would survive. Within a few years even more nations would

---

Box 25

A remarkable novel by Mohsin Hamid (2007), *The Reluctant Fundamentalist*, shows how constructive a role the US could play in defusing nuclear tensions between these two nations: "Surely, all America had to do was to inform India that an attack on Pakistan . . . would be responded to by the overwhelming force of America's military" (p. 143). It also portrays how tense the last confrontation between India and Pakistan was, what with spouses and children leaving the country (pp. 127, 161, 177). And finally, it shows how someone with deep roots in America's way of life was eventually overcome with rage at near absolute power and its abuse: "your constant interference in the affairs of others was insufferable" (p. 156); "the lives of those of us who lived in lands in which such killers [terrorists] also lived had no meaning except as collateral damage" (p. 178): "[when the twin towers collapsed] my thoughts were not with the victims . . . I was caught up with the symbolism of it all, the fact that someone had so visibly brought America to her knees" (p. 73).

---

have them than at present – newcomers would be encouraged by the fact that they were not already hopelessly outgunned. Realistic steps toward control of such weapons are, first, that America acquire an effective monopoly; and second, that its weapons be internationalized rather than destroyed. Postponing the second step, we will discuss the first.

What might reduce the number of those who currently have nuclear weapons? The first priority should be in South Asia where both India and Pakistan have weapons of mass destruction and a history of conflict. America should ascertain whether they are willing to at least let their systems atrophy, in return for an American guarantee of their security (see Box 25). It would have to be established that both are willing to (tacitly) accept that the present division of Kashmir is tolerable, when weighed against the possibility of nuclear devastation and the waste of ever-expanding nuclear establishments.

America would have to guarantee that it would automatically come to the aid of whichever side was attacked – and probably be the spearhead of a force that would take over border control if incursions by irregulars were a problem. India could hardly disarm unless she was also guaranteed her border with China – and China should be asked to give firm assurances (as distinct from being asked to disarm).

We now see why the preservation of the US deterrent is essential. It must be there to give guarantees to those who might forsake their own. It must be there so that the US can seek the pacification that is the essence of the role of a world sovereign: "Covenants, without the sword, are but words."

North Korea was willing to let its nuclear program wither thanks to its implicit non-aggression treaty with the US (the "Agreed framework between US and the Democratic People's Republic of Korea" 1994). It now wants ratification of a formal non-aggression treaty by the US Senate – and the US should jump at this chance to demonstrate that it truly is pursuing a pacific policy. There is supposed to be a special relationship with Britain, which might, for the first time, be turned to some use. How salutary it would be if Britain were to unilaterally forgo nuclear weapons to prove to the world that US policy is not merely to disarm non-whites.

It may be that the time is not yet ripe for real steps toward nuclear disarmament. That is not a prescription for inaction. The intervention in Bosnia not only had humane consequences but also showed that America really did care about saving Muslim lives (Halberstein, 2001, chs. 27–31). It would also be good if America offered the world some kind of leadership in energy conservation and climate control. Submitting to the jurisdiction of the International Criminal Court would provide other nations an example of good citizenship. Until the US takes itself seriously as a world sovereign, it can hardly expect anyone else to do so.

Even the best policies may take some time to build the necessary faith that America is sincere and that she is committed in a way that would survive a change of administrations. That is no excuse for what we have got. The rhetoric being used to justify war against Iraq is so false as to make one weep. It is true that Hussein has delusions of grandeur about leading a united Arab nation to world power. But we must see him in the light of reality. He has little standing in the Arab world. He has had to settle for aspiring to be the Arab hero who has tried to develop a deterrent to counter that of Israel. Although he has offered financial rewards to Palestinian terrorists, he is hated by Islamic fundamentalists of the sort that have links to al-Qaeda. He faces an Israel with a huge military advantage (Feldman and Shapir, 2004). This is the person who is supposed to pose a threat to US security. Neighbors, like Turkey, seem blissfully unaware they are at the mercy of a madman who may at any time unleash toxins that will kill them all.

As for the "war on terror," Iraq pales into insignificance compared to America's ally, Saudi Arabia. That nation's citizens supplied most of the al-Qaeda cadre who attacked the Twin Towers. It makes little effort to restrict the recruitment of terrorists within its own territory and allows "Islamic charities" to divert millions to international terrorists. How can anyone trust America's sincerity for decades – after it has debased its high purpose into propaganda, simply to panic its citizens into a war pursued for other reasons.

Then there is the Korean debacle. Oddly, naming North Korea as one of the three most wicked nations in the world, and proceeding to attack another of the nations so named, made North Korea think it might be next (Bush, 2002). So they have flexed their nuclear muscles, and what message has America sent to the world? If a state does not in fact have the weapons or delivery systems to threaten US interests, it is subject to invasion on moral grounds. While if a state actually has them, it will be treated with great circumspection. What an incentive system to offer nations (like Iran) who are unsure of America's intentions.

As for the struggle against organizations who have powerful weapons and are beyond the control of nation-states, and who therefore cannot be deterred by threatening a nation-state, they will have to be weakened mainly behind the scenes by cloak and dagger operations. These groups are such a threat to France, Germany, etc., as well as America, that those nations will not withhold cooperation despite the extraordinary language the American administration has directed at them over their unwillingness to invade Iraq.

Nonetheless, who would have thought America could have sowed so much disunity among nations who, after the events of 9/11, were united in a common cause. The great harm that has been done is that none of these nations, nations who should have been among the easiest to bind together, is likely to feel for decades that they can trust American probity or continuity of purpose. None of them is likely to develop a consensus that real leadership can be expected from America as world sovereign – as distinct from merely tolerating her as the world power that emerged triumphant (thank heaven) from the struggle with the Soviet Union. This alone would have been a good enough reason to alter the Iraq policy for a nation who would be king.

While international cooperation has the best chance of minimizing the threat to America from the above networks, nothing can guarantee security. Hopefully, the next attack on the US homeland will not bring a witless invasion somewhere to prove to the American public that "something is being done." The Byzantine Empire had to live for a thousand years without hysterical response to cities being periodically taken out by plague, the Bulgars, the Arabs, the Turks. An empire worth its salt will learn to respond rationally rather than by the politics of theater.

A sovereign should not be so evil as to always do good

Individuals can kill to do good whenever they can square it with their consciences. Great powers operating within their sphere of influence can usually do whatever they have convinced themselves is good (it rarely is, of course). A world sovereign does not have a license to do good indiscriminately. Saddam Hussein is a tyrant. Is it not a good thing to depose a tyrant? That depends on when and where and, above all, whether it detracts from consensus for the sovereign's power.

The Middle East is one of those agonizing cases where both sides have an overwhelming moral case. Any Jew at the end of World War II, witnessing the extermination of the 6 million after Western nations denied them escape, would believe that only if Jews had their own state could they give themselves the protection others had denied them. And you would not be too fastidious in securing that state: were Jews to be the only people in human history who never inconvenienced anyone in nation building?

On the other hand, a Palestinian Arab would say: fair enough – but *we* did nothing to you – this is not going to happen at our expense. I am not condemning with hindsight: America was not a world sovereign when she made her choice but a victorious great power acting out of sympathy for a people who had done much to win a place in our hearts. And I am not saying that US policy is now to be altered without guarantees for Israeli survival.

Still, the fact remains: by siding with Israel, America long ago took sides in a morally ambiguous dispute. This is something the world sovereign should avoid. The rule: when the sovereign chooses an ethical goal, it should be one that commands an almost universal moral consensus – like control of weapons of mass destruction. When you break this rule, a new rule takes hold: recognize that you have forfeited the right to do good. The rule only applies to the area concerned, of course: the Middle East. And even there, there are exceptions. The fact that America is morally compromised in the Middle East could be trumped by events so significant that they provide an overriding justification. If Iraq really posed a danger of universal destruction, that would suffice – which is why, no doubt, America has debased its true mission by rhetoric claiming as much. Another exception: you can intervene if a nation attacks across an international boundary and all look upon you as an enforcer of the peace – as in the case of the 1990–91 Gulf War.

Nations find it hard enough to reconcile themselves to the world sovereign's exercise of its power. It is absurd to expect Arabs to view America as a morally neutral sovereign playing a legitimate role. America is in the position of a ruler who has licensed one person in a neighborhood divided by hate to carry a gun. I refer to its huge unpaid loans that have helped Israel create a nuclear strike force (Washington Report). Is it odd that other residents try to sneak in unlicensed weapons to redress the balance? Syria may have weapons of mass destruction. Iraq was more open about it because it wanted to be recognized as the Arab state that could prevent Israel from using its first-strike capacity to dictate terms. Israel should have been left to deter Iraq's weapons, tolerating them if it must, crippling them if it could.

There is much talk of "regime change" as a justification of American military intervention. This is indicative of how little America understands the rational priorities of a world sovereign. If someone is trying to bring order to a primitive political system, reforming behavior is near the bottom of the list. A sheriff in a town where everyone carries a gun does not expend his political capital to reform the town drunk, despite the fact that it would be ideally desirable is help his wife and children.

This is particularly true in that America cannot tolerate real democracy in Iraq. Expression of the popular will would almost certainly divide Iraq into three states composed of Kurds, Sunni Arabs, and Shia Arabs respectively. An independent Kurdish state would destabilize Turkey (Phillips, 2004). An independent Shia state (or a united Iraq controlled by the Shia majority) would be an ally of "evil" Iran. Such political developments will have to be frustrated by force exercised either by America or by the very Sunnis who sustained Saddam Hussein in power.

At best, Iraq will get a more polite tyranny. At worst, America will be drawn into a series of interventions in a region in which it is hated. Is this an example of how America intends to exercise its power as world sovereign? Nothing could do more to create alarm – and undermine the confidence and consensus necessary for the sovereign to do its proper job: make peace wherever possible.

A sovereign must live down its history as a great power

Let us set aside what cannot be set aside, America's compromised position in the Middle East, in order to make a more general point. Any nation that history promoted to the role of world sovereign would have something to live down: its record as a great power. The excuse of every great power throughout history for invading weaker nations has been concern for the welfare of their peoples. Oddly, that concern is never much manifest ten years before the invasion and usually dissipates shortly after.

America's past is fairly typical. The Spanish–American War began with the goal of freeing the Spanish colonies and ended with their annexation. Since 1945, no misery has been too great, no government too awful, to merit much concern as long as America's strategic interests were served (Blum, 2002). America's outrage at Saddam Hussein's brutality was missing in the 1980s when it gave him the satellite intelligence he used to better target Iranian troops with chemical weapons. The world has every right to believe that if the sufferings of the Iraqi people are lessened, it will only be as an accident of US policy.

Well, are not such historical accidents to be welcomed – why look a gift horse in the mouth? Even if all that results in Iraq is a more polite tyranny, better that than a tyrant whose grandiose fantasies have inflicted so much misery. Who cares about the depth of America's concern so long as the consequences are good? The answer is that a world sovereign must care about the world's perception of its aims. Invading people for their own good is calculated to reinforce the perception that America has not really abandoned the

rhetoric and behavior of a great power. Other nations fear that grant-
ing America a license to interfere whenever there is a suffering
people really means giving America a license to kill. Surely the task
of the sovereign is to reassure, not to create alarm.

The sovereign must earn the right to use war to do good by
compiling a record that inspires confidence. It inspires confidence by
showing that it really does want a world made safer by the taming
of weapons of mass destruction. That may take a very long time.
Indeed, it may be only at that distant day when the first priority of
the sovereign, a safer world, has been attained that the next priority,
using force to promote the general welfare, can be persistently
pursued. As usual, there will be exceptional cases. The sovereign may
intervene when suffering is so great (Somalia) or slaughter so great
(Bosnia) that much of the world forgets its suspicions. But when it is
clear that suspicion is endemic, the sovereign, however great its dis-
interested passion to do good, must show moral restraint.

A world sovereign should watch its tongue

We have seen the harm done by the rhetoric of the Bush administration in the case of North Korea and its suspect rhetoric in the case
of Iraq. Worse still is the rhetoric of the so-called "war on terror,"
which has become almost universal. That rhetoric creates enemies
that are not true enemies and friends that are not true friends. It has
systematically mis-educated the American people about the true
state of the world.

Terror occurs when people both suffer from a burning sense
of injustice and cannot compete with whomever they see as their
oppressor in terms of conventional military tactics. Those are prerequisites rather than sufficient conditions: things like oil money
and favorable terrain help turn discontent into action. The alternative to terror is massive civil disobedience after the manner of
Gandhi and Martin Luther King. Sadly, circumstances rarely allow
for a pacifist response.

American irregulars were denounced as terrorists at the time of the American Revolution. Those loyal to the Crown who fled to Canada were not seeking a more temperate climate. American patriots could not get at English living in England. It would be interesting to know what would have happened if they had possessed the means. Two Prime Ministers of Israel, Menachem Begin and Yitzhak Shamir, were once members of terrorist organizations, namely, the Irgun and the Stern gang (Tessler, 1994, p. 207; Quandt, 1993, p. 349). The only way to stop terror everywhere would be to eliminate a sense of injustice or grievances everywhere. That is beyond the power of any world sovereign.

Therefore, the American people have been mis-educated about the true state of the world: they have been told that it can be divided into normal human beings and crazy people who out of sheer wickedness use terror. That premise entails the conclusion that everyone who is threatened by terrorists must be worthy of support, whether it is Israel fighting Palestinians, Russia fighting Chechens, the Philippines fighting Muslim rebels. America's recent knee-jerk response, that it will help the Philippine government "because they have a terrorist problem," shows how such absurd rhetoric can be hijacked by states the justice of whose cause America should carefully evaluate (Bush, 2003).

The only terror America should oppose is terror that threatens America and those nations whose hands are relatively clean. In passing, America has some cleansing of its own hands to do. Those who speak of America showing resolve against Iraq show a curious lack of resolve in one quarter: telling Israel privately but firmly that removal of the settlements on the West Bank must proceed with vigor (after all, they violate the UN resolutions that are so sacred to America) or American aid will be phased out. Israel should also be told that if they resist by mobilizing support within America, the President will address the nation and, for the first time, offer a full and honest presentation of the facts.

It may be said that there was no alternative to the rhetoric of the war on terror to energize the American public. That is nonsense. The Twin Towers was an attempt to destroy America's moral and political autonomy by inflicting cruel loss. It threatened the capacity of a free people to seek any goal abroad that anyone might resent. For domestic consumption, the fight against al-Qaeda should have been called "The Second War for American Independence." Other nations should have been asked whether they wanted America to be so crippled and whether they wanted to circumscribe their own autonomy out of fear. For international consumption, the objective of the joint effort against al-Qaeda could be called "freedom from fear" (note the alliteration).

No member of the Bush administration really believes what they say about terrorism – or at least let us pray to God that this is so. And no sovereign should give its subjects a fundamentally false picture of the world. A short-term gain in terms of emotive language is not worth the price. The farther the people are from a true apprehension of reality, the harder to sell policies that attack real evils.

A world sovereign should be prudent when pursuing self-interest

No one expects America to be a saint, if only because a saint cannot play the role of world sovereign. Naturally, the US feels threatened with collapse because of lack of oil. Does she fear that developments in the Middle East are in the offing that may put all of that oil in hostile hands? It would be refreshing if something so clearly within the spectrum of normal great-power behavior were the true objective of the war against Iraq.

America talks as if she wants democracy in the Middle East. The notion that, given the present mood, more popular governments would serve America's interests is too silly to merit discussion. So perhaps that is mere window dressing and the real objective is to set up an oil protectorate in Iraq supported by American arms and largesse. However, an assessment of consequences shows that this may well not be the best way to ensure a flow of oil to the West.

The dangers are:

1 Such a Western military enclave might become even more hated than Israel.
2 Every regime in the area would be forced to take sides and, if they remained US allies, the very regimes America fears may be overthrown would be overthrown.
3 Militants may make determined efforts to sabotage oil fields, refineries, and pipelines with incendiary devices.

Would it not be better to moderate American policy in the Middle East and depend on the desire of even regimes with limited sympathy for America to make money? That means selling oil on the international market for the best price you can get – with America having the advantage of being the biggest customer with the best hard currency.

However, let us assume that the pros and cons are evenly balanced on whether war or moderation is the best bet. If that is so, and if the world sovereign sees that war is undermining the consensus necessary to gain respect as world sovereign, that should tip the balance in favor of moderation. There is no sign that the present administration believes that such consensus counts as even a feather in the scales. For them, lining up support is a grudging concession to the fact that a lot of people, quite inexplicably, seem to either withhold support or at least care about the extent of support. After all, support should come automatically because US policy is so admirable; if a majority of nations disagree, well so much worse for them. The recalcitrant have already been told that ways will be found to punish them for their cowardice and cupidity.

A world sovereign should seek to internationalize its power

America has long treated the UN as a mere instrument of national policy. When it could not get its way in the 1980s, it crippled the UN by withholding funds. Now the US wishes to do the UN a great favor: take enforcement of that body's own resolutions out of its hands without its consent. In fact, as everyone knows, vigilante justice is the most direct path to undermining a government's authority and the one thing no government that wishes to survive can tolerate. Americans have been told that France and Germany are cool toward the current US posture toward the UN. In fact, they think America is behaving like an outlaw that threatens the international system. Their mouths are shut by fear. The world cannot afford to insult the only nation that can play a dominant and constructive role in world affairs (Dyer, 2002).

The US should be obsessed with an overriding objective: how to render world sovereignty tolerable and productive. It must somehow sugar the bitter pill of a single nation acting as world sovereign. Therefore, above all, it should be solicitous toward the UN. Showing respect for the UN is a heaven-sent opportunity to offer proof that America looks forward to the day, however distant, perhaps a century away, of putting its power under international control. That depends, of course, on its having met the test of slowly pacifying the world through use of its nuclear and military superiority, persuading other nations to give up weapons of mass destruction and neutralizing those who would privatize them, thereby creating a world that it can trust and that reciprocates that trust. It can justify its pursuit of a nuclear monopoly only by sending a consistent message that those arms are a heavy burden it will someday be willing to share: that it will move to international control of its weapons of mass destruction once their pacifying purpose has been achieved.

Current arms policy aims at winning miserable small-scale advantages. I refer to America's refusal to ratify the Comprehensive Nuclear Test Ban Treaty, the sabotage of the Biological and Toxic Weapons Convention, and worst of all, the announcement that America considers itself free to use nuclear weapons against states that do not possess them (Nye, 2002). The weapons named are tactical rather than weapons of mass destruction. But no tactical advantage is worth the anxieties that have been aroused.

All of the lessons rolled up into one

The one lesson: practice moral restraint to achieve a higher moral purpose. There is precedent for America playing the sovereign role of offering security to nations who forgo weapons. America has said that an attack on non-nuclear Japan will be deemed to be an attack on itself; America has long guaranteed the security of weaponless Iceland.

If that policy is to be extended, with great caution, to other states, fears must be alleviated. The greatest fear is that as America comes closer and closer to total dominance and others come closer and closer to being at its mercy, it will abuse its power to impose its own self-interest or self-defined moral goals. The roles of world sovereign and Don Quixote are incompatible. Every lesser moral goal must be assessed in the light of the overriding goal of a safer world. Is that not good enough to satisfy the most voracious moral appetite? (See Box 26.)

The problem with American foreign policy is not so much that Bush and his advisors are acting out their own peculiar version of the role of a great power, national interest modified by idealism, with the familiar mix of intelligence and stupidity, genuine moral purpose and blind moral arrogance. It is that America is playing the role of a great power at all. Rather than the role history has assigned it, namely, that of world sovereign.

Things could be worse. What if the USSR had won the Cold War? What if history had nominated France, a nation whose intelligent cynicism forbids any long-term objective of a better world order? Then there is Britain, a nation so addled by its "special relationship" with America that it has lost any capacity for independent thought. To be fair, Britain is experiencing that prolonged nervous breakdown that afflicted Sweden in the eighteenth and early nine-

---

Box 26

One cannot accuse Bush of not wanting to do good things according to his own lights. Shortly after the invasion, we were presented with the "Vision for a New Iraq" whose draft constitution contained an anti-abortion clause. Evidence of a happy correspondence between Islam and the President's moral principles.

---

teenth centuries when it had to face the fact that it was no longer a great power. It is a pity that Britain has developed no higher goal than to be the jackal that runs at the lion's feet.

America must choose. It can exploit its position as the sole great power, treating the entire world as a sphere of influence, baffled by the world's failure to applaud its good intent (when it exists). Or it can play the role of world sovereign. To settle for the former is to settle for being a dwarf in giant's clothing. To choose the latter means being a good and prudent king, unloved, envied, resented, but acknowledged by all to be essential to security and well-being.

• • •

This concludes the sermon given prior to the invasion of Iraq. The second half of this chapter develops themes only adumbrated above: the long-term security of Israel; America's self-image; and American military power.

A tale of two nations

Two nations bound together like Siamese twins: Israel and the United States. At present, they are interacting in a way that undermines both the security of one and the interests of the other. In the long run, events are likely to force a choice no one wants to make. The temptations of imperialism are affecting both in terms of what they do within and outside their borders. I will set the consequences for Israeli society aside, but no American can ignore how

America's conception of its security affects its own quest for the good life.

Israel and the left bank

One momentous event has occurred since the invasion of Iraq: President Bush's statement of April 14, 2004 accepting that "already existing population centers" on the West Bank may have to remain in Israeli hands (Bush, 2004). The following day, John Kerry, his Democratic opponent for President, added his endorsement (Zogby, 2004).

Bush and Kerry have sent entirely the wrong message to Israel. It is not in Israel's interests to effectively annex sections of the left bank. Israel is in denial. She will not face the fact that maximizing her chances of survival depends on Palestinian public opinion. I will argue for four propositions: Israel will always need American support; America cannot support Israel if the Arab governments of the Middle East unite against America; that will occur unless a majority of Palestinians are willing to tolerate the existence of Israel; and that is dependent on the creation of a viable Palestinian state.

Israel and America

Israel would not have the military advantage she enjoys in the Middle East without the enormous American military and financial aid she has received. From 1949 to 1997, foreign aid grants and loans totaled $74 billion and unpaid interest totaled $50 billion (Washington Report). She is an American protectorate. The only alternative to American aid is the one that I have suggested: that America gives her the protection she gives Japan and Iceland by taking her under America's nuclear umbrella and maintaining a symbolic military presence in Israel. The fanatics among the Palestinians, and throughout the Middle East in general, will never accept Israel no matter what she does. Therefore, she will always remain in need of American support.

America and the Middle East

Any Palestinian leader willing to make a formal peace with Israel, even one that included the West Bank and East Jerusalem, would probably be assassinated or at best overthrown. America has always totally misconstrued its role in the Israeli–Palestinian dispute. To broker a real and lasting peace agreement may be impossible and America's prestige should not be dependent on doing the impossible. The mania of every American President to leave office with a "Middle East peace settlement" to his credit exposes us to ridicule.

The building of the wall is the most intelligent and realistic thing done in the Middle East in over sixty years of posturing. It should have been a vehicle for presenting the Palestinians with a state as a fait accompli, a state they could live with and within well enough so that moderate opinion would evolve toward tolerance of Israel. That will take time and Israel has to accept that there will be attacks (against which she will retaliate) from the territory of the new state for a long time. The demand that some "leader" deliver peace along her border is an absurdity. The creation of a viable Palestinian state is in her interests and peace must be a gradual evolution, not some immediate reward.

But the Israelis cannot bear to liquidate their settlements on the West Bank. They speak of only absorbing 20 or 30 percent of the West Bank. That is not moderation. If they had built the wall around more than they have, it would leave a huge Arab fifth column behind their lines. The territory Israel is annexing is the most fertile and viable portion of the West Bank in terms of water supply. The Palestinians are being consigned to something like the American Southwest without irrigation. Not even moderate Palestinian opinion can accept this – ever.

As popular (not democratic) government comes to the Middle East, the moderates will be hard pressed by the not moderate masses. Without the existence of a viable Palestinian state, they cannot possibly tolerate American support for Israel. When peak oil arrives, they will be forced to play the oil card. America's only choices will be to try to dominate militarily the major oil producing states, which will prove impossible, or abandon Israel. Those "friends" of Israel who scream every time there is a hint that the US government might rein her in are pushing her toward disaster. Her survival is dependent on a moderate Arab public opinion that is being systematically alienated. The easy political victories they win at present blind them to the rage building up inside American intellectuals coerced into silence. And if the price of supporting Israel hits the Americans in the pocket, they will find how quickly public opinion can shift.

A viable Palestinian state

This poses the question of whether it is economically possible for Israel to leave the entire West Bank in hostile hands for some years. At present, Israel could not survive without water from the West Bank. However, by phasing out the water-thirsty sectors of her horticulture, eliminating the absurdity of growing apricots and so forth, and initiating desalinization projects, this could be overcome. "Making the desert bloom" does not help make Israel self-sufficient, as if that were an attainable goal (she cannot do without a host of imports). It makes her dependent on West Bank water, with all the baggage that carries.

The possibility of giving up East Jerusalem is gaining ground in Israeli public opinion. The Orthodox, who wish to get rid of secular Israelis in Jerusalem only slightly less than they wish to be rid of Arabs, are causing many Israelis to leave the city. The result of this exodus and high Arab birth rates, and the dependence of industry on Arab labor, is that Jerusalem is edging ever closer to an Arab majority. A political boundary that cut off the Arab East would solve many problems.

Can Israel resist the temptation to maximize her territory and take on the wrath of the settlers on the West Bank? Whatever the answer to that question, it is not in anyone's interest for the American government to "accept" the permanence of the West Bank settlements. That is the road to three great disasters: America's eventual betrayal of Israel; counterproductive American meddling in the affairs of the Middle East; and forfeiting America's opportunity to play the role of world sovereign.

Given the bipartisan support for Bush's declaration, there is little hope of a more sensible policy in the near future. But at least, idealists who are also realists in America now have a sharp focus: if they cannot moderate US policy toward Israel, other foreign policy victories (mere withdrawal from Iraq) will be drained of substance. The long-term prospects are not hopeless. In 1945, there was another great power that espoused an irrational foreign policy. George Kennan advocated educating the USSR about political reality by way of a policy of containment. They were to be forced, time after time, to moderate their behavior when they ran into the countervailing force of American power – so that eventually they would realize that the world was not theirs for the making without the good will of others.

Political reality is a wonderful educator even when those who teach its lessons are many and weak rather than one and strong. Time after time, it is likely to sober America by conjoining its behavior with consequences unforeseen and unwelcome. America may come to realize that there is something better than trying to coerce the world into playing the role of a sphere of influence. It took Russia forty years to moderate its behavior. America's friends must hope that she is not a slow learner.

The roots of American exceptionalism

Every nation suffers from the delusion that it is an exception to the veniality of all others. But few are so far removed from reality as to assume that the rest of the world shares that opinion. When students ask about the ideological roots of current US policy, I am reluctant to respond, in that such speculation is not far removed from psychoanalysis of an only quasi-existent group mind. However, I have an opinion.

President Bush and his advisors are no more exotic than the Mandarins of China, unusual perhaps only in the depth of their patriotism. American history has dictated the contents of their minds and, like most Americans, they are too ahistorical to assess their heritage. Two huge nations, isolated and virtually self-sufficient, nineteenth century America and imperial China. Both self-obsessed, each looked into the mirror and saw a unique human experiment with a people and institutions specially blessed. The Chinese court could not imagine why anyone would want to visit the barbarians and 60 percent of US Congressmen see no reason to possess a passport.

After World War I, the view that America was the center of the universe split into two ideologies. American liberals tended to espouse Wilsonian idealism, that is, they believed that America had a mission to democratize the world beyond its borders. If this failed, the presumption was that other great powers were too wicked to lay their interests on the altar of a better world (Krock, 1992). However, there was at least the breath of a psychological constraint: that there was something odd about attempting to impose a democratic world order by undemocratic means, that is, through force rather than a consensus that embraced at least a fair swag of other nations.

American conservatives tended to be isolationists. They found the rest of the world so wicked as to be hopeless. And here, there was a very powerful psychological constraint: America should not risk contamination by associating with bad company but should concentrate on perfecting its own society within its own borders (Cole, 1962).

The world-view of the present administration combines the worst features of both ideologies. The conviction that the world is wicked is held with all of the fervor of the conservatives. This erases the liberal constraint (never very strong) that other nations should be persuaded. The crusade to improve the world is espoused with all of the fervor of the liberals. This erases the conservative constraint that America should focus on perfection within. The result is something rather incredible. The very definition of sovereignty is control over the means of organized violence. In asserting the right to license who may carry weapons of mass destruction, America has asserted a claim to world sovereignty. And the stated rationale for this claim – American exceptionalism. The rest of the world should simply acknowledge America's unique virtue.

Thus, we have a nation drunk on self-esteem and uninhibited in its pursuit of its mission. It would, of course, prefer others to endorse its actions, if only because that would speak well of them and would enhance America's strength. But that does not affect the moral equation: America has the right to act unilaterally because its motives are pure and failure to do so is moral cowardice.

I would be the last to object to the fact that America's psychology has a moral dimension. But there is a kind of self-esteem that easily translates into moral arrogance, particularly when a nation becomes aware that it possesses great power. Self-esteem is a virtue only when it has a solid foundation. A combination of idealism and realism brings self-esteem under control. It implies a balance sheet that weighs up when we have put our ideals into practice with self-restraint and rationality against when we have ignored them or made cheap moral gestures. That is usually a humbling experience. Otherwise, you are likely to get the worst possible combination: moral arrogance endlessly expanding to fill a cognitive vacuum.

America's global empire

An assessment of America's military posture poses two problems: whether America's global empire serves its true interests; and how to deal with terror without hysteria. Most Americans reject the existence of an American empire. Colin Powell has characterized

America as a nation unlike others that seeks to annex no foreign territory. Rather it sends its sons and daughters to be killed in defense of freedom, asking only for a few square feet of earth in which to bury its dead. As we wipe away the tear in our eye, we would do well to compare two maps: one from 1897 showing the British Empire under Queen Victoria; and one showing the present-day American empire as defined by a military presence.

In terms of military presence abroad, America dwarfs Britain's global reach. Even when not involved in a shooting war like Iraq, America maintains over 250,000 army and naval personnel abroad in about 1,000 bases in over 130 countries; if one adds spies, technicians, teachers, dependents, and civilian contractors, the total is over 500,000 (Johnson, 2004). Britain at its height had 96,000 soldiers overseas (about 73 percent of whom were in India) and 90,000 naval personnel. They were located in thirty-three countries and that figure includes those hosting naval bases only (Porter, 1991).

In terms of military dominance, Britain had rivals in every area of weaponry. The US has 9,000 M1 Abrams tanks, a weapon so formidable that it has suffered only three battle casualties in its twenty years of combat use. The rest of the world has nothing that can compete. The US has nine super-carrier battle groups at sea, the rest of the world none. The US has three different kinds of stealth aircraft, the rest of the world none. The US is also far ahead in terms of smart missiles and unmanned high-altitude drones (Ferguson, 2004) – see Box 27.

The difference between America as dominant world power in the twenty-first century and Britain as dominant world power in the nineteenth century is that it is no longer worth the cost of actually acquiring colonies in the classical sense. Britain "annexed" territories that were either settled by its own people or sparsely populated by pre-industrial peoples, or that had weak national identity because modern nationalism had not yet taken root. America was not capable of pacifying Vietnam and cannot pacify Iraq. Imagine making India a colony today. America has the kind of global empire

---

Box 27

The American arms advantage will escalate over at least the next twenty years. The US military has realistic plans to miniaturize its unmanned aerial vehicles, first to the size of birds and then to the size of bees with full intelligence and combat capabilities. Eventually, they will have something even tinier, called "smart dust," to be deployed in huge swarms that can identify targets and persons and release nano-weapons. Indeed, by 2025, combat troops will be phased out in favor of a fighting force that is largely robotic, a drone army permeating ground, water, and air (Kurzweil, 2005). Without the risk of casualties that might alienate public opinion, America can launch numerous military interventions whether they make any sense or not.

Before leaving the maps, just locate Iran on the US bases map. Clearly, any right-thinking person can see that this nation is a plausible threat to America and that its people could not possibly feel threatened by the United States.

---

it is possible to have in our century and Britain had the kind of global empire it was possible to have a century or so ago.

However, it is foolish to argue about whether to use the word "empire" as if that had the capacity to alter reality. The central questions are: what are the political relationships between America and the nations that host its troops; and what strategic purposes do its bases serve? These are intertwined. I will discuss only those nations and bases that are most significant.

There is the strategic purpose of encircling continental America with bases that afford an early warning system, so as to destroy incoming missiles and retaliate more quickly. This is served by the bases in the western hemisphere inclusive of Greenland and Iceland plus those in Hawaii and Alaska. Whether all of these are really necessary, what with satellite surveillance and nuclear subs at sea, can be questioned, but there is no significant political cost in terms of antagonizing host nations or making others nations feel

The British Empire in 1897

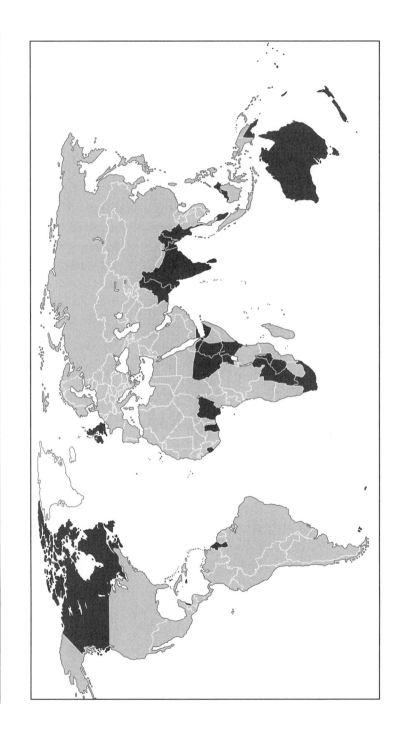

America, its allies, and bases abroad

threatened. The exception, of course, is the Panama Canal Zone but that has a real and legitimate strategic purpose. Iceland is a protectorate in the sense that the US defends it in the absence of its own armed forces, but, as we have seen, that is not always a bad thing.

The bases in Western Europe are residues of the Cold War and even the US Congress has limited troop numbers in that area to 100,000. But the world has got used to them, no one perceives them as a real threat, and no host nation is politically compromised by their presence. The extension of early warning bases into Eastern Europe to intercept missiles launched by "rogue states" is absurd in strategic terms. Stalin never dared attack the US and neither North Korea nor Iran will risk certain extermination. If they did have sophisticated missiles, the system would not work. It is purely a matter of pork barrel politics, that is, US corporations located in electorally important states see money in it. Whatever the eagerness of Eastern European nations who hate their former master, it is stupid to insult Russia by stationing US bases there.

One good thing has come of it by pure accident. Russia has proposed, as a sign that America is sincere when it says the system is not directed against her, that the bases be erected on her territory. This would be a wonderful signal to the world that America is genuinely interested in cooperation to pacify the world, rather than the posturing traditional to great powers. It would be well worth the waste of resources. That America cannot see the opportunity shows how far away it is from being worthy of the role of world sovereign.

The strategic purpose of encircling and saturating the oil producing area of the Middle East with bases located in the Arabian peninsula, Iraq, Afghanistan, Pakistan, and Islamic states that were once part of the USSR is disastrous from every point of view. Most of the people of the area are anti-American for what they deem to be very good reasons. To think that military force can guarantee the flow of oil to America thanks to bases surrounded by a hostile population is the height of folly. All it guarantees is sabotage and costly attempts to maintain in power governments whose legitimacy is undermined by the very fact that they tolerate American bases. Thanks to its history of Western military domination, no Middle Eastern people will tolerate a Western military force on its soil except as a desperate expedient to be liquidated as soon as possible.

I will review some host nations of US bases. Kuwait was traumatized by its recent invasion from Iraq, but even she is appalled by the prospect of America's control of 23 percent of her territory. The governments of the anti-democratic autocracies of the Persian Gulf seem confident of their viability for the time being and are willing to be American satraps. Saudi Arabia is less sure and was not entirely displeased when America withdrew most of its forces to punish her for not supporting the Iraq war strongly enough. The word "satrap" is appropriate, I think. The word was originally applied to the ruler of a Persian province, and today often carries the implication of a local tyrant.

Americans may object to the notion that the US has diminished the sovereignty of these nations. Let us imagine that America had foreign bases on its soil, whose firepower was greater than all of its own forces combined, whose soldiers were immune to prosecution in US courts, and who were exempted by a "Status of Forces Agreement" from any responsibility for environmental damage caused (Johnson, 2004).

The enrollment of Kyrgyzstan, Georgia, and Uzbekistan (a tyranny if there ever was one) as satraps is pointless and irritating to the Russians. They have already reacted by completing a base only 40 miles from the US base in Kyrgyzstan at Bishkek (Ferguson, 2004). More serious, does America have any real intention of restoring full sovereignty to either Iraq or Afghanistan? It has established at least four bases in Iraq that it refuses to designate as temporary. A fifth base has been established in Afghanistan.

In mid-2007, Iraqi oil workers struck, partially because of outrage at the fact that America has made it a non-negotiable demand that the entire Iraqi oil industry be leased on favorable terms to US corporations for thirty years (Parker, 2007). Does America think that any truly independent Iraqi government will honor these contracts? When peak oil hits, does America really think it can extract more than its market share by saturating the Middle East with bases that drive the locals wild with rage?

There is the strategic purpose of encircling China. This is to be served by a military alliance with India plus the crescent of bases extending from Pakistan through Southeast Asia up through the Philippines, Japan, and Korea. The most serious mistake is the nuclear alliance with India. Why, exactly, do we want to antagonize China needlessly? She has no serious overseas territorial ambitions. Her military forces are third rate. The excuse usually given is that, thanks to her rate of growth, China will match the US economically sometime after 2030 and the US had better get ready to "contain" her now. America should be nice to China in the hope it can cooperate with her as joint world sovereign when the time comes. A pity America is not winning her trust by behaving like a world sovereign today.

The American bases in the Far East have not been seen as too provocative thus far. China understands the historical reasons that have made Taiwan into an American protectorate and is willing to wait for the inevitable "Hong Kong" solution. The fact that Japan is an American protectorate in return for not being a nuclear power itself is actually reassuring to China. The US itself would like to reduce its commitment in Korea. The danger is that the alliance with India signals a whole new strategic role for these bases that will embitter China. When Spain encircled France in the sixteenth century, France did not rest until the circle was broken. Can America never look at the world through the eyes of anyone else? Imagine a circle of Chinese bases that ran from Central America through the Caribbean through Long Island into Canada. But of course the US has no aggressive intent.

In sum, a critique of the strategic rationale of US bases dictates removal of at least half of them. All bases in the Middle East should be removed, there is no sense putting more bases in Europe, and there should be an unspoken agreement with China about what bases are to be retained in the Far East. Most of the bases within the

US have little military value and exist simply to create jobs and profits. The early warning system has no military value at all. The so-called war on terror is necessary but the part that makes sense, cloak and dagger work, is cheap.

Making good on a promise

Remember my promissory note: to show that American security would not suffer by deep cuts in military spending. I hope I have redeemed it (see Box 28).

I have one misgiving, namely, that my analysis of America's global empire exaggerates the rationality of its design. The real policy seems to be, whenever history hands us a base, keep it for a rainy day. The most frightening thing is an imperial power whose behavior is circumscribed by no rational limits. Everyone fears an actor driven purely by primitive forces such as the lust for power. A strategy can be tempered by critique but expansion with no strategy can be combated only by the shock of defeat. During the worst days of the Cold War, America seemed to have lost all sense of a rational policy of deterrence and was amassing more and more weapons of mass destruction simply because it could. Even as good a friend as New Zealand was dismayed and sent a message by declaring itself nuclear free.

Perhaps the shock of Iraq will bring a reappraisal of present policy in the Middle East. The outcome might conjoin the best, rather than the worst, from the isolationist and Wilsonian traditions: be wary of foreign commitments that are pointless and corrupting; be alert to opportunities to do good where there is a genuine consensus. There was a genuine consensus for the Marshall Plan and NATO. Where is the consensus for a base in Uzbekistan?

America afraid

The difficulty America is having extracting its troops from Iraq is obscuring the emergence of a more intractable problem: how to

Box 28

I have not touched on possible savings from what America spends on military aid. Her record in the Middle East is too fantastic for a Gilbert and Sullivan comic opera. First, billions were given to Saddam Hussein in Iraq to arm him against Iran, then billions to Israel to arm her against Saddam Hussein, then millions to the Taliban to arm them against the Russians, then billions to invade Afghanistan to overthrow the Taliban, now $20 billion to Saudi Arabia and $30 billion to Israel to arm them against who – Iran or one another? It is true the Saudis will pay for their arms although Israel will not.

America keeps trying to pick winners in an area where no nation has guaranteed stability of regime except Israel and Turkey. Reflect for a moment as to how much better off everyone (including America) would be if it had never sent any arms whatsoever to the Middle East (or overthrown any regime in the Middle East). It is not too late to change. We could save a lot of money just by admitting that pumping arms into the Middle East has only one predictable consequence: everyone will feel they need more.

No one whose friendship we buy will stay bought. Whatever accommodation a ruling elite may make, the people of every Arab nation hate America as an ally of Israel. The Israelis half-hate us because everyone dislikes being dependent on a foreign power. The only objective worthy of active pursuit in the Middle East is the preservation of Israel. The only military aid that makes any sense is what we give Israel to maintain her army. She would not have had to spend so much if we had not spent billions to arm states all of which are her enemies or potential enemies. Taking her under our nuclear umbrella might, in the long run, allow her to spend less even on her nuclear establishment.

extract itself from Afghanistan. A worst-case scenario looms in which the Taliban gains ground so that it controls significant territory. I doubt whether the US public would wear the transfer of 100,000 troops from Iraq to Afghanistan. What if whatever forces it is tolerable to commit cannot suppress the rebels? You can declare victory and quit Iraq (we got rid of Saddam Hussein), but the whole point of Afghanistan was to depose the Taliban. Leaving them in control, defiant and openly allowing al-Qaeda to operate, appears to involve an intolerable loss of face.

And yet, America is tolerating this very thing. Pakistan has taken no serious steps to prevent al-Qaeda from establishing camps along its western frontier. There is a certain irony here. Americans needs Pakistan as an ally to fight a war in Iraq (a country in which al-Qaeda never existed) and therefore gives al-Qaeda a safe haven from which to operate. This tolerance, of course, will not survive the duration of the war in Iraq. So what is to be done about nations that defy the US by openly permitting al-Qaeda to base camps on their territories?

Hopefully, we have learned that invading countries is both too costly and counterproductive. If only fear and hysteria can be controlled, we may actually try what is more effective. Locate the camps through intelligence (satellite and otherwise) and follow the Israeli example of liquidating their physical structure. When they are rebuilt, do it again. This will allow individuals to escape but it is rather inefficient to hunt scattered individuals with an army. Armies are large and make a lot of noise and the pursued have plenty of time to run and hide. You use private detectives to locate individuals, that is, you use your secret service. This may seem unspectacular but it will have to do.

PART IV

A history of moral confusion

8   William James and Leo Strauss

The recognition of cultural relativity carries its own values . . .
As soon as the new opinion is embraced as customary belief, it
will be another trusted bulwark of the good life.
> (Ruth Benedict, 1934)

Socrates's last word was that he knew that he knew nothing.
> (Allan Bloom, 1987)

Now for the most interesting part: the quest for a philosophical foundation for Jefferson's ideals. The students that Bloom and I criticized for their relativism are not really to blame. They are merely the latest manifestation of a tradition whose deep roots in America's intellectual thought go back over a hundred years. By 1900, American intellectuals knew that Jefferson's ideals could no longer be based on Locke and were seeking a foundation on the best that modern science and critical philosophy could offer. That attempt is not viable, but they were trying to do something necessary and deserve to be treated with respect. Their thinking is so deeply engrained in our minds that contemporary intellectuals of postmodern persuasion recreate their arguments. It is indeed true that those who despise history are doomed to repeat it.

    This chapter will fall into three sections: showing why relativism is a false friend; a quick rejection of Rawls; and an analysis of the followers of Leo Strauss.

Ruth Benedict and cultural relativism

To put Benedict into context, we must recapitulate the battle of ideas in America fought by the generation in ascendancy after the Civil War. Everyone was now a Darwinian. The conservative Social Darwinists used Darwin (William Graham Sumner was more sophisticated) to defend the elitist excesses of late nineteenth-century capitalism as the "survival of the fittest." Cut-throat economic competition was the equivalent of the struggle for survival, and the elites who had prevailed represented the highest level of social progress ever attained. Those who were alarmed by the excesses of the industrial rich and the emergence of the trusts needed an ideology to break the "steel chain of ideas" that lent dignity to the power and privileges of the plutocracy. They found their ideology in reform Darwinism (Goldman, 1956, pp. 66–72).

The reform Darwinists emphasized the environmental side of Darwin's theory, that is, the fact that changing environment was the crucial factor in promoting new evolutionary developments. They attacked the conservatives as actually being pre-Darwinian (the worst of epithets) in that they wanted to freeze in time the social system of late nineteenth-century America. They went further: the thinking of those who supported that system, the laissez-faire economics, Spencer's sociology, legalistic jurisprudence, and most of all the savagely competitive ideals, were merely social products of the time. Walter Lippmann (1913) was convinced that reformers should greet thoroughgoing ethical relativism with jubilation. He said that any belief in an "intrinsic" good would be used to bolster the cause of reaction and the status quo (he later changed his mind).

Franz Boas was pioneering the new science of anthropology and Ruth Benedict was one of his best pupils. She anticipated the modern temper by making tolerance the supreme virtue and believed that cross-cultural anthropology could give it an unassailable foundation. Her greatest book, *Patterns of Culture*, closes with a rejection of "absolute definitions of morality" and "categorical imperatives." But that, we are told, does not forbid "rationally selected goals." Benedict (1934, ch. 8) says that social relativity should not be construed as a doctrine of despair but carries with it its own values, namely, "tolerance for coexisting and equally valid patterns of life."

The implicit connecting argument appears to be: all values are sociologically relative; therefore, we have no reason to favor one value over another; therefore, we have an obligation to be tolerant and treat all values as equally valid.

The argument self-destructs as soon as it is realized that an obligation to be tolerant is itself a moral principle or value and not something else, say, a turnip. Therefore, it too is sociologically relative, and, according to the terms of the argument, we have no reason to favor it over intolerance. Some may think that while tolerance is not logically entailed by sociological relativism, it is an obviously appropriate psychological reaction. But actually, the reaction depends on the person: psychology sets no limits on itself. When it breaks free of logic, it can move anywhere from appreciation of diversity and tolerance to disgust for the "primitive" and a sense of arrogant self-approval.

William James and epistemological relativism

William James (1897, pp. 199–210) anticipated Benedict. However, he based his version of egalitarian ethics not on sociological relativism but on our lack of knowledge of the good (epistemological relativism). The argument: there is no defensible criterion of objectivity in ethics; therefore, we cannot label certain human demands or the demands of certain people as objective, thus putting them ahead of the demands of other people; therefore, we should treat all human demands as worthy of satisfaction without reference to what they are or whose they are.

Once again, the argument self-destructs, this time when it is realized that treating the demands of people in general as worthy of satisfaction, even though I hold no moral principle to that effect, is to accept the objective status of those demands. Objectivity in ethics can be stated as follows: an ideal or demand has objective status if all humanity ought to respect it whether they actually find it attractive or not. Therefore, James' conclusion amounts to asserting that literally all human demands have objective status. If we lack a criterion of objectivity in ethics, we can hardly go from saying that certain human demands cannot be labeled objective to saying that all human demands have objective status.

Do contemporary postmodern thinkers commit what I call the "tolerance school error"? I think so, although since many of them eschew the use of reasoned debate about ethics, you have to look for implicit argument. Yeatman (1992, p. 7) says that different social groups generate distinct perspectives on justice; there is a Maori view and a Pakeha view but no "God's-eye view." This means that "all then that is possible" is a mutual dialogue on "how they should decide and manage their life conditions." If the assertion about the relativity of justice is supposed to logically entail mutual respect and negotiating a mutually acceptable compromise, then this is the tolerance school error.

Young believes that the fact that two groups define themselves, after mutual interaction, as both similar to and dissimilar from one another is something from which "we can *derive* [emphasis mine] a social and political ideal of togetherness in difference." This is later defined as a "mutual recognition" of "group related rights." Actually, there is no bridge whatsoever linking the fact that two ethnic groups define themselves in terms of similarities and dissimilarities with the ideal of mutual regard for one another's rights. Or at least there is no bridge unless some middle term is inserted in the argument, namely, something that asserts group equality. This could be either the tolerance school argument (group differences themselves entail valuing groups equally) or a moral principle (when confronted with differences, we ought to extend mutual regard). Since Young (1992, pp. 16, 21) provides no connecting link, we are left in doubt.

It is interesting that Haggis (1992, p. 75) interprets Young as rejecting a "universal moral point of view" and as positing the claim that "I want" can be translated into "I am entitled to." Such a claim is operationally identical with William James' conclusion that all human demands are worthy of satisfaction. The rejection of moral objectivity is identical with James' premise. All of these thinkers are from the English-speaking world but only Iris Marion Young is influential on the American scene. I do not know if she was aware of her debt to James.

In any event, enough has been said to show that when today's youth base their humane-egalitarian ideals on relativism, they are building on sand. The notion that relativism justifies ideals like tolerance or equality is logically incoherent. When humane values are given preferment over their opposites on the grounds that no one's values merit preferment, something has gone wrong. Tolerance and equality, group chauvinism and elitism, all are values and must share a common fate. The former do not pop out of a pit that has swallowed all values unless a conjuror is at work,

A detour into Rawls

I will not spend much time on John Rawls, but wish to acknowledge his attempt to provide an alternative to cultural relativism "as a bulwark of the good life." In 1972, he offered a theory of justice as a philosophical foundation for the ideals of American liberals. It won over many scholars. Evaluating his theory raises the question of what he was trying to do. If he was trying to systematize liberal ideals into a coherent whole, he did a good job. But that is not the same as what Jefferson thought he had or what the Straussites are concerned about. They want something to show that humane ideals are in accord with knowledge of the good, something that would justify them versus anti-humane ideals and banish ethical skepticism.

Rawls may well never have envisioned that more ambitious role, but in any event his theory of justice cannot play it. His theory posits people in an original position, that is, people not yet conceived and not yet reared in a particular place at a particular time. Therefore, they have no particular genetic endowment, or personal traits, or social status, and, indeed, a veil of ignorance forbids them knowledge of any particularity they may eventually attain. They calculate what would serve their interests and, not surprisingly, decide in favor of social arrangements that protect even the most unfortunate from misery, that is, social arrangements with a strong humane-egalitarian flavor.

An elitist like Nietzsche would quite rightly argue that the original position begs the question. The issue is whether all qualify for moral concern or whether that must be earned by exhibiting an excellence (being a superman or a creative genius). All Nietzsche need say is that, as long as people are in the original position, they know too little about themselves (or others) to assess whether their interests are worth taking into account. And the fact that Rawls sets them calculating their interests in such a state of ignorance merely shows his bias: that whether or not someone exhibits excellence is irrelevant. In a word, the original position is simply an arbitrary leveler. In stripping people of differences in genetic potential and developed talent, it obliterates the distinction between the great (who merit concern for their fate) and the herd (who merit no concern). Every human being has been transformed into an everyman who therefore takes every man's interests into account. The original position covertly gives all human beings a ticket of admission into the circle of moral concern without regard to merit.

Using this method, an animal rights advocate could simply posit that those in the original position were ignorant of whether they would be born animals, and have them calculate that self-interest dictated a social order that valued the welfare of human beings and animals equally. This is too easy a road to the justification of animal rights.

In 1985, Rawls initiated an approach to justification called wide reflective equilibrium, which has been elaborated by Kai Nielsen

216

(1994). Nielsen sees a trend in pluralist democracies toward achieving a liberal-left consensus about justice. He believes that modernization makes the trend likely but not inevitable; for example, it could be reversed by economic crisis or deteriorating educational systems. However, at present, this trend can be furthered by philosophers promoting a rational scrutiny of conflicting ideals along these lines: seeking coherence between our considered moral convictions and our moral principles; and relating these to social theory, a scientific account of human nature, and a wide range of factual considerations. The objective is a rational consensus. It will be rational within the context of what is known at a particular time in a particular evolving democracy, and that will marginalize racism, sexism, and class elitism.

Here we must distinguish between a historical trend and a trend based on reason. We all hope that history is on the side of humane ideals, in that the more people who become humane, the easier the task of building a humane society. But only a rational enterprise, a logical and evidential argument that shows that all of us should accept humane ideals, would count as a justification. Even if history for some reason secured the domination of humane-egalitarian ideals, were those ideals as rationally indefensible as classical racism, they would hardly have been vindicated. Moreover, we must face the fact that any actual social consensus will always be protective of falsehoods, not just truths.

The emerging American liberal-left consensus is no exception. It regards as indecent questioning beliefs no sane person can hold. Blacks are said to suffer from great environmental handicaps when below average achievement is explained, and yet blacks are supposed to emerge from that environment without crippling intellectual or character deficiencies (Flynn, 1980). There are supposed to be no intellectual group differences that are of genetic origin, something unlikely to be true of the huge gap between Chinese and white Americans in visuo-spatial skills (Flynn, 1991). There is supposed to be no tension between raising wages, either by legislation or by collective bargaining, and job creation. Unemployment is supposed to be the major cause of crime. Although a member of the Socialist left, I am conducting no vendetta against the liberal left. A list at least as long could be compiled for the right. The point is that no social process is really very good at truth-testing. No social trend will ever replace the lonely individual as the assessor of truth.

Perhaps wide reflective equilibrium comes down to something fairly simple? Every one of us should test conflicting ideals in the light of all we know to be true at the moment. Perhaps we can show that humane-egalitarian ideals do not require sweeping the truths of social or biological science under the carpet while anti-humane ones do. To show that, we will have to come down from the heights and get our minds dirty by using social science to refute our anti-humane opponents in detail. If that is what wide reflective equilibrium is all about, I will eventually endorse wide reflective equilibrium. But that is getting ahead of the story.

Bloom and the Straussites

In my opinion, the only serious attempt to "save" Americans from cultural relativism has come from the students of Leo Strauss. The book by Allan Bloom, *The Closing of the American Mind* (1987) is virtually a Straussite primer. We were both students of Strauss, whose own lineage of academic mentors begins with Max Weber, and I will use Bloom's book as a vehicle to interpret what the Straussite crusade is all about. As will become clear, even if Bloom were still alive, and even if he agreed with my interpretation, he might feel forced to deny it. At any rate, what I offer may explain to academics all over the world why the presence of a Straussite in their department often means accommodating someone who believes that every one of his colleagues is an enemy of the good. See Box 29.

Bloom puts eloquently the universal Straussite message. First, that ethical skepticism, the view that no rational case can be made for any particular set of ideals (including humane ideals) vis-à-vis others, has pernicious effects on the social order. At best, it leaves

---

Box 29 Strauss and the hidden text

The followers of Strauss can be irritating for other reasons. Strauss was convinced that the great works of political philosophy were never to be taken at face value. Hidden behind the words was a message for the initiated or the perceptive, which sometimes could be extracted only by using the methods of code breaking or cryptography. The true messages were sometimes reassuring: it appears that Shakespeare really did write his own plays. Now what does that mean? Of course, he wrote what he wrote. Does that conceal the fact that I disbelieve that Shakespeare wrote the plays attributed to him? Is what I will say about the Inner Circle of Straussites to be taken literally, or merely an invitation to his other students to adopt my own state of mind?

The eminent chemist T. J. C. Lark suffered from a peculiar obsession that forced him to read and reread endlessly every word of the Straussite literature. Shortly before his self-inflicted blindness, he wrote these lines:

> Sage after sage so much learning
>   Sage after sage so little said
> Page after page can't stop turning
>   Page after page wish I were dead.

(To save chemists from harassment, I had better add that Lark is only loosely based on a real person and that the person's fate was not quite so magic.)

---

us with a witless and rudderless cultural relativism that undermines knowledge of the good, destroys the ardor we have for humane ideals, and leaves us unable to defend and operationalize them. At worst, it creates an abyss of nihilism in which all reverence for the good disappears and monsters emerge who think they are supermen beyond good and evil. Second, that Nietzsche best illustrates the problem of ethical skepticism and we need, above all, an antidote to his blend of elitism and cruelty.

Box 30

We will not have time to include the remaining great premodern thinker, St. Thomas Aquinas. He made what stands as the best attempt to give humane ideals a religious justification. This is not to say he was without flaw. He committed the sin of gluttony and was very corpulent. He was one of those medieval people for whom a semi-circle had to be cut out of the dining table so that they could reach their food. He was also very reserved. A famous incident has been passed down over the ages. One night at supper the other students were deriding him, calling him the dumb ox. From the head of the table, their teacher Albertus Magnus called out, "One day the braying of this ox will be heard throughout the world." St. Thomas said, "Pass the potatoes."

What then follows is curious. Rather than a refutation of Nietzsche or ethical skepticism, we get bland assertions that ethical skepticism is "a dogma" and "unproven" with absolutely no accompanying argument. We are simply told to read the classics, particularly Plato and Aristotle, and that the wisdom found there will provide the precious antidote. There are also many scattered positive references to Aristotle, who saw that each thing including man has its own unique excellence or perfection. In sum, the Straussites seem completely bankrupt with nothing to say beyond "ethical skepticism is so awful that we must simply reject it as false even though no one can actually show that it is false."

However, before we dismiss them as lacking the courage to follow truth wherever it may lead, let us do what they advise and turn to the classics. All of us want a justification of humane ideals, and if there is one hidden in Plato or Aristotle it is too precious to be overlooked. So let us set the Straussites aside for the moment and enter into a dialogue between Plato, Aristotle, and ourselves. Whether or not we find what we seek, those who have never read these great thinkers will discover delight (see Box 30).

Plato and the divided line

In Plato's *Republic*, the enemy of the good is the sophist named Thrasymachus, who is identical to some modern social scientists. The only road to truth is the scientific method and a cross-cultural survey shows that various societies have no ethics in common, in fact, they are all ordered by the struggle for power, which divides society into winners and losers. The stronger party take office and rules in its own interests, so "justice" is actually rule in the interests of the stronger party. Alternately, "justice" is the principle of might makes right. There are rational people who see all of this and are creatures of enlightened self-interest and they seek to be the stronger party or at least hangers on in the role of advisors. They are unencumbered by moral scruples. Then there are the fools who still take morality seriously and handicap themselves in the struggle for power. The more the better for those who think clearly – because they are enfeebled competitors.

Plato uses Socrates as his mouthpiece. Why is that? Are we being told that what Socrates says conceals at least something of what Plato really believes? At any rate, Socrates launches a devastating critique of the principle of might makes right. It leads to logical problems. Who is the stronger: is it whoever wins the struggle for rule or whoever's will prevails in a given situation? If the latter, Thrasymachus is undermining the ruler's power because every time I can get away with breaking his law (say evade taxes), I am the stronger (and no tax system can operate without general voluntary compliance). If you dogmatically say the ruler is always the stronger simply because he has won the struggle for rule, you have abandoned what the social science tells of political reality. Thrasymachus cannot face up to what his slogan means in practice. He wants the ruler to be simply a tyrant and yet wants people to respect him as if he had a moral title to rule.

Socrates drives the point home with the analogy of the band of thieves. Even they could not operate effectively to rob the rest of us without an ethical code they took seriously. The leader must sleep and could be killed for his share of the booty. They must respect his fairness in dividing the spoils and the sharing of risks. Politics or the struggle for power can never order a human society unless diluted by ethics.

That is why every effective tyrant's rule has rested on a moralistic ideology. Stalin was worthy of regard because he was history's instrument toward a better world. That is why Rubashov agrees to confess in *Darkness at Noon* despite his awareness of all the lies and madness that surround Stalin's rule. Could anyone less mad have forced the peasants to sacrifice themselves for industrialization? Hitler was worthy of regard because he was the only person who could defend European civilization from contamination. The idealism that supported his regime is brilliantly displayed in the film *Cabaret*. The scene in the beer garden in which a handsome Hitler Youth sings "Tomorrow belongs to me" brings everyone to their feet, save three elderly cloth-capped workers who are undoubtedly Social Democrats or Communists.

Adeimantus and Glaucon, the idealistic youths that Socrates must save from Thrasymachus' clutches, demand something better than he has given them thus far. They cannot worship the good if it is just honor among thieves. They use the fable of the ring to indicate that if all we want is the minimum ethical glue to hold society together, we could "invent" ethics by way of a social contract that is a mere mutual defense treaty. Since we realize that an unregulated struggle for power would throw us into a state of nature in which life was "nasty, brutish, and short," we agree to refrain from mutual hostilities to the degree necessary to allow us to cheat each other in non-lethal ways. We now have a "morality" but it is a let's pretend morality. No one really respects the "good," it is merely a loathed set of regulations. What everyone would really like is a ring that made them invisible, so that without risk they could be an exception to the social contract and steal, rape, and murder at will.

What Adeimantus and Glaucon say is confused. They seem to assume that we could organize a human society with an ethics based on enlightened self-interest but need a justification of the good in order to love it. In fact, no society could function effectively if politics were only tempered by a morality of enlightened self-interest. No soldier would obey a suicidal order dictated by the need to save his nation's army from destruction. Parents would put no more into raising a child than was convenient for their own preferred life style. So we do need to love the good. However, it is not self-evident that one can love the good only if it has some objectivity that transcends personal commitment.

Socrates expresses some reservation about saying more in defense of the good than he has said up to that point. However, he tries to satisfy their desire for a case that shows that morality is worthy of regard by all rational people, that is, has an objective status in which reason can command commitment even when it is absent. He offers them a theory of ethical knowledge that vindicates humane-egalitarian ideals in the light of ethical truth.

It will have to be a non-scientific way of knowing, of course, and there follows the wonderful divided line. Science can explore only the bottom half of the divided line, the realm of physical nature or, in this case, actual human societies. Cephalus, the elderly merchant whose home hosts the dialogue, does not even observe actual human societies systematically. When asked, what is justice, he simply lists duties acknowledged by an Athenian gentleman such as telling the truth and paying one's debts. Thrasymachus, as we have seen, does a systematic cross-cultural survey and extracts the generalization that might makes right. There is a reason why his method gives him the opposite of justice, namely, everything in the physical world is to some degree defective.

Therefore, when we generalize what all actual societies have in common, we are describing an ordering principle of human society that introduces defect, rather than justice or its perfecting ordering principle. This means we must transcend the physical word and proceed to the top half of the divided line, which is the world of general ideas or forms.

The demonstration that we all have general ideas latent in our minds arises out of something quite fundamental: human beings can classify things. We can all tell the difference between chairs and tables despite the fact that particular chairs differ greatly from one another. Therefore, we must have in our minds a general idea of chair, one that is truly general and cannot be reduced to a sense image. After all, if the general idea was of a blue chair, or one four feet tall, or one made of wood, it would exclude from the class things we know to be chairs. It must be broad enough to cover all of the particulars chairs we see around us in the physical world.

Plato thought that just as we get our sense-images of chairs from physical objects, we must get our general ideas from an objectively existing world, which includes not only the Form of Chair but also a Form for every class of thing, including the Form of Human Society. After all, we can distinguish human societies from insect societies. But we need not be concerned about the existence of the World of Forms. In terms of refuting the ethical skeptic, the salient feature of the general ideas or Forms is their perfection. No chair in the physical world is perfect, only the carpenter's concept of chair. No straight line I draw on the blackboard is perfect, only the geometer's concept of a straight line as the shortest distance between two points.

All human societies share defect, which is what misled Thrasymachus. But now we can give Adeimantus and Glaucon what they wanted: an account of what truly perfects human society, that is, the perfecting ordering principle that we call justice. All we need do is to ascend the divided line into the World of Forms and read off the contents of the Form of Human Society. Then we will have knowledge of the good. Or more accurately, we will have knowledge of one kind of good. There are other goods like beauty and truth and the perfect state of the human individual that would require exhaustive knowledge of the World of Forms. And that is impossible without knowledge of the Chief Good. It is an all-embracing concept of perfection broad enough to cover all of the particular kinds of perfection we have listed, that is, justice, beauty, truth, the harmonious soul, and so forth.

Aristotle and the divided line

Plato's thought has a sublime elegance. However, Aristotle puts a series of objections to Plato's doctrine of Forms that are devastating. For economy's sake, I will put what seems to me the strongest objection and use my own words. It has to do with an ambiguity about what the Forms are supposed to be.

The only reason we posted the Form of Human Society was because we needed a general idea broad enough to cover all of the particular societies in that class. And yet, we then make it so specific that it can tell us that one human society is better than all others, namely, a human society in which the struggle for power is eliminated by a whole series of social arrangements. These are highly specific. They spell out the detail of an educational system, the way of life of the rulers, the status of women, and so forth. Clearly our use of the Form to refute ethical skepticism, and argue that humane-egalitarian ideals have objective status, is completely inconsistent with our argument for the very existence of the Forms. A concept of human society specific enough to give moral advice can no more have the breadth needed to cover all of the differing human societies we see around us than a blue chair would be broad enough to cover all of the objects in the class chair.

Plato's mathematical analogies were misleading. If a line is not perfectly straight, it is not a straight line at all. Therefore, a single concept can capture both the perfection of a straight line and still be broad enough to include all the members of its class. Human societies are different. A society need not be perfect to be a human society rather than an insect society. Therefore, the concept that we posited to cover the class would lose its necessary breadth were it to represent a perfect state.

When we pretended to read off our ideal society from the content of the Form, we were really reading our ideals in. Plato's image of an ideal society is a noble one. How wonderful to replace politics by ethics. Rulers selected by merit, free from greed and nepotism, who give simple proof of their virtues to the masses (no personal property or families), run an educational system that diagnoses and trains the best in everyone, and mold a society in which all feel valuable because they all play a role benefiting both themselves and others. There is no sexism or privilege. There are no extremes of rich and poor. But it is purely personal without a shred of objectivity. To demonstrate this, all Nietzsche need say is that it would fail to produce artists of genius who are free to exercise their creativity at the expense of the herd. There is no rebuttal. If there is anything to which Plato's ideal society is unfriendly, it is great art.

Aristotle and mental health

Therefore, Aristotle must make a new case for ethical objectivity. He replaces a separately existing World of Forms with formal and final causes. By that, he means that when we observe the world around us, we see that every kind of thing has its own excellence. Acorns tend to grow into healthy oak trees. Human beings do not have a built-in tendency to realize their perfect state; rather they have to be habituated to virtue by their upbringing. But nonetheless, there is a passive grain in human nature such that if society (and our own free choices) cuts in accord with that grain (rather than against it), we will experience the difference. Those whose lives follow the optimum road for man have a sense of psychic well-being called eudaimonia (a sort of happiness plus, as we shall see). Those whose societies cause them to deviate from the optimum road lack eudaimonia.

An athlete whose body is trained properly will delight in its use, while an unfit person will find physical exertion a trial. So with human character. Recall what Aristotle said about Sparta and Carthage. Sparta confused the good man with the good soldier.

While efficient in war, they know nothing of the satisfactions that attend philosophy, art, music; their women are despised as non-warriors and given rule of the household, which means that the men experience none of the good things that come with love between equals or child-rearing. Carthage confuses the good man with the good entrepreneur or businessman. They consume philosophy and art rather than create it and have no higher purpose to their lives than the acquisition of wealth, which is destructive of civic virtue and means that they must depend on mercenaries rather than citizen soldiers.

In sum, the perfecting life evidences its existence by a broad and vivid range of fulfilling experiences set in a harmonious emotional world (harmony of soul). Other lives lead to a narrow range of satisfactions, a deadening of the spirit, often a sense of inward turmoil or anxiety, and a half-conscious sense of unrealized potential. This need not become pathological; after all, every society lends its ideal person reinforcement, and in a savagely competitive society some can congratulate themselves on having won whatever contest they enter. But it can become pathological. Witness the suburban neurosis that afflicted many housewives in America after World War II when they were assigned a role that left their potential undeveloped.

This way of justifying humane ideals, that they have objective status in the sense that they realize the peculiar excellence of human nature, is attractive to modern thinkers. With a few alterations, it can be turned into propositions that are empirically verifiable.

Look at the suicide rate in classical Kwakiutl Indian society, a sort of parody on Nietzsche plus materialism, in which status was gained by showing that you could destroy more goods than your opponent, thus reinforcing your own sense of triumph and sending him into despair. Indeed, you selected a wife solely so as to target her father for destruction. Clearly, this is a way of life that cuts against the grain. That humans have no built-in tendency toward their perfect state is shown by the fact that the Kwakiutls have no difficulty socializing their children, that is, human nature does not resist this kind of socialization. The empirical flavor of Aristotle explains his appeal to thinkers as diverse as Erich Fromm and Aldous Huxley.

From a Straussite point of view, those who see no flaw in the Aristotelian attempt at justification of the good life are the better off for it. They will not fall into the abyss of ethical skepticism. But just as Aristotle saw the flaw in Plato, Plato was aware of a fatal defect in Aristotle's case. It has to do with an ambiguity about the kind of goodness Aristotle uses to justify the good life.

In presenting Aristotle, I have used medical language, speaking, for example, of man's perfect state as psychic well-being and using an analogy with the physical well-being of a properly trained athlete. As to the warrant for this, there is a key passage in Aristotle (Ethics, III, 1113a, 22–30) in which he rejects ethical skepticism:

> Different persons have different views of what is good and
> clearly this will not do . . . It is what the perfected man
> values that is properly valued, while the defective man
> may value virtually anything. It is the same as in the case
> of the body. Things that are truly wholesome are
> wholesome if you are in good health but if you are
> diseased other things appear wholesome You will get the
> same result with things that are bitter or sweet or hot or
> heavy and so forth.

It is suggestive that when Bloom wants a clear exception to relativism, he refers to bodily health (Bloom, 1987, p. 77).

Aristotle's reference to health cannot be discounted as an isolated instance. Even if he had made no such reference, he had no choice but to clarify what he meant by the perfect state of a human being, that is, he had to give the meaningless general term "perfect" some clarity by identifying it with a specific kind of goodness.

Aristotle (Ethics, I, 1096a, 11–34) underlines this necessity in his critique of Plato's concept of the Chief Good. The concept of the

Chief Good had to be broad enough to cover all kinds of goodness, whether they fell under the rubric of justice or beauty or truth. He notes that "good" has many senses, depending on what we are referring to, whether God (divine) or reason (sound) or a means to an end (useful) or war (victory) or the body (health) or athletics (fitness). The sciences of these things, theology or logic or prudence or military tactics or medicine or gymnastics, can give us advice. But this is only because they have criteria that are specific enough to tell us to do this (eat wholesome food) rather than that (eat sweets). Otherwise, their notion of good would be non-operational. It is vacuous to simply tell someone to be "good," which is why "knowledge" of the Chief Good has never been embodied in a science.

Similarly, if Aristotle's advice to live a life that realizes our excellence or our perfect state is to have any meaning, it too must be classified under one of the kinds of goodness. And if the appeal to eudaimonia (psychic well-being) is to be significant, it falls under the category of medical goodness or psychological health. The fatal ambiguity in Aristotle is the fact that moral goodness or duty is only contingently connected to medical goodness. Even if there is an objective standard as to what perfects a human being in terms of psychological health, health cannot provide a foundation for moral goodness. Therefore, its objectivity does not translate into ethical objectivity. Truth about ethics cannot be based on health.

Imagine we had evolved so that we had to catch an eye disease to have good vision. Then the diseased eye would tell us the truth about the world around us, not healthy eyes. Yet, Aristotle (*Ethics*, III, 1113a, 32–33) tells us that the perfected man "sees the truth in every department of conduct, being as it were the norm and measure of them." Imagine that psychological health required a bit of viciousness; for example, to have a sense of complete psychic well-being, men had to be petty tyrants over their families. None of us would concede that this was moral conduct. We would acknowledge that there is a trade-off between moral goodness and psychological health. There are many specific cases in which individuals must choose between duty and their own perfection.

Assume that you are an 18–year-old youth in Vietnam in 1945 and believe that, until your nation is free of foreign domination and united, it cannot prosper. Your father offers to send you to Paris to study philosophy, but you choose to do your duty and go into the jungle for almost thirty years to cut throats, first the French, then the Americans. No one will seriously argue that you will emerge an undamaged person, which is to say that the path of duty diverged from the path of perfection. A young woman in rural Maine in 1930 is the youngest daughter and the rest have left home while she remains with her aging and infirm parents. She gives up education and marriage. She knows very well that she will not experience eudaimonia but will be warped at least to some degree by bitterness. But it is her duty.

These two cases have to do with a conflict between what would perfect the individual in terms of psychic health and duty to others or the larger society. Perhaps we can resolve them by using the health of society as our yardstick of excellence? Even were that possible, still looming over everything is the logical gap between medical goodness and moral goodness. But setting that aside, the appeal to the health of society is not an option.

Society as a whole must have a moral dimension, as we have seen. An idealistic morality is required as a social glue; and the glue that may bring the greatest happiness to the greatest number is a humane-egalitarian morality. But society is real only as a web of relationships between individuals. It does not exist as some giant physical body that can be healthy or as a huge individual that can experience eudaimonia in any literal sense. As Bloom (1987, p. 113) concedes, these are mere images. If there is no such thing as the health of society, the category of medical goodness has no real application. The conflict between perfecting oneself and duty is the crucial real-world dilemma and completes the destruction of the Aristotelian justification.

Plato and the inner circle

Plato was fully aware of the flaw in Aristotle's attempt to justify the good life. It is true that he thought it vitally important to show that a virtuous man, under normal circumstances, was psychologically healthy and that a vicious man was mentally ill. But only because anything else would be ugly. What an irony if moral wickedness and psychological health were in fact correlated. He shows that in a society in which the struggle for power has been eliminated, the ruler has as much eudaimonia or harmony of soul as a ruler can have. He can play the role of social architect rather than the role of politician, which means he can create something beautiful while being loved and respected by all members of society.

The tyrant is the ultimate politician. He is loathed by the losers of the struggle for power and envied by the winners, who get a lesser share of the spoils than he gets. Haunted by fear, he must eliminate any worthwhile person in his inner circle, kill his children as possible rivals, and flatter the head of the secret police. He is insane but shows no clinical symptoms because his life is given order, not by goodness, but by one all-consuming master passion, that is, the lust for power.

Despite all of this, Plato does not offer the contingent connection between moral goodness and mental health as a justification of humane-egalitarian ideals. Virtuous people usually enjoy mental health but they are not good because they have mental health. That is why we must seek the objective status of the good life elsewhere by ascending to the World of Forms. So Aristotle saw the defect in Plato's approach and Plato saw the defect in Aristotle's approach and they were both correct. I hope that this dialogue between ourselves and the ancients has been pleasant enough to provide an incentive to read them.

But is it possible that Plato was also aware that his own approach was invalid? He wrote a dialogue called the *Parmenides* in which he put all of Aristotle's objections against his World of Forms and indeed put most of them with even greater force. Is Plato telling us that he knows that there is a void at the top of the divided line and that true wisdom means knowing that there is no knowledge of the good? Recall that the divided line was introduced as a concession to the idealism of Adeimantus and Glaucon; and that Plato confesses dismay that they were not convinced by what he had already said against Thrasymachus.

Whatever Plato's reservations, the students of Strauss have read both of the ancients with care. This divides them into two groups and determines their strategy, one group toward the other, both toward that all-important third group, the masses. We can best analyze the behavior of these three by appropriating a hierarchy from Plato. He distinguished three classes: the inner circle of the Philosopher Kings who have wisdom and know the good; the Auxiliaries who lack full wisdom and merely love the good as presented to them by the inner circle; and the masses who have been given traditions and myths that persuade them that decent conduct is an objective duty.

The members of the inner circle of Straussites have ascended the divided line and know the truth about the vacuum that lies there. There is no knowledge of the good. It is enough for them that humane-egalitarian ideals are theirs and that these are the best antidote to the principle of might makes right. When humane idealism glues a society together, ethics realizes its full potential to moderate the savagery of the struggle for power. The Auxiliaries are those who take the flawed Aristotelian solution seriously, either because they have not studied it deeply enough or because, like Adeimantus and Glaucon, they are simply not able to retain their idealism without a case for ethical objectivity. The masses are at risk because, in an age of science, loss of faith in humane traditions is an ever-present danger.

These considerations dictate strategy. The inner circle must never disabuse the Auxiliaries. On the contrary, reverent noises must always be made about Aristotle and no flaw made explicit. Who knows if they would be able to survive wisdom? Therefore, the inner circle can never recruit. People must find their own way, from the masses to the Auxiliaries by being encouraged to study the ancients in general and Aristotle in particular, from the Auxiliaries to the inner circle by the self-discovery of full wisdom. Two Straussites may have offices next door to one another and not know whether both are Auxiliaries or whether both are members of the inner circle. Indeed, you might be the only member of the inner circle alive at this moment. Who said philosophy was boring! But hints dropped in conversation, subtle suggestions about what might be read, could allow you to become aware of one another.

Both the inner circle and the Auxiliaries will behave the same toward the masses. You will be most influential if you play the role of an academic or a minister of religion. Where there is a tradition of ethical truth as in America, emphasize the wickedness of ethical skepticism. For many people, the mere fact something is wicked will make them eschew the possibility that it is true. Encourage them to stand by their tradition rather than to turn to cultural relativism. The latter is simply too mindless and counter-productive and is always likely to evolve into complete skepticism. Always bolster authentic religious faith. A believer in God's law cannot think it less than objective. Encourage your students to study the ancients. They will never be the worse for it and that is how you recruit Auxiliaries.

The inner circle will always strive to preserve goodness within a society wherever it exists, but I want to set the record straight on one point. The neo-conservatives who advised Bush to invade Iraq are often referred to in the press as "students of Leo Strauss." There was a streak of conservatism in Strauss's domestic politics. He admired English country gentlemen with a tradition of public service, which is to say Tories. However, nothing he ever said implied an adventurous foreign policy. Like all of us, he hoped that liberal democracy would eventually win the day. But he was skeptical of attempts to export goodness, and certainly he never endorsed conversion by the sword.

Box 31

Pythagoras invented science in the sense that science explains the qualitative differences we see around us as quantitative differences. For example, we see different colors of light and optics tells us that they can be explained by their various wavelengths. He found that the note we hear when a string is plucked is purely a consequence of the length of the string. This amazing discovery convinced him that the entire universe was made of shapes that could be represented as numbers. For example, three was the smallest triangular number, four was the smallest square number, and so forth. Today, when we say that four is two squared or that eight is two cubed, we are speaking language inherited from Pythagoras.

Then they discovered something terrible. A right-angled triangle (a triangle with one angle equal to 90 degrees) is one of the most important shapes. Yet, one of its sides (the hypotenuse) cannot by represented as a ratio between numbers. Since the hypotenuse of a right-angled triangle can be represented as the square root of two, all you have to do is prove that the square root of two is an "irrational" number, that is, cannot be represented as a ratio. This was proven but kept a secret because, were it revealed, people might lose faith in Pythagoras and his followers.

That the masses revere them was important because they used their prestige to establish themselves as the ruling elite in Greek city-states located in Italy. Sadly, one of their rules was that people must never eat beans. As Russell says, more often than once, the people, maddened by their hankering after beans, rose up and deposed them.

Breaking the Pythagorean oath

Since it is forbidden to reveal the nakedness of the good, I am clearly a traitor. In the ancient world, there was a Pythagorean brotherhood whose members swore an oath that none of them would reveal the terrible secret that the square root of two was an irrational number.

The one who finally did was executed (see Box 31). I have sworn no formal oath but the inner circle knows that formalities are not important. What is of concern to an honorable man is not what penalties others might levy but whether he must indict himself in his own heart. I will defend my choice.

The inner circle can never be fully honest except with one another. They must withhold the full truth from their students, their colleagues, their spouse, and their most intimate friend. But that would be a threadbare defense. Plato makes us aware that telling the whole truth can be a deception, if what you say leaves your audience further from the truth than they were before. To tell the masses that there is no knowledge of the good, when there is no chance of their achieving full understanding, is simply to impel them toward the abyss of ethical skepticism.

The only possible defense is that I can improve on the usual strategy. That implies: that I have a message that offers an antidote to ethical skepticism; that acknowledging the truth of ethical skepticism is necessary to make my case; and that this direct approach may win over more converts to the good life than subterfuge. After all, the masses are getting better educated and less pious. They may start abandoning their traditions and churches and see through Aristotle and any other approach not fully defensible in the light of truth. The next chapter is my brief before the court.

9   The status of the good life

There is something divine about you if you can put the case for injustice so strongly, and yet believe that right is better than wrong . . . But I do not see how I am to help you, witness my failure to convince you just now, when I thought I had demonstrated the superiority of justice in my conversation with Thrasymachus.

(Plato, *Republic*, II, 368)

Without Nature or Plato or Aristotle or God to hand us our ideals, how do we know how to view good and evil? We must do what every thinking human being has done both before and after the rise of philosophy. You do not just accept whatever most people in your culture happen to believe. When I recommend Jefferson's ideals, they should carry no weight at all simply because you are an American and they were formulated by a revered American. Unless you find that they resonate with you, you have no good reason to adopt them or take pride in your nation's moral heritage. You should read widely, survey the diversity of ideals that human kind has developed, try to put yourself in their shoes, and reflect. Then you look within and ask certain questions.

Who am I?

You ask yourself, what kind of behavior overwhelms me with moral revulsion, for example reading the diary of Anne Frank and identifying with the people that Hitler systematically exterminated simply because they were Jewish? You ask yourself, who most excites my moral admiration, someone like Debs or my boss who never looks beyond a bigger car and a bigger house? Do I have a friend who lives the kind of life I admire? What kind of ideals do I want to see my children use to give substance to their lives? All of these questions are ways of clarifying what you hold dear and isolating the deepest moral principles to which you are committed. Other people (like Nietzsche) will get results contrary to our own. We will get to that later. But here we learn an important lesson: your ideals define who you are. And living up to who they are is rather important for some people.

If you find that you resonate with all the ideals that various cultures hold, anti-Semitism and tolerance, female circumcision and women's liberation, that is the only good reason to value them all equally. I doubt anyone has ever been that strange; at best they resonate with the ideal of treating all human ideals as equal despite how cruel and repugnant some are. Well, if that really comes ahead of doing the most humane thing, promoting equality, and so forth, you know yourself best. But do not think some kind of logic forces you to feel that way.

If you look within and find nothing, then you *are* looking into an abyss. But it is not philosophy that positions you there; it is your poverty of soul. If you want an antidote, begin by reading some great novels: Singer's *The Slave*, Remark's *Spark of Life*, Wilder's *The Bridge of San Luis Rey*. Or read some great poetry – Yeats's *The Second Coming* or Arnold's *Dover Beach* – or attend some great films and plays, and see if you cannot sink some roots in the human condition.

Discovering what moral principles you hold dear is not the end of the story, of course. Nietzsche will do us the service of challenging us as to whether our ideals commit us to logical inconsistencies, or myths about the real world that we are too cowardly to acknowledge. Indeed, every bit of knowledge we get has the potential to force us to adjust our ideals in the light of reality.

The nihilist fallacy

Dostoyevsky in *The Brothers Karamazov* says that if God is dead, anything is allowable. God for him was the only source of knowledge of the good, and he meant that if the good was not objective all moral ideals were trivialized because they collapse into the category of mere whim or desire. Risking one's life to pull a child out of the path of an oncoming car becomes indistinguishable from van Gogh's mad whim to cut off his ear. In other words, ethical skepticism entails nihilism in the sense that it becomes irrational to take duties seriously, both duties in general and humane ideals in particular. We may be passionately committed to principles that tell us that we should act humanely, but the message of those principles is deceptive. They are like hallucinations whose content deceives. This is the kind of abyss to which the Straussites refer.

This argument is logically incoherent and should be labeled the nihilist fallacy. Commitment to a moral principle is a commitment to a duty, and it is far more serious than a mere preference for one soft drink over another, which no one confuses with a self-imposed duty. In the absence of an ethical truth-test of some sort, a humane person cannot tell Nietzsche he ought to accept humane ideals. However, to say that we ourselves ought to abandon humane ideals is to claim more than that they lack objective status. It is to claim that they have subjective status, that we should discount them as if they were hallucinations. But why do we discount a hallucination? It is because it has *failed* a truth-test. It is deceptive about something: we saw an oasis in the desert, and when we ran to get there we got a mouth full of sand rather than a mouth full of water.

If there is no test of objectivity in ethics, humane ideals can neither pass nor fail – there is no test to fail. What are they supposed to be deceptive about? They are not deceptive about our deepest selves. In the absence of objectivity, there is also no such thing as subjectivity. It may be foolish to say humane ideals ought to be accepted by those who loathe them, but it would be equally absurd to say they ought to be dismissed by those who cherish them.

A self-imposed duty to be humane may seem worthless to the anti-humane, but for us it is worth precisely what it is worth to us. That may be a great deal. It may demand that we lay down our lives to avoid anti-humane consequences. To do otherwise would be false to our principles. The fact that lack of ethical objectivity does not logically entail nihilism does not, of course, forbid nihilism as a psychological reaction. When people lost faith that the world rested on a turtle, some of them panicked. Someone reared in an atmosphere of faith, and whose life has been entirely God-centered, may find that loss of faith robs the world of all that engaged his or her passions. Similarly, someone who has always presumed that humane ideals were in accord with some kind of ethical truth may find lack of objective status unbearable, and his or her commitment to humane ideals may wither. Self-imposed duties may seem too pale a shadow of truth-imposed duties.

People must, I fear, come to terms with such a loss, just as they must come to terms with the death of a loved one, and philosophical analysis cannot dictate the outcome. What philosophy can do is make certain that a logical mistake does not influence our psychology. No one needs to sink into despair because she mistakenly believes that logic entails nihilism

The darker side of ethical objectivity

What would knowledge of the good or establishing its objective status entail? It would entail that we can give reasons for humane ideals that are valid for all human kind, Nietzsche as well as ourselves. We can hardly tell Nietzsche to adopt them simply because they take the welfare of all human beings into account, any more than he can tell us to adopt his ideals simply because they favor an elite of creative geniuses over herd men. Both of us would be giving purely partisan reasons for our ideals. You need non-partisan reasons. These would have to somehow bridge the divide between Nietzsche and myself, the gulf between the humane and the anti-humane. So the reasons would have to be neutral ones, neither distinctively humane nor elitist. That is why "neutral" concepts such as nature (Jefferson) or psychological health (Aristotle) are appealing.

But do we really want to substitute neutral reasons for calling actions good for partisan humane reasons? If you justify humane behavior as the dictates of nature or what perfects man, you have to mean it. You cannot tell your opponents that humane ideals ought to be accepted because those ideals are in accord with nature without adopting that reason yourself. Otherwise, your opponent could accuse you of bad faith: "I thought you told me that the real reason for accepting these ideals was that they are in accord with nature. Do you mean to tell me that is not your reason?" He would be quite correct. If that is the right way to reason about what is good, it cannot be set aside like a best room used for company only. You must live in it yourself. This extracts a heavy price: you can no longer give your true reasons for the ideals you accept, namely, that you hold them precisely because they are humane.

I will try to dramatize this point, by recourse to a great humanist. In *Les Misérables*, Victor Hugo introduces us to Sister Simplice and prepares us for a moving climax. Sister Simplice has always believed that lying is an absolute form of evil and took her name after Simplice of Sicily, who was martyred rather than lie about her place of birth. Hugo shows her resisting the temptation to tell lies out of kindness. She meets Jean Valjean and recognizes his essential goodness. Finally, she is approached by Javert, who seeks to arrest Jean Valjean for a trivial offense and restore him to the horrors of the galleys.

She has never told a lie in her life, but to save Jean Valjean she "lied twice in succession, without hesitation, promptly, as a person does when sacrificing herself." Victor Hugo adds, "O sainted maid! You left this world many years ago; you have rejoined your sisters, the virgins, and your brothers, the angels, in the light; may this lie be counted to your credit in paradise." Hugo wanted to say that her benevolent lie was right precisely because it was benevolent. It is hard to see him settling for something else. Here we see the darker side of ethical objectivity fully revealed. It forces us to set aside the reasons we want to give for the goodness of our acts and substitute the kind of reasons it puts into our mouth. For example, that it is right to tell a benevolent lie because this is in accord with nature.

Imagine that Hugo had added a bit to his account. Sister Simplice tells her lie, Javert leaves, and she says to Jean Valjean: "I can see that you are surprised. But over the last few months, I have been thinking about the purposes of nature. I now see that the natural purpose of communication does not require that we always convey our thoughts accurately. Just as there are exceptions to everything in nature, we can make exceptions here." Or that she says: "I have been reading Aristotle lately and thinking about what perfects human nature in the sense of maximizing psychological health. I have decided that the tension caused by always telling the truth is too great for human beings to bear and that I am no exception. At any rate, be reassured that I did not allow any thought of benevolence to enter in while I thought this question out."

My point is that humanism is not simply a set of conclusions about what is right; it has its reasons. If we are honest, we will admit that neutral concepts thrust upon us a whole range of reasons we do not really care about, to the detriment of reasons about which we really do. The latter may seem "subjective," but they are our own. Ask yourself this: would you really give up humane ideals if they were not in accord with nature, or if less humane behavior would contribute to your psychological health (remember the woman with the aged parents to care for)? If so, I can only assume you care more about nature than you do about the humane content of your ideals. (For a supposed exception, see Box 32.)

Box 32

A religious person may say that they put God ahead of their own distinctive reasons for calling acts right or wrong. They are happy to adopt as their reason "God wills it." Imagine that God was like the God of the Old Testament and commanded a revenge ethic. You may think it to your credit if you set your humane ideals aside in favor of God's will but I do not. God is still all-powerful but He is no longer benevolent. Might does not make right. I might obey Him out of fear but I would have no sense of doing the right thing.

If you think God benevolent, you may find it easier to resist the temptation to give up because you have a powerful ally, just as Marxists feel heartened by having history on their side. Well, that may be a prop to morale, but for me it is not the central question as to why I resist temptation. Giving in would call into question my image of myself. Rather than reading the Old Testament to refresh my commitment, I read Ginger's biography of Debs. Which is why it gets so many pages in chapter 2. Secular people have their heroes (Debs' hero was John Brown) just as Christians have their saints.

The good and the beautiful

Granted that the objectivity of humane ideals would have a darker side, we must still face the fact that there is no such thing as knowledge of the good. Can we love humane ideals wholeheartedly without that? There is an outstanding example of a love affair with something that cannot be known: we love beauty, and yet there is no knowledge of it either. Since what is beautiful is a matter of social convention, this may seem to be a trap. However, there is an important difference between the good and the beautiful concerning whether their contents can transcend convention or ethnocentrism.

In ethics that is an achievement in which we can rejoice. A cosmopolitan ethic must of course be sustained by a tradition (that may be present only in one or a few nations). This book is an attempt to nurture such a tradition in America. But while the roots of ethics are inevitably culture bound, its content can transcend the ethnocentrism with which we all began: human being means the same as a fellow tribesman. Its content can expand to embrace all humanity as worthy of entry into the circle of moral concern. And the reason its content can be universal is that we need not appreciate all humanity to endow them with moral worth. I never much liked the dour, Bible-quoting, killjoy Scandinavian Americans I met in Minnesota, certainly not as much as my own Irish Americans. But I admit into my circle of moral concern not only them but also billions of people I have never met.

Standards of beauty will have roots in a tradition but no standard can expand to call the art of all other cultures beautiful. Here appreciation is central. Let us start with something humble, that is, the appreciation of good food. No one could rejoice in an attempt to like every food that any culinary tradition has produced, grubs as well as practically raw steaks, chocolate grasshoppers as well as pecan pie. We may want to expand our palate beyond the limits of our mother's (or father's – what a minefield language is today) home cooking, but aspiring to a universal taste would seem bizarre. Who could possibly want to do such a thing? There is no merit in such an eccentric objective.

Art is the same. Music, painting, theater, architecture, dance, all have their roots in a tradition and no person can expand the content of his or her standard of *appreciated* beauty to encompass what is beautiful in the context of all human traditions. I do not appreciate the rococo in either art, architecture, or music. It is just too ornamental for me and the best of their compositions does not give me as much as the worst of Mozart. I appreciate classical Chinese music even less. Others may have a wider range of appreciation. They may claim to enjoy the entire tradition of Western classical music, folk music, jazz, blues, Chinese and Indian classical music, and so forth. But sooner or later they reach a limit, perhaps with hillbilly, Western, rap, yodeling, crooners, Morris dancing, the nose flute, endless African chants, sea shanties, what have you. Even if it were possible, the quest for such a universal taste would seem bizarre. Creative artists borrow from many traditions but none of them dissipate their talent by a quest for universal creativity. When Shostakovich was asked why he did not explore the modern idiom more fully, he said, "but there are so many beautiful things that have not been composed in the key of C."

In a word, a quest for a cosmopolitan appreciation of beauty would be pointless. It has nothing to do with loving beauty as much as beauty can be loved. Ethics is different. If you do transcend ethnocentrism, you have not drained your ethic of significance. When everyone counts in everyone's eyes, the content is still meaningful and represents a triumphant expansion of one's moral perspective. In art, the best you can do is to make a paper concession and say that you are sure that whatever some alien tradition counts as beautiful sounds beautiful to them, although it is just noise to you. That is analogous to saying that you are sure that the Hitler Youth were idealists and truly believed in blood and iron. In art, you can say that you respect the integrity of all traditions, however little you can appreciate them. That is analogous to saying that all human beings are worthy of regard, however little you happen to like some of them. That is, it gains universality by being a moral proposition about respect for art and not an aesthetic proposition about what counts with you as beautiful. Beauty inevitably divides humanity; only ethics can unite it.

There is no sleight of hand here. No demonstration has been given that it is more rational to be a cosmopolitan humanist than a tribesman. To the tribesman, there is no merit whatsoever in cosmopolitanism; it is an absurd and trivial goal and he may prefer an ethic that puts his own people ahead of all of the rest of humanity. But the fact we have not shown that our cosmopolitanism has objective status (and therefore should be seen as worthy in his eyes) need not devalue it in our eyes. To us, it is a great triumph that we have transcended mere ethnocentrism.

Two qualifications. First, note that I have taken pains not to deny the practical importance of a moral tradition. No ethics will have much impact unless embodied in such a tradition. That is why cosmopolitan humanists need not feel guilt when they choose maintaining the health of their society over the attempt to relieve the miseries of the entire population of the world. As we have said, if every humane society undermined its own viability in a futile attempt to provide an instant fix for world poverty, there would be no home for humane ideals left. Every such home is infinitely precious. America must remain the home of the Jeffersonian ideal rather than give it up due to an atmosphere of frustration and confusion.

Second, Nietzsche is still standing at our shoulder. He too has an international cosmopolitan ethic that can be universalized: people everywhere should accept that only creative geniuses are worthy of being admitted to the circle of moral concern. He does not ask them to revert to crude ethnocentrism but holds up a criterion of the good that is in no way diluted by crossing national boundaries. Herd men and humane cosmopolitans are unlikely to appreciate it, of course, but that merely shows that they have bad taste. It devalues most people by excluding them from the circle of moral concern but that is the whole point: they merit exclusion.

Granted that humane-egalitarian ethics is not the only way to transcend ethnocentrism. Nonetheless it does so and we can be thrilled at the achievement and value the vehicle that has carried us there. The fact that Nietzsche considers our vehicle a poor thing does not mean that we must do so.

Logic and science

The content of our ideals transcends ethnocentrism. But let us go beyond their content to their status. I will argue that humane ideals are unique in that they allow us to look logic and science full in the face. But that raises the question of the status of logic and science. Do they transcend mere ethnocentrism or convention?

Logic and science have a universal character. Aristotelian logic was not the invention of a Greek elite that wanted to be one up on the way ordinary people thought. The scientific method is not peculiarly Western and valued because it elevates us above pre-industrial peoples. In the Stone Age culture of New Guinea, an elderly person may say to a child, "that is a gumquat, so don't eat it." If the child asks why, the answer is "because gumquats are poisonous." So we have a perfect syllogism: All G are p, that is a G, therefore it is p. They use experience to decide when to hunt; for example, if they discover that an animal is nocturnal, they hunt it at night. They use an empirical method and the scientific method is simply a refinement that gives observation its maximum dividends. It is hard to see how these people could survive if they turned their backs on logic and "science."

Postmodernists like Derrida say that reality is a text. No one is quite sure what this means but it appears to mean that the world is a blank slate on which we can impose whatever subjective interpretation we like (Flynn, 1993). The assertion that all theories are equally explanatory/non-explanatory was refuted every time Derrida put on his spectacles. The theory of optics explains why they worked and nothing else does so. If all of this sounds silly, that is not my fault. As Konrad Adenauer said in 1949: "In view of the fact that God limited the intelligence of man, it seems unfair that he did not also limit his stupidity." The philosophy of science poses logical problems concerning the foundations of the scientific method but none of these reveals any alternative that would better enhance our understanding of reality (see Box 33).

Nietzsche and his supermen

At last, we are face to face with our eternal adversary. As the Straussites point out, Nietzsche is the opponent who gives those of us with humane ideals our worst nightmares. To demonstrate his strengths and eventually his weaknesses, I will undertake four tasks: describe the foundation or core propositions of his ethics; show how

Box 33 Can we say anything reasonable about anything?

One logical problem about science is the problem of induction. Science is about prediction. Because every prediction is based on past experience, it assumes some continuity between the future and the past. Yet, we can give no good reason why the future should resemble the past: no time machine allows us to look at the future; logic cannot establish facts about the future because it cannot establish the facts about anything; cause–effect laws are no good because even if the cause is occurring at this moment, how do I know the effect will follow merely because it has always followed in the past? We cannot even assume that objects will retain their identity. Bertrand Russell sums up neatly: the lunatic's suspicion that his egg is about to turn into a snake is as rational as my assumption that it will remain an egg.

But this same line of reasoning shows that we cannot defend any particular account of the past. To simplify, I will speak of a past more distant than living memory. If there was no continuity of cause–effect laws beyond that point and no such thing as stable identity, any reconstruction of the past is as reasonable as any other. Beyond the memory of the oldest living astronomer, the heavenly bodies may have moved in accord with other laws and leapt into position to begin to obey the law of gravity at the moment he began his observations. Records of previous observations carry no weight because the symbols on the page may have altered at that time. If I am the oldest person alive that remembers seeing my father, he may have been an egg up to the moment of my first memory. Not as disturbing as no expectations about the future, but still, my image of my father is not improved by the notion that he spent virtually his entire life as an egg with only a brief day of humanity at the end.

If we take the problem of induction seriously, we are caught in the bubble of the present with no rational expectations about the future and no rational account of the past. I have not "solved" the problem but have reassessed its importance by classifying it. It belongs to a class of dilemmas that arise when we assume radical discontinuity over time (the universe might have been created ten seconds ago looking as if it were very old). The problem threatens science less than sanity, including the sanity of those who reject the objectivity of science. They too do not want their eggs to bite them. If the future ever does break radically with the past, we will all have more to worry about than an unsolved philosophical paradox.

these obviate arguments effective against opponents like racists; summarize his thought more fully, with emphasis on how his ideals are to be operationalized; and show what weapons logic and science give us to use against him.

Nietzsche's ethics rests on three propositions: only supermen merit moral concern; therefore, worrying about what people deserve applies only to supermen; therefore, supermen can treat "herd men" as means to their own ends, with the proviso that supermen should not do anything that would demean themselves in their own eyes. I believe that Nietzsche is correct in contending that before we apply moral categories we must make a prior assessment. We must decide for ourselves just what creatures are a form of life significant enough to merit moral concern. This can be shown by using a ladder of being running from insects, through higher animals, through ordinary human beings, to supermen or people of creative genius.

The minority sect of Hindus called Jainists brush the path in front of them to avoid stepping on insects and wear masks to avoid breathing in microbes. Moving up the ladder (or down if you prefer), most animal rights advocates do not worry much about insects. They would spray mosquito larvae to prevent malaria. But they draw the line under the higher animals (do not countenance medical experiments on them). Most humanists draw the line for possessing things like rights below the species Homo sapiens. Nietzsche chooses to draw the line for moral concern below supermen, according ordinary people only the derivative consideration (sadism is demeaning) humanists accord animals (Kaufmann, 1962, p. 24). In the absence of ethical objectivity, where anyone draws the line is a matter of personal commitment, and Nietzsche can argue that his delineation is no more or less arbitrary than our own.

The fact that Nietzsche uses merit to delineate his concern, a standard of merit only the great can meet, robs many of our arguments of their normal force. Vulgar racists flatly assert that whites are entitled to exploit blacks. If we ask them whether they too would deserve exploitation were their skins to turn black, they have to choose between two impossible alternatives: abandoning logic or saying that none of their valued personal traits count against sheer blackness. But why are they caught in this dilemma? Because imagining that your skin color changes does not entail imagining any change whatsoever in your personal traits.

When Nietzsche asserts that those who possess creative genius are entitled to use ordinary people as a means to their ends, we can ask him to imagine he was a herd man. Would he then still say that supermen were entitled to use herd men as a means to their ends, even if this meant a total lack of concern for his own welfare?

But why should he hesitate? Unlike the racist, Nietzsche is being asked to imagine a revolution in his personal traits. He is being asked to imagine himself of no more than average intelligence rather than brilliant, enjoying pedestrian work rather than the ecstasy of creation, with a pedestrian sense of humor rather than a keen wit. He is being asked to imagine his core personality so altered that he has changed into someone radically different from the sort of person he actually is; indeed, he has changed into the kind of person he loathes. He can simply reply that if he were that sort of person, he certainly should be exploited, while reminding us that he is not really like that at all.

It may be said that this misses the point. It is a black mark against your ideals if you must shut your eyes to some feature of the real world in order to hold them. If Nietzsche attained true empathy with ordinary people and felt the sufferings he might inflict upon them as if they were his own sufferings, would that not necessarily awaken sympathy? The best way to test whether empathy and sympathy are necessarily conjoined is to imagine Nietzsche making empathetic demands on us. He might ask us whether we have ever fully identified with the sheer awfulness of ordinary people.

Have we ever made an honest effort to access the minds of a family convulsed with mirth at a female impersonator or weeping sentimentally at endless reruns of *This Is Your Life*; to merge with a mob mindlessly baying for blood at a Nuremberg rally; to duplicate the psyche of a bullying husband; to appreciate the idiot vanity of someone who offers the world no more than a pretty face and a cloying manner? He might assert that if we truly did all of this, we could not hold on to our egalitarian ideals, at least not while under the spell of these experiences, at least not if we repeated the experiment time after time. And he might argue that if the tactic did not work, that merely showed we were incapable of true empathy.

If determining whether a series of empathetic experiments can weaken moral commitment is a legitimate test of commitment, we should not wait for Nietzsche. We should make such demands on ourselves and push them on others. If some of our humane comrades seem to falter in their commitment, we should urge them to immerse themselves in the awfulness of ordinary people, perhaps beginning with a close reading of the section on the common man in Philip Wylie's *Generation of Vipers*. I doubt any of us would feel obliged to do this.

There is a core of validity here: if someone can only sustain a humane-egalitarian commitment by falsifying what people are like, turning workers into proletarian heroes or farmers into peasants sitting under an oak tree always deciding wisely, or believing that everybody is "essentially good at heart," then his or her commitment is built on sand. But if we have faced up to what people are like, warts and all, and still feel a lively sympathy, we need not undertake a concerted campaign to weaken our commitment by wallowing in human awfulness. Indeed, if some of our comrades approached us and said that under the spell of such experiences they doubted their ideals, we might say that this was a temptation to be resisted. We might say that this was no state of mind in which to make a binding decision, any more than one should decide on the existence of God when terrified of death. We might advise our comrades to calm down, reflect soberly, and see whether their commitment to humane ideals, despite what ordinary people can be like, was not still alive and meaningful.

If that is our view of empathy as a test of moral commitment, we can hardly object if Nietzsche adopts it. Imagine that Nietzsche, at our urging, did close the distance between himself and a herd man suffused with suffering, not impossible because suffering probably serves as a psychic leveler, and experienced what? The self-sympathy of the herd man perhaps, because if Nietzsche had truly become that person, it would not be the distinctive Nietzsche experiencing anything. When he emerged from total empathy and recovered his own psyche, he might lose any feeling of sympathy at all. It is quite possible to attain real empathy with someone and then, when the spell is broken, be disgusted by the personality entered into, as every actor who has played Uriah Heep will know.

But let us assume that the resurrected Nietzsche did feel some lingering sympathy. I suspect he would react much as we would if empathy left us with a residual loss of sympathy for ordinary people. His psychological distance restored, he would soberly assess his feelings. He would find he still had a lively contempt for herd men, would be disgusted that for a moment he had felt sympathy for a creature so unworthy of sympathy, would deny that he was obliged to accept as final any decision he was tempted to make while captive of that emotion. He would contemplate anew the glory of the great, the awfulness of the masses, and assess with a cool head whether he still believed the sufferings of herd men should not inhibit the goals of the great. Certainly, he would feel under no obligation to undertake a concerted campaign to weaken his commitment by constant or repeated identification with ordinary human suffering.

Those committed to humane ideals are obliged to try to convert others, particularly when reason fails, by inducing conversion experiences. But those with opposing ideals, so long as they have not hidden behind false assumptions about people or hidden from the human consequences of their ideals, have no obligation to cooperate. Sympathy for ordinary people is our best card, contempt for ordinary people is Nietzsche's best card: we are each obliged to play our own card by the ideals we hold, but neither of us is obligated to play both cards evenhandedly because neither of us holds both humane and Nietzschean ideals.

Having demonstrated why Nietzsche is a formidable opponent, it is time to let him develop the detail of his ethics. Toward the end of *Beyond Good and Evil*, Nietzsche tells us that a "distinguished soul" first clarifies for itself the question of rank. Who are its equals to whom it will accord respect and equal rights, and who are its natural inferiors who should sacrifice themselves to a being such as "we are"? If such sacrifices mean that the lot of the latter is hard, that after all "is justice itself." Extending fairness to people in general is to treat them as the equals of their superiors, and this is unfair to supermen. The herd possesses a powerful herd need to obey. It was a sort of kindness when Napoleon stepped forward as absolute commander of the herd Europeans; indeed, he was the high point of the whole nineteenth century and created its most valuable men and moments.

Between unequals morality is no more than a kind of weapon. History shows the master moralities of rulers confident enough to despise the ruled and a slave morality espoused by the ruled or slaves or dependents of all kinds. It is the intrinsic right of masters to create values, and they create moralities of self-glorification. Although one may act toward lower beings as one sees fit, this does not mean sadism (Morgan, 1965, p. 371). The distinguished man may even aid the miserable, not out of compassion but out of a consciousness of riches to lavish.

Slaves defend themselves against their superiors by identifying good with the slavish traits of ordinary people, compliance, patience, diligence, and humility. Whenever slave morality predominates, there is a tendency to reconcile the meanings of the word "good" and the word "dumb" (Nietzsche, *Beyond Good and Evil*, secs. 199, 201, 226, 228, 260–261, 265; *Genealogy of Morals*, I, sec. 13; *Thus Spoke Zarathustra*, II, On the Tarantulas; *Twilight of the Idols*, Skirmishes of an Untimely Man, sec. 48).

Christianity above all is a slave morality, one that attempts to give the best a guilty conscience. It holds up the ideal of a sublime abortion, a herd animal of good will, sickliness, and mediocrity (blessed are the meek). Christianity is a popularized Platonism that turns pure form and moral absolutes into all souls equal before God. God learned Greek to write the New Testament and learned it badly. Supermen must avoid self-deception, be too strong to be disarmed by guilt, and persist with their unique mission: they are the only ones who have the right to mold humanity for a higher purpose as artists do when they use their materials.

They must go beyond good and evil, beyond the herd animal morality of compassion and neighborly love that is conventional European morality, to experiments with both "good" and "evil," embrace everything evil, frightful, tyrannical, brutal, and snakelike in man. A superman has no right to waste a superior, rare, and privileged nature out of concern for others. Even God could not become perfect if he were not permitted to sin (Nietzsche, *Beyond Good and Evil*, Preface, secs. 2, 23, 41, 44, 62, 65a, 121, 199, 219, 221).

Nietzsche endorses caste societies, particularly those established by barbarian conquest, because a ruling caste knows that society exists only so that a select kind of creature can raise itself to a higher task. It also accepts the reduction of an enormous number of people to incomplete human beings, to slaves, to tools. The Germans must take the blame for inventing the printing press, thus the prevalence of newspaper reading, thus democratic "enlightenment." The result has been equality before the law, flattering the desires of herd animals, the socialist demand for social equality, the very rejection of the concepts "master" and "servant."

Worst of all, compulsory education and universal literacy have corrupted not only writing but thinking, and this has reduced rare spirits to rabble (Kaufmann, 1954). The Brahmans of India knew how to educate the masses; they used religion as it should be used, to influence and control the ruled and sanctify their suffering. They even used religion to avoid the dirt of politicking by annexing the power to nominate kings. The problem for the future, the serious problem, is how to breed a new caste to rule Europe. The Jews could have the ascendancy, literally the supremacy, because they are beyond doubt the strongest, toughest, and purest race in Europe. But they do not want it; all they want is assimilation. Perhaps we can interbreed Jews and the officers of the Prussian landed gentry, adding some intellectuality to a hereditary art of command (Nietzsche, *Beyond Good and Evil*, Preface, secs. 22, 61, 251, 257–258; *Thus Spoke Zarathustra*, I, On Reading and Writing; *Twilight of the Idols*, Skirmishes of an Untimely Man, sec. 40).

For those who have read garbled accounts of Nietzsche, he would have despised the Nazis with their Führer and anti-Semitism and vulgar German nationalism. Hitler would not qualify as a super-man against a standard that goes beyond military virtues to embrace the creative genius of Leonardo, and Goethe, and Beethoven. Nietzsche wants to banish the anti-Semitic crybabies, the Germans who are so weak that they fear the Jews as a stronger race. It is time to stop the literary obscenity of leading Jews to the slaughter as scapegoats of every conceivable public and internal misfortune. Germans should look at themselves with a clearer eye unclouded by patriotic drivel: they are a monstrous conglomeration of races, perhaps not even predominantly Aryan. France is the seat of the most intellectual and sophisticated culture of Europe (Nietzsche, *Beyond Good and Evil*, secs. 241, 244, 251, 254; *Genealogy of Morals*, III, sec. 26; *Human, All-Too-Human*, sec. 475).

Nietzsche mounts a strong attack on those who say they hold humane ideals. Humane intellectuals exhibit a total disso-nance between their metaphysics and their ethics. They would ridicule anyone who still believed in Plato's Forms or the Christian God, but they cling to a morality that makes sense only for believers. Love for mankind in general because everyone has a soul dear to God is a notion that makes some kind of sense, but love of mankind without this is simply stupidity and brutishness.

Humane intellectuals suffer from "soul superstition." How could anyone love ordinary people without some concept that sanctifies them? Nietzsche is challenging us to review our commitments, look within ourselves and face what is really there, ask ourselves whether we would really be committed to egalitarian principles if our minds were not infected by a disreputable metaphysical residue. Utilitarianism, pasture-happiness for the herd, insipid and sentimental compassion, are these really what we admire most? The English do because they are not a philosophical race. After all, what are English people like? Cattle taught to raise their voices in moral "mooing" by the Methodists and the Salvation Army, a penitential fit their highest level of achievement. Just look at how even the most beautiful English woman walks.

Nietzsche feels that history is on his side. As more thinking people have the clarity and courage to face up to the moral implications of the demise of Platonic and Christian metaphysics, they will abandon an ethics that, its ontological foundations gone, rests on nothing except bad taste. Those with the right breeding will become "new philosophers" and hammer out a new conscience, a conscience that appreciates that a whole people is only nature's detour to six or seven great men (Nietzsche, *Beyond Good and Evil*, Preface, secs. 44, 60, 126, 186, 203, 213, 225, 252).

The case against Nietzsche

Before attempting to diagnose where Nietzsche is truly vulnerable, recall that he has taught us something: unless you can face without flinching every sad and silly manifestation of human behavior, your commitment to humane ideals is untested. However, George Orwell was not alone in passing that test. And whatever historical debt we may owe to the Greeks and to Christianity, plenty of us find our commitment to humane ideals enough without the prop of Plato's Forms or the notion of equality before God.

The absence of ethical truth affects all moral ideals and poses no special problems for humane ones. As to whether we are plants bound to wither when torn from our original metaphysical soil, the future will decide that. But I suspect that our roots go deep into human psychology, just as deep as those that feed the superman. In most societies, children internalize other-regarding oughts within the family, and some tend to generalize their moral concern outside that small circle, unless the struggle for existence is too intense, or unless social myths convince them that only a certain race, or class, or caste is fully human. The prevalence of humane ideals probably depends on things like mutual respect within families, reasonable access to a good life, and visible examples of blacks and poor people and untouchables with the kind of traits the myths tell us cannot be.

Bloom (1987) argues that the family is less likely to nurture humane ideals in the future because of the increasing number of children who feel betrayed by the divorce of their parents. It is true that young people today are more likely to come to maturity without that trust in others, even in those who claim to love them the most, that would encourage them to enlarge their circle of moral concern. But at least they are less likely to get from their elders the active racist and class and nationalistic and gender biases that once circumscribed the tendency to identify with human kind. A significant minority of youth has always loved to get drunk on ideals, often precisely because the moral landscape in which they have been reared was so barren. No one can foresee, as yet, the full impact on morals of the new childhood environment that is evolving. I hope Bloom's pessimism is proved wrong.

This brings us to the core of Nietzsche's ideals. Operationalizing them assumes that we can locate supermen in the real world or at least provide a plausible scenario for their emergence.

Nietzsche recommends the caste societies that have been imposed by barbarian conquests. He says that these provide a vehicle by which rare creatures can rise to perform a higher task.

However, the barbarian conquests he so admires did not really do anything to impose a genetic or cultural elite on a mass of herd men. Until about AD 1500, the date when Europeans achieved a technology potent enough to withstand nomadic cavalry, the horse was the greatest instrument of conquest in Eurasia. The only superiority required to be a barbarian conqueror was a homeland with abundant horses and pasture, agriculture not developed enough for large permanent settlements, and proximity to a civilization with advanced metallurgy. It may appear that Nietzsche has handicapped his thesis by not endorsing more civilized conquerors, but the Romans showed no signs of genetic superiority to the Etruscans, Celts, or Greeks.

As for the European conquest of the Americas, this was largely an accident of biogeography. The Europeans had dense populations, large centralized states with ocean-going ships, and iron tools. This advantage in population growth and development was enormously enhanced by the fact that Europe's indigenous animals, such as horses, oxen, mouflon sheep, pigs, and cows, and Europe's indigenous cereals, such as wheat, barley, oats, and rye, are relatively easy to domesticate.

The indigenous animals of the western hemisphere, such as tapirs, bighorn sheep, peccaries, and bisons, and the indigenous plants, such as annual teosinte, maygrass, little barley, and wild millet, are very difficult to domesticate. The absence of pack animals and draft animals crippled transport, and therefore trade, communications, and the beneficial flow of technology from one distant group to another (Diamond, 1991, chs. 14 and 15; Sowell, 1998, ch. 5). I am not taking a dogmatic stance on the possibility of some genetic differences between conquering and conquered peoples, but whatever gap may have existed, it was light-years short of the gap posited between supermen and herd men.

Setting aside conquerors, whether barbarian or otherwise, Nietzsche's hopes for caste are based on illusion. Caste freezes in place an elite with no clear superiority. Indeed, it impedes the evolution of a significant correlation between rank and merit more effectively than any other social experiment humanity has ever tried. Mascie-Taylor has said the last word about Sir Cyril Burt's sins in fabricating data, but this does not detract from the validity of Burt's pioneering social models. If one wants to sustain even a moderate correlation between rank and merit, social mobility must be high, that is, 20 to 30 percent must shift class in every generation. Burt's description of the historical prerequisites of a meritocracy has never been bettered: an elite established by force and blood relationship must give way to an aristocracy of property or wealth; finally, that must give way to an open society stratified by talent free to make its way (Burt, 1959; 1961).

Caste must be abolished to achieve another of Nietzsche's objectives, that is, the maximization of great achievement. The best means to that goal is to tap the reservoir of talent existent throughout the whole of society. Only because Nietzsche's ban on education or literacy for the masses has been ignored do we have our own century's explosion of scientific and mathematical achievement.

Look at the wonderful things dancing before our eyes, the prospect of a grand unified theory of all the forces of nature, the bold cosmological speculations about the origins of the universe, the solution of Faltings's theorem, the solution of Fermat's last theorem, the answer to Hilbert's question about Diophantine equations, the exciting and elegant progress on curves of genus 2 and above. The Brahmans of India were a dead hand on great achievement as much as any other caste. If education and literacy had been restricted to them, much of post-independence India's contribution to the arts, literature, film, science, and mathematics would never have occurred. As Nielsen (1985, p. 33) says, improving the lot of the masses revealed that they had always contained many creative people, unsung Miltons, undiscovered Goethes, quasi-Goethes, and mini-Goethes.

The real world confronts Nietzsche with a choice between two options: either caste without merit or merit with social mobility. The first option would mean jettisoning the ideal of excellence and tear the heart out of his value system. The second option retains that ideal but levies several demoralizing prices.

First, an open society, one that forces all to compete with some kind of equal opportunity, eliminates the social distance between the elite and the herd so dear to Nietzsche's heart. The select man will find that he, and particularly his children, can no longer simply issue commands, avoid the bad company of dwarfed beasts with pretensions to equal rights and demands, confine the ill-smelling task of studying the many to reading books (Nietzsche, *Beyond Good and Evil*, secs, 26, 203, 257). Second, the prerogatives of supermen cannot be transplanted into a socially mobile society. Even bosses cannot use their secretaries as mere means to ends, much less a scientist a lab assistant, when the lab assistant might be a scientist tomorrow or when the scientist's son or daughter is likely to serve an apprenticeship as a lab assistant.

No matter whether one posits an open society or a caste society, there remains an additional problem. There is no way of providing a mechanism for conferring rule on supermen. Some individuals will scale the heights of achievement, but no one has ever found a way to give creative geniuses political or social control. Even in his own day, Nietzsche could not specify any social group likely to become a superman ruling elite. His proposal to breed Jews with the Prussian military to seize control of a united Europe is surely tongue-in-cheek, a delicious slap at German pretensions and anti-Semitism. Military conquest promises nothing better for the future than it delivered in the past; witness Hitler and the imperial rule of Stalin.

Bertrand Russell (1946, p. 789) opines that Nietzsche had a romantic ideal, perhaps best represented by someone like Pope Julius II, fighting for Bologna one day and employing Michelangelo the next. If so, his ideal is truly consigned to the dustbin of history.

No general today rides a horse around the field of battle and doubles as a munificent head of state. During Operation Desert Storm, General Colin Powell never got closer to Iraq than Saudi Arabia, and his job as head of the chiefs of staff was rather like that of a top executive at General Motors. General Norman Schwarzkopf, the commander in the field, played a role akin to someone running a complex computerized dating service operating under pressure. Total automation of reconnaissance and weaponry may soon mean that no "soldier," much less general, gets within 500 miles of the enemy until the battle is over. General Powell knew he could not avoid the "dirt" of politics if he wanted to be President, and he found it not to his taste.

As for a group like the Brahmans influencing popular culture behind the scenes, advertising executives, film producers, and pop stars play that role today. There is nothing in Nietzsche's writings to save him from the fate of Miniver Cheevy, child of scorn, who grew lean as he assailed the seasons. Someone who could not face loss of the "medieval grace" of iron clothing.

If Nietzsche can specify no actual or emerging elite that has been staffed by a "select kind of creature," what of the conscious creation of an ideal elite? This poses the problem of identification. It is hard to imagine any institutional method of stamping credentials, a sort of self-perpetuating fraternity plus sorority accepting or blackballing candidates, which could operate without self-destructive controversy. After all, the prerogatives of membership include control, enslavement, and sacrifice of those rejected.

Nietzsche's own attempts at screening for creative genius do not inspire confidence. He does not provide a list of supermen (they belong to the future), but he does tell us whom he admires and rejects (Nietzsche, *Beyond Good and Evil*, secs. 199–200, 224, 245, 252–256, 269). Those approved include some of the great names we would expect, although Alcibiades and Frederick the Great give pause. He likes Shakespeare despite the revolting vapors and the closeness of the English rabble. Gogol is no better than Byron or Poe, a great stylist but child-brained. Rejected are Bacon, Hobbes, Locke, and Hume as unphilosophical, Darwin and Spencer as mediocre intellects, Schumann because of petty taste. Bach, Newton, Leibniz, and Gauss go, as far as I can see, unmentioned. All of this suggests that no one can identify supermen except idiosyncratically.

Although Nietzsche has no plausible scenario for a public role for supermen, his ideals have implications for personal conduct or private ethics. Even here, the lack of an institutional method of identifying creative geniuses is significant because it leaves open only the alternative of personal identification. This leaves every fool in Greenwich Village who paints himself or herself blue and rolls across a canvas free to claim the prerogatives of a superman. It conjures up the specter of these so-called artists murdering "ordinary" people in alleys to get money for paint and materials or even simply for inspiration. In other words, the only real-world consequence of putting Nietzsche's ethics into practice would probably be an increase in New York City's already robust random murder rate. What contribution this would make to great achievement is unclear.

Nietzsche ignores real geniuses: "Love and knowledge and delight in beauty . . . are enough to fill the lives of the greatest men who have ever lived" (Russell 1946, p. 800). How many artists today believe that embracing "everything evil, frightful, tyrannical, brutal, and snake-like in man" would enhance their talent? Even if some were to adopt the psychology of the superman, the results would be rather humdrum. They would not want to command an army because that would be boring. They would not run for office because that would be demeaning, witness Obama and Clinton. They could not attempt to manipulate the American psyche because they would have to debase their art beyond recognition. They could rob herd people when broke. That would hardly give then a sense of "high distinction." People on drugs do that every day.

Nietzsche gives us analytic brilliance, the wonderful style, and the challenge we must accept for our own peace of mind, namely, whether we have the courage to look humanity full in the face.

However, those committed to humane ideals concede him too much: they imagine a group of creative geniuses in power demanding the right to use everyone else and lament our lack of a refutation of that demand. In fact, Nietzsche had no concept that could perform the most fundamental task of justice: since he could not operationalize his ideals, he had no ordering principle for human society.

The truth is that we can beat Nietzsche at his own game. A humane-egalitarian open society with social mobility will produce far more creative geniuses than the strange, frozen, largely pre-literate, semi-medieval society Nietzsche admires. If creative geniuses have political wisdom as well as their own special talent, and they care to enter the ring, they usually punch above their weight – look at the atomic scientists. They do far better than they would as a self-selected secret cabal trying to imitate the Brahmans. As far as the individual of creative potential goes, there is no evidence that a humane character structure is an impediment or that indulging in a sense of God-like superiority is necessary. Nietzsche gives self-deluded artists a license to kill and we cannot use reason to coerce him into being more humane. That is sad but it should not cast us into an abyss.

Here I stand

I have tried to give reasons as to why those of us who are committed to humane-egalitarian ideals should suffer no crisis of morale. First, those ideals define who we are. They are precious precisely because they are our own: an idea of the good to which we are deeply committed. Second, we know that ethical objectivity is not only an illusion but also undesirable. If something alien hands us our ideals, we pay the price that they have become distorted in the process. Even if something like God hands us our ideals, we allow Him to do so only because we recreate Him in our image (make him benevolent). How curious to regard that as a valuable gift.

Third, the content of our ideals is a cause of special pride.

Their content transcends the dross of ethnocentrism or tribal morality to include all humanity as worthy of moral concern. Fourth, our ideals have a special relationship with truth. We can render them logically coherent, face up to their consequences in practice, show how they can order a human society, face up to everything that science teaches us about ourselves and the world, things that our opponents like racists and Nietzsche cannot do.

Have I really parted company with Leo Strauss? In Plato's *Republic*, the emptiness at the top of the divided line is not the whole story. Remember that before that whole enterprise gets underway, in the very first book of the dialogue, Socrates defends his ideal of justice against Thrasymachus. There it is established that anyone's concept of justice must past the test of being able to order a human society, that it must not involve logical inconsistencies, that we must be willing to accept the consequences of putting it into practice, and that it must not require ignoring what we know about man and society. Thrasymachus' concept of justice as "might makes right" fails on all counts. In other words, Plato's refutation of Thrasymachus is identical in kind to the one I have offered against Nietzsche.

I hope the members of the inner circle will feel they have what they need to fill the void at the top of the divided line. To ask for more is the mark of an Auxiliary. That may be too harsh: the very idealism of Adeimantus and Glaucon, the noble sons of Ariston, made them want more. They may be upset that here is no knowledge of the good, but honesty is best. Playing games with Aristotle holds its own dangers. A candidate may be bright enough to see through the words and get lost along the way. Worst of all, raising false hopes about what Aristotle or Plato can do spreads the "objectivity disease": the notion that our ideals are worthless unless God or nature or truth or a moral reality saves them from "subjectivity."

10   Choosing to be free

It matters not how straight the gate
  How charged with punishment the scroll,
I am the master of my fate,
  I am the captain of my soul
    (William Ernest Henley, *Invictus*, 1875)

In a surprisingly strict and technical sense the American radical
tradition has been based on a philosophy of free will.
  (Straughton Lynd, 1969, pp. 168–169)

Besides the motives felt, and besides the formed habits or past
self, is there not a *present self* that has a part to perform in
reference to them both? Is there not a causal self, over and
above the caused self (the character) that has been left as a
deposit from previous behaviour?
  (Michael Maher, SJ, 1940, p. 410)

I have always had to struggle to live up to my ideals, and on occasion
they have cost me some sacrifice of safety and liberty. I would like to
have a license to believe that the important decisions were free
choices for which I deserve either moral praise or moral blame. If you
are someone for whom that is a matter of indifference, you can skip
this chapter. If not, you will find herein a case that free will is an
open option.

  I fear that this means arguing for no less than ten propositions:

1 We presume free will when deciding what to do.

2 The concept of free will is coherent.

3 We must ask whether or not that presumption corresponds to reality.

4 Viewed from that perspective, free will is not compatible with determinism.

5 Free will alone renders moral praise and blame appropriate.

6 Whether we are truly free or determined is testable in theory but unlikely to be decided in practice.

7 Nonetheless the necessity of either allocating or withholding moral praise and blame forces us to choose between them.

8 This must be done without rational guidance.

9 However, it is a moral choice and therefore subject to the rules of moral reasoning.

10 A humane person may well adopt a policy of praise/blame in personal relationships and eschew such in other circumstances such as the legal code.

The present self as uncaused first cause

The odd thing about the supposed ambiguity of the concept of free will is that it arises out of a universal human experience. As both Kant (Flynn, 1986) and Pinker (2002) point out, if I am torn between visiting a sick friend and going to see an escapist film, and I wait for a billiard ball to knock me toward the hospital or the theater, I will wait forever. That is to say that all of us face situations in which we must choose and nothing else will do it for us. Therefore, I take the following as common ground: the human mind is a functional system with both unconscious (whatever is going on in the brain) and conscious components; and the latter sometimes operates as a present self that must act under the presumption of free choice.

The concept of free choice is perfectly coherent and easily stated. Free choice, to the extent that it is real, would be an uncaused cause. It is the opposite of what we call an epiphenomenon. A good example of the latter is the reflection of a tree in a pond: if you cut down the tree, the reflection disappears; but if you drop a rock on the reflection, the tree is unmoved. An epiphenomenon is all effect and no cause. If free choice exists, the present self has a genuine choice between (at least) two alternatives and creates a future that would not otherwise have existed. If we decide to pick up hitchhikers as an act of charity at a greater risk to our lives, the world will be different: more hitchhikers will get to their destinations quicker and some extra lives will be lost. Free choice breaks the flow of the world from past to future and thus the result is what philosophers call "metaphysical discontinuity."

Free will is not, of course, a God-like necessary being. It came into existence when I reached the age of reason and will go out of existence when I die. But so long as the present self exists, it is self-generating. That is to say that it affects itself over time. The more good choices I make, the more I enhance "will power," that is, the more the present self will find it easier to choose good over evil. It also affects character. When I act out of regard for moral principles, I enliven my commitment to them.

Dennett (2003) and others argue against the dignity of free will on the grounds that it is irrelevant to what we admire most: someone who always does good. We do indeed, but that is because these people deserve *credit* for what *they have become*. Their present selves over time made a whole series of choices rightly and the result was the strength of will to do what moral principles (more and more deeply ingrained) entail. Thanks to the present self, these decisions are today virtually automatic. Note the word "virtually." Even the saint does not attain the perfect or Holy Will Kant attributed to God and it is hubris for anyone to believe that like God they are beyond temptation. Those who do believe that are likely to find themselves suddenly at risk, say in old age as the prospect of death engenders a sense of indifference.

However, the point is this. We all know the hard road to sanctity, that is, how hard it is to record a life history of choosing good over evil that renders the present self's choices virtually automatic. The saint deserves credit both for those choices as they were made and for the kind of present self they have engendered. But if none of them had been free, what credit would he deserve? Shortly, I will argue that the answer is none at all. For now, it is enough to suggest that the fact that the road to sanctity is paved with free choices is crucial. We take this into account when we give the highest praise to those who had the most difficult path. For some, raised humanely with few temptations, the road is, well, not easy, because it is never easy. But we admire most those who became outstandingly good despite adversity.

Does that lead to the odd conclusion that we should not create a good society in which virtue comes more easily? Of course not. The fact that moral praiseworthiness is a great good does not mean it is the only great good. If moral praiseworthiness is diminished by a social dynamic that makes humane actions more frequent, then the trade-off is worthwhile. Would we want to create a society in which sanctity was a certain outcome for everyone? That amounts to wishing we were angels rather than human beings, which is as absurd as wishing we were social insects. Human nature is the foundation of the value of moral praiseworthiness and if you abolish our humanity, of course, it loses its *raison d'être*. Given what we are, we need all the help in becoming good we can get.

Note that one of the absurdities supposed to attend free will has been shown to be absurd. The question is often put: If I am an agent acting in a void beyond the reach of character, a sort of loose cannon, a ghost in a machine, etc., etc., then to whom would we give whatever credit may be due? To some sort of characterless abstraction?

The answer, of course, is that moral credit is due to my present self and my present self is a rather important part of me. It has been my faithful companion throughout life, the part of me that has had to make choices, the part of me that has recorded a history with (at least some) good choices for each of which it deserves credit, the part of me that deserves some credit for my virtuous (on balance,

I hope) character, though only in so far as it has played a role in the evolution of my character. I deserve no credit for influences that molded my character if they were beyond my control.

It may be objected that even my concept of the present self is a mysterious entity isolated from my psychological make-up. That I am, in effect, positing a meta-character beyond and apart from what most people would call character. This is just a matter of labeling. I have distinguished the present self from my character (in the sense of the repository of my principles) simply to emphasize its unique role. If you wish, it is that part of my character that must make free choices and record a history of good choices and strengthen my will thereby. Incoherence does not shadow the concept of free choice. It can be stated more clearly than many (say beauty or empathy).

A word of explanation

Most readers may think, as I do, that it is virtually self-evident that the central question is whether our experience of being free whenever we make a decision is mere illusion or corresponds to reality. They will find, perhaps to their surprise, that most philosophers deny this and call themselves "compatibilists." They think that we can both explain all human behavior scientifically and still believe in free will. Therefore, I must argue in favor of what seems self-evident. I do not wish to discourage non-philosophers from following the argument of the next section, but if they skim it I will understand.

Reality trumps appearance

No good reason can be given for evading the question of whether the appearance of free will matches reality. Reality always trumps appearance. The only way to determine whether appearance can be trusted in the light of reality is to open your mind to the possibility of either a positive or a negative outcome.

The compatibilists and I have some common ground. We both assert that clocks differ from people. Clocks are unconscious while people are aware of certain thought processes when we make decisions, that is, we have considerations, weigh them, know that nothing will happen unless we make a decision, and so forth. But I believe that the next step is to show that our sense of having real alternatives from among which we choose corresponds to a reality in which those *very same* alternatives are open.

If I return a borrowed book to a friend, the universe is such that he can read it that night; if I do not return it, the universe is different in the sense that he cannot. Which is to say that there is a radical discontinuity from one state of the universe to the next; indeed, the discontinuity is so radical it must accommodate all of the free choices people are making throughout the world. Which is to say that much human behavior and its effects escape causality in the radical sense that they escape all scientific explanation.

The compatibilists think they can evade the task of showing that open alternatives correspond to reality, and the unwelcome consequence that scientific explanation is limited, by qualifying the nature of causality. They have three arguments, though not all use all three. The first is that Hume showed that causal connections are contingent rather than necessary. Actually, Hume did not qualify causality but undermined it completely. He showed that we cannot justify positing any causal connection between events, however feeble (this is another way of putting the problem of induction which we solved in Box 33).

It is important to note that Hume's analysis applies to *all* causal explanations, those that explain the behavior of a clock as much as those that explain the behavior of people. Therefore, it cannot differentiate between clocks and people. And yet, that is what we must do if we are to justify blaming people in a way in which we do not blame clocks, that is, we must show that alternatives are truly open for people in a way in which they are not open for clocks. Simply citing our conscious ratiocination as a difference will not do.

What if our sense of having more than one alternative open is an illusion rather than grounded in reality?

Mirages deceive us about where things are. Hallucinations deceive us about what things exist. Who is to say that our experience of decision-making does not deceive us when it implies that more than one alternative is open? Astrologers think it deceptive. So do orthodox Freudians. So does virtually every physiologist I know.

The first two do not trouble me but the third does. Does anyone really believe that the antidote is to tell them all to read Hume? Exactly how would that obviate the anticipation of the outcomes of all of our decisions from brain states? And does not "ought imply can"? When we blame someone for a choice, we say you ought not to have done that, meaning you should have chosen differently. What sense would this make if the choice they made was the only one open? Compatibilism is lazy: it thinks that it can evade these questions. Or better, it hates the notion of setting limits on scientific explanation so much that it will not face the fact that blameworthy freedom and causal explanation are incompatible.

Sometimes compatibilists appeal to indeterminacy, either on the subatomic level (electrons unpredictably jump from one place to another), or in the context of chaos theory (where thousands of chaotic trends make the timing and occurrence of an event only probable). But actually, indeterminacy takes us no farther than Hume. The electrons of a clock are just as unpredictable in their jumps as those of a human being. Chaos theory applies to things like predicting the weather (where thousands of chaotic variables come into play), but no one uses it to give a causal analysis of either clocks or the behavior of an individual human being. So no kind of indeterminacy differentiates clocks and people. Chanting "indeterminacy" no more justifies evading the central question than chanting "Hume" (see Box 34).

A point for reflection. Remember that when I make a decision, I rule out alternative universes in favor of a certain state of affairs: if I do not return a borrowed book to someone, I dictate a uni-

Box 34

To show how irrelevant indeterminacy is to the central question, whether we truly have choices subject to moral praise and blame, Kant's distinction between positive and negative freedom is apt. Something can be indeterminate and not worthy of praise or blame. A random event like an electron jump cannot be praised or blamed because no present self exists faced with open alternatives and choosing freely between them. The same is true of a clock. The existence of a present self of this sort is the crux of the matter. You do not praise or blame a Mexican jumping bean simply because it is unpredictable.

I have had my position described in jumping bean terms. Critics have said that when I posit an alternative to determinism, I must think that my free will just pops into existence, which is hardly consistent with my being in control of it. The reader now knows that this is not the case. The present self does not pop into existence. It has many causal antecedents (including its own choices) and it is my constant companion. Its choices do not pop into existence. My present self makes them. And it experiences them as if they were free, the question being, are they really?

verse in which he cannot read that book tonight. That happens despite all the talk of indeterminacy. The only way in which this radical discontinuity between past and future can be avoided is by saying that the outcome of my choice was determined, whatever quibbles about electrons or chaos theory are added.

Other compatibilists emphasize the distinction between causes acting from without and those acting from within. Causes acting from without like gravity produce behavior for which I cannot be blamed (falling on someone after being pushed out of a window). But the behavior of human beings is caused by forces acting from within their psyches. There is a real distinction here. A stone is at the mercy of causes outside itself. If someone hits me with one, it is silly to call it a bad stone. It is no different from any other stone, including "innocent" stones. But a clock acts in response to forces influencing it from within and if it deceives me about the time, it makes sense to call it a bad clock. But note that this is merely a condemnation of its bad "character," not moral blame of its choices – it has no real choices.

Dennett (2003) is better than many compatibilists (also see Gribben, 2005). He notes indeterminacy and cites Hume but this does not keep him from conceding two points. First, scientific (or naturalist) explanations of how the world works leave no room for radical free will, that is, leave no room for a reality that includes free choices as breaking the continuity of the universe from one state to the next. Note in passing the implication of this: in order to refute compatibilism, "all" we need do is show that only radical free will renders moral praise and blame appropriate.

Second, he rejects the reality of radical free will on the grounds that it cannot be reconciled with scientific explanation. But that does not justify salvaging science at the expense of free will. Why assume that we must reject the reality of free choice if that renders part of reality beyond scientific explanation? Why not assume the reverse: that we must recognize a limitation on science if uncaused causes are part of reality. Dennett has a field day demolishing those who try to fit free choice into some niche created by scientific explanation (such as indeterminacy). They are mistaken to try. Science excites our admiration because of the wonderful explanations it has given us about the world thus far. But no one has evidenced the hypothesis that all of reality is susceptible to scientific explanation.

Perhaps science itself could suggest that the contrary is the case. Before judging that to be absurd, wait for a discussion of how free will versus determinism might be decided by evidence, at least in theory. For now, note that on one level it is generally accepted that science may have limits: we may not be bright enough to discover all of the laws that govern the universe. That is not the same as concluding that certain facets of the universe are not susceptible to scientific explanation even by an omniscient mind. But let us keep an open mind even if omniscience is beyond us.

Dennett (2003, p. 85) also analyzes the flip of a coin. He rightly notes that the practical significance of this event is not illuminated by its causal determination in reality. No doubt, the speed and vector of the spin, the density of the air, and the effects of gravity determine whether it falls as heads or tails. But there is no pattern in its outcomes that we can predict. That is the whole point of using a coin as a device for making random choices. As far as we are concerned, it is a fair way of giving two alternatives an even chance of selection. Is this not a case of where an undetermined "appearance" trumps a deterministic "reality"?

Let us imagine that the coin was an agent and we leveled an indictment of moral irresponsibility. Assume that the two alternatives were whether to visit our sick friend or go to an escapist film. We say: "You have chosen to make this decision in a way that ignores the significance of the two alternatives. One act is dictated by a moral principle, the other by your own pleasure of the moment. What you have done is not as bad as simply giving in to the temptation to enjoy yourself at the expense of your friend. But even so, to make the outcome a matter of chance was totally irresponsible." The coin replies: "But I had no control over the situation. It is true that I have to bear causal responsibility for this decision in the sense that I was a necessary participant in the events that led to it. But others manufactured my character (neither head nor tail is the heavier side) and once I was in motion, forces determined the outcome. You can pass a moral judgment on my behavior as bad behavior but you cannot pass a moral judgment on me for behaving badly."

The coin has a case. The missing element in the real-world situation, however described, whether as random or determined, is a present self that is playing the role of an uncaused cause. Let me underline that point. If the present self cast in such a role is merely a necessary presumption for action (cannot wait for a billiard ball), and we find that it has no basis in reality, then reality trumps appearance. The presumption of a free choice is illusion and one does not base judgments on illusions.

Assume a person decided to make this decision by flipping a coin and we passed judgment on him or her. The person replies: "I know I seem to control such situations and I do in the causal sense in that I am a necessary participant in the events that lead to an outcome. But in fact, myself as uncaused cause is an illusion. No free choice ever entered into the formation of my character. And my character dictated that I would run away from this decision by flipping a coin. You can pass a moral judgment on my bad behavior but not on me for behaving badly."

I see no weakness in the person's case as compared to the coin's case. Unless of course, the reality was different. Coins do not have a present self even on the level of appearance, so the question of whether they can act as uncaused causes in reality does not arise. People do act under the presumption of free choice, and therefore the key question is whether that presumption is illusion or real. It is just that simple. As foreshadowed, compatibilism is now refuted. Scientific explanation, if it extends to the whole of reality including the choices of the present self, banishes free will and renders moral praise and blame inappropriate. I should warn the reader that every time I argue with a compatibilist, they name another thinker that I have not read. None thus far has said anything sensible, so I ran out of patience (see Box 35).

From this point on, I will use "determinism" to refer to hard determinism, that is, I will assume that it is incompatible with free will and allocating moral praise or blame.

Two labels

Note the concession that both the coin and the person grant: we can make a moral judgment of their behavior in terms of humane moral principles. That kind of moral judgment is at the very core of morality and is appropriate whether we are really free or not (Flynn,

Box 35

The last straw (no pun intended) was reading the iconic paper by Peter Strawson (1962) entitled "Freedom and resentment." The argument is a breathtaking evasion of the central questions. He points to the reactions we have when someone does us an injury, such as feeling resentful, expecting them to be sorry, falling out of love with them, and so forth. Should we give these up if we believe in determinism? His first answer is that we cannot because they are too deeply engrained. He anticipates that this will only spark the reply: even if that is so, it evades the question of whether, if rational, we will see that they are no basis for a *judgment* of moral condemnation. His rebuttal is that whether we give up our reactions is a practical question in no way dependent on theoretical questions like the truth of determinism. We should assess whether we would benefit from giving up our reactions and look at how this would impoverish our lives.

Holton (2008) suggests interpreting Strawson as saying that the words "a person is free" is not a description of what people are. It is just a way of signaling that we are prepared to react to them with indignation and so forth. Holton then points out the flaw. This makes it legitimate to assess my belief in God in terms of whether I benefit from it; and when I say "I believe in God" that merely signals that I am prepared to be worshipful and so forth.

We must hope that we never encounter a people who deeply value blaming (or worshiping) clocks. In sum, like other compatibilists, Strawson evades the two central questions: what makes people different from clocks; if it is only the experience of freedom (having purposes, reasons for what we do, a conscious need to make a choice), why should we not distrust that experience as mere appearance and probe for the reality beneath?

2000a). Even if the agent is not free, we can indict his or her character as productive of bad acts, force him to assume ownership of his acts in the sense of admitting that his character is responsible for them, and do something to ensure he does not replicate his conduct.

But we cannot indict him as agent for behaving badly if he in fact played no role as uncaused cause. That kind of moral judgment is equally central to morality. For clarity's sake, I will give each of these two kinds of judgments its own label. Assessing good or bad behavior is moral approval or condemnation. Assessing behaving well or ill is to allocate moral praise and blame. The two are quite different. When a person deceives us about the time and when a clock does, we pass a judgment of blame on the former that we do not on the latter.

It may be said that humane behavior has a moral significance that takes priority over the exercise of virtue. As noted, if social reforms make it easier to become good, diminishing the role of the present self in choosing to be good, the prospect of more good acts outweighs the loss of virtue. But given the stuff of human nature, both have their moral value. A utopia is a travesty if populated by angels (all choosing well automatically) rather than people (struggling to perfect their characters by a series of free choices). Admittedly, eliminating good behavior in favor of behaving well would be even more odd. It would have to be a society of "people" whose free choices were the sole influence on their character formation; and in which the outcome of benevolent acts did no one any good because (unknown to the actors) everyone was self-sufficient in terms of what they needed to live a full life. We can see why theologians argue that God's Holy Will would be "objectless" without lesser beings to benefit from its exercise.

Wittgenstein (1989) confuses this issue, as he does so many others, and that confusion has carried over to those like Dilman (1999, p. 251) who follow in his wake. Wittgenstein asked what cash value being free has in the sense of being able to do other than one does. For example, a man refuses to take a bribe. What would it mean to say that he could have accepted it? One could do so only if one were morally corrupt, and who would welcome that option?

In rebuttal, this is a case in which we have done something right. The sterility of being able to do other than one does is less clear if we have done something wrong. Let us say I have kept something borrowed. Would no one welcome the possibility that he or she could have behaved like a more honest person? And would no one prefer to believe that the present self had some influence here, rather than to believe that this dishonest behavior was beyond its control? I set aside those who welcome the notion that they are not morally responsible (only causally responsible) for anything because it absolves them from the possibility of any moral blame.

Did Wittgenstein never regret anything he did? He was so arrogant that he turned every session of the Cambridge Philosophical Society he attended into a monologue, welcomed by his admirers but hardly respectful of anyone else. He was so obtuse that he ruined the lives of students by advising them to abandon philosophy (which was supposed to be worse than futile) to become laborers. He was so unreflective that he wished to add his personal bit of killing to World War I, a war above all that had little honor on any side. If he did not welcome the possibility of alternatives to his behavior, many others will wish that "his character" had been free to choose otherwise and that he had actually done so.

As a student, I once borrowed a blue tie from a friend. I never returned it. I had no tie, needed one on occasion, had little money, and really liked the look of that blue tie. My friend somehow sensed my reluctance and never embarrassed me by confronting me. Moral praise to him if he was free, moral blame to me if I was free. If we were not free, a good act by him for which he deserves no credit and a bad act by me for which I deserve no blame.

For those as yet unconvinced, I plead that they think carefully about the following, which is a typical example of moral discourse. Imagine that my friend had confronted me and said, "I am disappointed in you." Under the presumption of my freedom, the meaning is quite straightforward: "You and I both know you could have done the right thing." A clear indictment that I am morally blameworthy. From Wittgenstein's perspective, the assertion becomes convoluted, that is, it should read, "I am disappointed with myself." After all, if my friend had made a proper estimate of my character, he would have seen my failure to return the tie as predictable. That assumes omniscience, of course, but the point is that he is not disappointed in the *real* me at all. He is disappointed in the *illusory* me who never existed. He was only surprised at my decision because of self-deception about my character. Whose fault is that? Certainly not mine. This is not to say he was morally culpable: he merely went cognitively astray.

His assertion really means, "I now see you as you really are." He can soften his words by adding, "but one unreturned tie does not make you Jack the Ripper." However, this does not obviate the fact that he has purged his assertion of any indictment of moral blame. He now sees he can expect worse acts on my part than he had suspected but he has been robbed of the ability to say that I made the wrong choice. There was no free choice (see Box 36).

Pinker (2002) makes a point similar to that of Wittgenstein. He asks the question, would anyone want complete freedom to do anything? If all of us were free to do anything, how could reward or punishment affect human behavior? Nothing would be an effective incentive or disincentive. This ignores how the present self operates in making (what we will presume to be) free choices.

After being consistently fired for my Social Democratic politics in America in the early 1960s, I was free to do anything within my power: commit suicide; stay and keep getting fired; abandon academia; go overseas. I eventually eliminated all but the last option because of certain considerations, mainly that I wanted to live, had a family to support, and had an intellectual curiosity about certain things. As for going overseas, I earn my living through talking. So that left English-speaking nations, that is, Britain, Ireland, South Africa, Canada, Australia, and New Zealand. Alarmed about the possibility of nuclear war, it seemed to make sense to choose a remote area like New Zealand or Australasia. As a Social Democrat, I had a

Box 36

Free choice makes people praiseworthy. Frankfurt (1969) imagines people who are free to choose A or not-A and do so. But had I made any choices other than those I actually made, a meddler would have coerced me into making the choices I did. It never did, but it would have. Thus, it appears that we actually can praise or blame people who cannot choose to act other than they do. This argument loses plausibility as soon as we clarify when the meddler has the option of not doing anything.

1   Assume it has no foreknowledge. It observes the outcome of our free choices. If it likes what it sees, it allows the choices to stand; otherwise it reverses them the next instant. In either event, people are completely free to choose to do either A or not-A and the argument collapses.

2   It has foreknowledge but no agenda, that is, no plan for history it prefers over any other. Thus, it likes whatever it foresees and never even intends to interfere. People are completely free to do either A or not-A and the argument collapses.

3   It has foreknowledge and an agenda, but likes what it foresees. Every free choice that will ever be made is appealing. Therefore, it simply passes a law that what will be will be. Now we know the meddler's name: it is Time. Time dictated from the day it began that whatever free choices I will make will be set in concrete the moment I make them. The laws that pertain are: one cannot do two alternative things at the same instant; one cannot make time run backwards and redo a decision made. Once made a decision is history. We do not need a meddler to legislate that and so the argument collapses.

4   It has foreknowledge, an agenda, and does not like what it foresees, that is, it anticipates at least one free choice

that would be at variance with its plan for history. Then it has only two options. Either it must anticipate that choice and prevent it, in which case the choice is not truly free. Or it must reverse that choice the moment after it occurs, in which case the choice itself was free. As in number (1), the person was free to do either A or not-A and the argument collapses.

The argument works only if you assume that the meddler has the power (even if unexercised) to let me make a free choice, halt time, reverse time so that it can go back and replace that choice by another, and start time rolling again.

much better image of New Zealand than Australia (the white Australian policy).

My description of this process in no way implies that my formed character left the present self only an executive role. I had to choose between alternatives that both my character and the real world left open. In a way, it seemed cowardly to abandon the struggle for a better America given America's predominant power in the world. But might I not speak out more effectively abroad – and there was my family to consider – and so forth. Note that, even under the presumption of freedom, the outside world was not helpless to influence the choice. Universities kept firing me, certain nations had adopted English as their dominant language, some had done things to make themselves more likely targets for nuclear destruction than others, and Australia had compromised its social democracy more than New Zealand. What others do structures the considerations of free present selves even if they are true considerations, that is, things to be weighed rather than merely a matter of character dictating the choice between them.

I have tried to show that either free will or determinism is true and there is no third option. Free will makes moral praise and blame appropriate; determinism makes them inappropriate. And the reader knows what I mean by determinism: believing that a scientific explanation of all human behavior is possible, at least in theory.

Confronting the issue

I have argued that both free will and its absence are open options. That puts us in a position to take arguments for and against free will seriously. I believe that all of these arguments fail. In one chapter, the best I can do is select three arguments on both sides and criticize them. For simplicity's sake, when the various arguments are presented, I will allow their advocates to speak as if determinism meant that the universe had a predetermined history. No argument's persuasiveness would be enhanced by a more sophisticated picture of reality, that is, one that takes into account all of the subtleties of the present state of scientific explanation.

It will be clear that I am treating the question as an evidential one and it may be objected that it can be resolved by logic alone. Let thinkers bring forward their demonstrations that the existence of free will entails a logical contradiction. Logic alone cannot settle any question about what exists, so it would be odd if it could show that the universe is one way (its past was A rather than B thanks to certain choices) or another way (all choices merely had their role to play in contributing to A).

The case against free will unproven

First argument: That the whole drift of science in general and evolutionary biology in particular has been to banish intentions and design in favor of a chain of impersonal causes that maximize predictability. The attempt to preserve a "ghost in a machine" that has Godlike powers to break the chain of causality and design a self-created future is no more respectable than the rejection of science represented by the advocates of "intelligent design". Human beings want to believe that they are unique, and now that they have lost their place at the center of the universe and the right to claim that they are made in the image of God, they fight to retain a vestige of Godlike qualities that set them off from all else. Just as evolution has shown that the apparent design in nature is the result of laws and chance, so physiology will show that apparent "free choice" is an illusion.

Answer: No one is talking about machines, whether housing ghosts or untenanted. Once again, recall the common ground. The mind is not a spirit insulated from a brain. Consciousness and brain are interrelated in a system that produces human behavior, both are necessary, and whatever happens to one (whether new experiences or brain trauma) influences the other. No one denies the existence of the present self. New things happen in evolution. At one time, matter had not attained the complexity to be self-replicating but then living creatures emerged; at one time, no living creature was conscious but then fish and reptiles and mammals emerged; at one time, conscious creatures had no self-awareness but then the present self emerged in the higher primates. The whole issue is whether the present self acts under an illusion that has survival value as such, or whether it is truly free. Evolution has produced enough surprises to leave both possibilities open.

Second argument: Everything that occurs in consciousness is linked to a physiological state of affairs in the brain. The two interact and if causal discontinuity occurred on the level of consciousness there would be a corresponding causal discontinuity in brain physiology, which is absurd.

Answer: This is just dualism in a new garb. The old dualism had material body and immaterial mind as two unlike entities that could not interact. Since matter had to be a machine and since matter and mind were synchronized (when I will my arm to lift, it rises), mind had to be a machine as well. Events in the mind machine just happened to occur an instant before the corresponding events occurred in the matter machine. This was the famous two clocks theory. The new dualism concedes that mind and matter interact, but retains the notion of two clocks that must be synchronized. In fact, there is only one clock but part of it is not governed by clockwork. The brain influences consciousness and consciousness influences the brain, and the contents of consciousness do so regardless of whether the operative content is determined (a conditioned reflex) or undetermined (a free choice).

Third argument: Specific scientific results falsify free will. Grey Walter once lectured about an experiment he conducted in the early 1960s, although he has never published any account and this has led to speculation (Dennett, 2003, p. 240). Electrodes were inserted in the motor areas of the brains of epilepsy patients. He ran wires from the electrode leads to a slide carousel. Whenever a patient decided to move to the next slide, electrical activity in the brain beat them to it and changed slides. The patients were astonished. They felt that just as they were about to push the button, but had not yet quite decided to do so, their brains had made the decision for them.

Answer: The fact that the electric impulse from the brain changed the slide is sheer showmanship. It could just as easily have lit up a light bulb or simply have been detected without doing anything at all external to the brain. The significance of the fact that there is extra electrical activity in the brain just prior to the fruition of a decision is no more significant than if there were reduced electrical activity. All we know is that something distinctive happens in the brain just before a decision is consummated. It may well be that something distinctive occurs just before the decision-making process begins and just after the decision is made.

All the experiment shows is that the present-self state of consciousness is impossible without special brain states that underpin it. The electrical activity in question may well have shifted backward from its original position in the process. We know that when the eye blinks in response to a stimulus, it can be trained to blink at a percept that always precedes the stimulus – and which would not in itself cause a blink. It may be that the electrical activity in question has moved from being an accompaniment of the fruition of a decision backward to accompany the near fruition of a decision.

Here is another discovery from modern science: the decisions of identical twins raised apart (having only genes in common) tend to be more similar (say about whom they marry) than those of randomly selected people with no genes in common.

Answer: The Dickens/Flynn model shows that separated twins have not only genes in common but also, thanks to those identical genes, much more similar life histories than randomly selected individuals. Assume that when I was losing jobs as an academic in America, I had a separated identical twin who, thanks to the same genes for IQ and verbosity and thanks to similar post-graduate study, had become a lawyer defending radicals. He too might be targeted and boycotted and threatened with underemployment. He too might have considered leaving. But when the crunch came, he might decide not to leave, or to shift to northern Alberta as sufficiently remote or, sadly, to compromise his ideals and qualify as harmless. The fact that some people have genes and environments that are much more similar than those of randomly selected people certainly means that their decisions and behavior will be more alike. But it does not show that the present self is a null factor.

The case for free will unproven

First argument: I will paraphrase Jesuit psychologists who must square the science they teach with the moral praise and blame they allocate in the confessional. Once consciousness evolved, evolution would tend to produce a creature whose present self had free choice because of the obvious survival advantage. In situations where there was time for reflection, a creature that could choose from a huge range of responses to challenges from the environment would be more successful than one limited to a certain set of responses.

Answer: A deterministic system can also generate a huge range of responses. The best example is the immune system. It can

284

create an enormous number of antibodies that are unspecialized in the sense that they are not limited to fighting one kind of disease but are adaptable. They act as tiny "Darwin machines" (Wilson, 2002). When the body is attacked, those most suited to fighting the infection are selected out and, if one is fortunate, they prevail. Some of them become specialized in the form of an immunity to that particular kind of malady, but there are plenty more left unspecialized to fight the next unknown enemy. There is no reason to think that the possible responses of a determined mind are any less vast. Moreover, the Jesuit argument assumes that evolution is actually capable of producing free choice. The illusion of free choice probably has survival value or it would not have evolved. True free choice might be optimal. But perhaps the best matter can do is produce the illusion plus a huge range of determined responses.

Second argument: When commenting on Kant, Paton (1967) argues that a rational mind escapes causality. For example, when you use a syllogism to arrive at a decision, conscious reason is in control and you are not buffeted by factors external to consciousness. Telling the truth is a categorical imperative; X is the truth; therefore, I will say X – with the presumption that categorical imperatives (which provide the major premises) are also dictated by reason.

Answer: No doubt, a person who can reason has a sort of autonomy not enjoyed by a creature driven by instinct. But the process of reasoning does not in itself exhibit a present self that is capable of choosing to do this rather than that with both options open. A combination of genes and environment may produce a consciousness capable of reason and one so committed to reason that rejection of the irrational is automatic. Once adopted, the laws of reason dictate the choice. True freedom means that the present self commands in the sense that it decides to forgo the irrational, however tempting it may be, in favor of a commitment to reason; and that without that "effort of the will," the irrational could prevail. The possibility or impossibility of the present self in command in that sense is left open in Paton's scenario.

Third argument: If I could raise my right hand and then go back to that same moment and raise my left, the truth of free will would have been proved. We cannot do that, but we can come so very close, that is, raise the left hand after an infinitesimal amount of time has passed. Is it really plausible that something altered in the intervening 1/1,000th of a second that determined a different outcome? The determinist is driven to positing a mysterious factor X that just must have been added to the causal mix. What was it – the motion of Jupiter, some slight alteration in the blood supply to the prefrontal lobes?

Would we reject the outcome of an experiment in any other context on such grounds? After experimenting with mixing hydrogen and oxygen, we keep getting water, that is, we get the same outcome. Critics object that something may have happened between each experiment, that it was crucial in producing the results, and therefore we must not take the uniformity of the results seriously.

Who would take them seriously? Yet, when we repeat experiments that lead to differential outcomes (I can raise either my right or my left hand even though my brain physiology can hardly vary significantly during the interval), we are supposed to take factor X seriously. Why do we reject *differential* outcomes under the same experimental conditions in which we accept *same* outcomes, save that we have an irrational bias in favor of determinism? How could any science be done if the factor X objection is to be taken seriously?

Answer: Assuming that the mind is a determined system that produces set outcomes, there is no reason to think that it can dictate the pattern of a series of decisions any less than a free choice. It can dictate right, left, left, right at 10 pm; and right, right, left, left at just after 10. The alteration in brain physiology between the two times would hardly have to be great. The argument ridicules the possibility of a factor X – and then proposes one! The key thing that has changed in a fraction of a second is supposed to be an altered mental state (deciding to do A rather than B). Why should the credentials of this factor X be stamped as opposed to any other change that has taken place? Unless you are already predisposed in its favor.

This argument really adds nothing to the fact that the present self must act under the presumption of freedom. It begs the central question: is that presumption real or illusion? If all options are truly open, the assumption that an "altered free choice by the present self" is pivotal is just as problematic as the assumption that an altered causal mix is responsible.

Forever in limbo?

If no argument or evidence offered hitherto decides the status of free will, what might count as decisive evidence? How could science decide the question of whether its own sway is unlimited or circumscribed by the existence of personal selves acting as uncaused causes? I suspect that it could do this only if brain physiology became fully mature.

Someone sits in a room with all the readings imaginable from another person's brain. She notes the characteristic reading that signals the beginning of a decision-making process and follows the incoming data through to the reading that a decision has been made. Analysis of the data (which may take weeks) allows her to correctly describe the decision: he was pondering the borrowed blue tie and decided to return it after all; he decides to hold his tongue so that others would have a chance to speak at the Cambridge Philosophical Society meeting; etc.

It would be wrong to demand a 100 percent success rate. What would be interesting would be if most decisions could be predicted but that there seemed to be a boundary around a class of decisions difficult to breach: where the present self was really torn and had to make an effort of the will. If a "perfected" physiology found that it could post-predict most decisions outside that boundary and few within, free will would be more probable. If that boundary proved irrelevant to post-prediction and was consistently invaded, determinism would be the more probable.

This implies that only a perfected physiology can give either free will or determinism a rational warrant for belief. But there is a deeper problem here. The above scenario has our physiologist only receiving brain readings. We have assumed that the mind is more than the brain. It is posited to be a functional system with both brain and consciousness as components that influence one another. Therefore, in order to moderate a mind through the process of decision making, we would have to have consciousness readings as well as brain readings. The subject in question could hardly report to the physiologist as to what he or she was thinking. First, to do so up to and including the decision would give the game away. Moreover, can anyone accurately report all that is going on in his consciousness; and even if he could, this would be a strange addition to normal consciousness.

If knowing the present state of another's mind is impossible, and if that is a prerequisite for predicting apparently free choices, at least with the specificity necessary to falsify free will, we will never know the truth. We will know that either free will or determinism must be true but never have a rational guide as to which is true. Even if this is too pessimistic, we will be at a loss for the foreseeable future.

The necessity to choose

How are we to find our way about in this strange world in which what we need to know to live our lives is unknown? It may be asked whether we really need to know. I will argue that we do because we must all decide whether or not to play the blaming game. Let me describe our predicament.

Imagine three identical doors. Behind one is a universe where certain free decisions have been made (to pick up hitchhikers) so it is in state A; behind the next is a universe in which other free decisions have been made (too dangerous to pick up hitchhikers) so it is in state B; behind the third is a universe in which no decision is free (in the sense of creating causal discontinuity) and it is in state

288

X, that is, it is in whatever state causality has dictated. That could be A or B but, of course, it cannot be both. We have gone through one of those doors but see nothing to tell us which universe we live in, at least for the present. Therefore, on one level, we should suspend judgment as to whether we are in a free or determined universe.

But on another level we cannot: when we interact with other people, we must decide whether or not to play the blaming game. We must decide between two ways of judging people. Whether to approve or commend them only as causally responsible for good or bad conduct. "You have done something wicked and it was you that did it and not someone else" (other clocks chimed on time). Or whether to praise and blame them for the outcome of their free choices as well. "You know very well you could have chosen differently."

We must decide whether the moral indignation we feel when someone deceives us about the time is any more appropriate than when a clock deceives us about the time. And the blaming game makes sense only if our universe includes free choices. In sum, we know that the universe is indeed free or indeed determined; we have no notion of which; and yet, we must still choose despite the absence of rational guidance. We simply must *decide* either to play the blaming game or not.

As far as I can see, this choice is unique. It is the sole existentialist dilemma: we must choose "policies" based on one or the other of two pictures of reality without any rational guidance as to which pertains. I guess if you could never make up your mind about whether God or gods exist, you might be in an even worse position. Are there none such, a million such? Are they ill disposed or benevolent? Can they harm me or not? But most of us do make a decision based on something we consider a proper guide to the intellect, such as proofs of the existence of god(s) or faith or the mystical experience. I believe the proofs are invalid and that I can give reasons for denying either faith or the mystical experience epistemological status. Therefore, I use ordinary experience to vouch for what does or does not exist. There may be some true agnostics in the world but they are few.

However, if I am correct, every one of us faces this kind of choice: we have no choice but to posit either free will or determinism and must do so without any proper guide to the intellect.

Note that what evolution grants survival value is no guide. If it were shown that believing in God had survival value, I could not really believe on those grounds. If it were shown that moral indignation had survival value in the sense that its display convinced potential aggressors that I would take a terrible revenge, I could not really believe in free will on those grounds. The issue at hand is what judgments I pass in my mind that go unarticulated: do I really believe in God or not; do I really believe there is a case for either free will or determinism? If I do not, what is serviceable cannot make me think otherwise. That does not mean I cannot display moral indignation as theater to impress aggressors. Although I suspect it would be better to fashion a substitute for such displays, namely, compile a history of terrible retaliation against aggressors that might give any new enemy pause.

Moral reasoning into the breach

I must decide on a policy, at least an interim policy to be pursued until physiology decides the truth of free will on its merits. Note that I am not saying that this is a free choice. To do that I would have to know that determinism is false and I do not know that. It should be described as choice that is both open and necessary. It is necessary in the sense that I must either treat people as blameworthy or not – there is no third alternative. It is open in the sense that if it is made, it must be made in ignorance of the rational considerations relevant to the issue.

But this does not mean that the decision is subject to no regulation. Since it has consequences for myself, others, and society, it is a moral decision. I believe it would be dehumanizing to treat my intimates as actors beyond moral praise or blame. If my wife did something thoughtless and hurtful to me, without mitigating circumstances, I would judge her to have freely chosen to do something she could have refrained from doing and react accordingly. For all I know, that might be true. This policy does not of course rule out license for human frailty. We all choose wrongly sometimes. It would allow her to apologize in the sense of saying "I know I should not have done that and am sorry I did. I won't behave that way again."

My policy, however, is not the only option. It is just as rational to regard your intimates as determined and you may find that amenable. Both of you would know that a display of moral indignation should be interpreted as a strong intolerance of the substance of your wife's behavior. Both of you would know that her apology should be interpreted as a plea that the behavior in question is atypical of her character and is unlikely to occur again.

I frankly feel that to drain the dimension of praise for behaving well and blame for behaving badly from personal relationships would be a charade on my part: I could tell myself I was doing it, but only because I did not really feel that I was doing it. But I am not so arrogant as to foist my psychology on others and assume that those who adopt a different policy are acting in "bad faith." Human psychology is diverse and everyone has the right to choose in the absence of a rational limit on the choice.

Consistency and roles

When we choose to play the blaming game, morality imposes its own logic, namely, that we must apply moral rules with logical consistency. My wife has every right to demand that if I play the blaming game with her, I do not exempt myself and plead that all my choices were dictated by factors outside the control of my present self. But logical consistency does not forbid a different policy where the morally relevant circumstances differ. Our penal system in certain areas is evolving toward the elimination of fault in the moral sense. I refer to divorce where establishing whether husband or wife was at fault simply embitters proceedings and is set aside in favor of an equitable division of property and the welfare of children. From a humane point of view, we may wish to further this trend and seek only protection of the public and reformation of the criminal, with punishment for punishment's sake (punishment that matches the wickedness of the choice) set aside. For all we know, those who transgress really may be determined and moral blame is inappropriate.

On the other hand, we must be mindful of the feelings of others. When the evil consequences of behavior are very great or the personal damage horrific, it may be too much to ask the injured party to accept a legal system drained of righting the moral balance sheet. Should Jews treat Hitler as determined? Should I treat someone who raped and killed my daughter as determined? And it could be correct that the horrific acts in question were the products of free choice. The analysis developed herein allows maximum flexibility: since the truth of free will is unknown, we are free to include whatever mix in our legal code has the most humane consequences. Once again, we cannot change the mix from day to day in that people have a right to anticipate what penalties the law will apply.

Even though I play the blaming game with my intimates, I may not play it in other social roles. I may be a psychiatrist of the school that believes that personalization of the tie between alienist and patient is counterproductive. And therefore treat my patients as determined creatures to whom whatever I say should be weighed in terms of their chances of recovery. If I have a son who is showing psychopathic tendencies, I may decide that it is better to adopt the policy of the alienist rather than the one I apply to most of my personal relationships. When I play the role of social scientist, I will certainly assume that determinism is true. After all, it might really be true. Any other assumption would set limits on scientific explanation. Let reality set those limits; it is not the job of the scientist to anticipate them. As for judges, their role depends on whether the legal system deems balance sheet considerations relevant to sentencing in the case at hand.

Believers and agnostics

What of those who believe they know the truth about free will or determinism? I will describe their "natural" position and note the extent they can deviate from it on moral grounds.

The natural position of the believer in free will is that there is (or at least was before they totally debased their character) a sphere of free choice for all actors. And that subject to the usual qualifications (mental retardation, provocation, etc.) moral praise/blame is in order in all spheres. Therefore, with regard to the penal code, there will be an internal difference compared to an agnostic like myself: they will have to entertain a private moral blame of a criminal's choices that I can forgo. However, if they hold humane moral principles, they may make the same policy distinctions that I do. For example, they may say that maximizing benevolent consequences requires eliminating punishment for punishment's sake from the judicial system. The mere fact that it would be just to punish wrongdoers for their sins does not mean that strict justice has to be applied when it would have counterproductive consequences.

Someone who really believes in determinism (and is not seduced by compatibilism) is in the natural position of never entertaining a private judgment of moral praise or blame. Therefore, they would find it difficult to imitate my policy mix. If they want to express moral indignation in personal interactions, they can do so only as a form of theater. And those who are the audience for that theater would always be in a position to say: "you do not really mean it." As for the legal code, they can introduce an element of punishment for punishment's sake but they will have to justify it as a mere instrument to either the goal of reformation or the goal of protection of public order. They can say that, without this, although grievously injured parties have no logical basis to demand their pound of flesh they cannot be expected to feel that way; and might take the law into their own hands if sentences did not give them satisfaction.

The positions of the true believers are different from the position of the agnostics. We can decide to play the blaming game or not subject only to the strictures of moral reasoning. Our private judgments are, of course, always qualified by our ignorance of whether they are appropriate. On the other hand, we do not know they are inappropriate. Like all agnostics, we must put up with uncertainty and can only solace ourselves with the knowledge that we have no choice as to whether to play the blaming game or not. After all, not to play it because we are uncertain is to operationalize a determinism that may be false.

We can take satisfaction in knowing that what we do is in accord with our moral principles. But it is infuriating never to know the truth. Living the examined life is not always a piece of cake.

The believers are not in limbo. However, they do not escape scot-free. A believer in determinism may find it psychologically enervating to dismiss all sense of moral indignation as based on an illusion. Believers in free will may find punishment for punishment's sake repugnant; and while they can refrain from exercising it themselves, and even eliminate it from the legal code, they may find their children practicing it when disciplining their grandchildren. They can, of course, appeal to their offspring on moral grounds but they cannot fault their logic.

The humane and the non-humane

Not everyone is humane. Nietzsche anticipated me in concluding that the truth of free will was unknown. As for policy, he believed that any self-respecting superman would opt for having free choice in that it makes one feel Godlike. Most herd men would be attracted to determinism because it excuses their folly and mediocrity. Once the options of free will and determinism are open, various moralities are free to adopt or reject the blaming game according to their own moral rules. What an untidy conclusion! But you (I hope) and I are dedicated to humane-egalitarian ideals. Praise yourself when you live up to them and blame yourself when you do not. That is, I suspect, the option that any idealist will want to take.

My position may seem to indicate a certain lack of humanity on my own part. In fact, I believe I understand the force that drives compatibilism. There you are, struggling every day to do what is right, and winning at great cost. And then someone denies that you deserve moral praise simply because of some future discoveries about brain physiology. I am not unsympathetic. As long as we each focus on our own mental life, the denial seems fantastic. But focus on judging another, knowing full well that factors of which he is unaware are really in control. We would admire the sort of person he is. But we could not praise him for being that person.

Epilogue

So why read Greek books? . . . Practically no one even tries to read them as they were once read – for the sake of finding out whether they are true.

(Bloom, 1987)

They shall beat their swords into plowshares and their spears into pruning-hooks.

(Isaiah 2.4)

If the body of a book does not appeal, no last words will save the day, so I will be brief. There is fertile ground for a revival of American idealism. The tension between the market and the good life and what ought to be done persists; indeed, it is more powerful than ever, given current corporate power and behavior. The issues are there: the transfer of resources from war to peace, the creation of a welfare state that will foster civic virtue, the creation of a commonwealth that will give everyone including black Americans access to what makes America a wonderful place to live, and the redemption of America's good name abroad. Despite all of the angst, the philosophical foundations of the Jeffersonian ideal are solid.

Leaders may be lacking but as Debs said, "I would not lead you into the promised land if I could, because if I could lead you in, someone else could lead you out" (Ginger, 1962, p. 260). It is best that the people lead and that leaders follow, and it is the people I hope to convince. Before a final plea on behalf of my version of humane-egalitarian ideals, I want to issue another plea: read the best of those who disagree with me. Start with Charles Murray and Thomas Sowell.

Living a good life is essentially the same task today as it was a century ago, or even a millennium or two ago. Our time may be more complex and confused, but the problems of confronting group differences, treating others justly, what makes human life worthwhile, whether our society promotes excellence, how to tame violence between nations, what turns ordinary people into "terrorists," whether our ideals are worthy of zealous pursuit, and whether people are free or simply subject to the causality of the natural world are the same questions that confronted the Greeks. We are much more powerful than they and can do far more harm; and we are making history spin so fast we have less time to learn how to think.

The logic of the liberal/left program has been stated. It runs from American foreign policy to American military policy to a society that offers all its citizens participation in the good life.

(1) Foreign policy: If acting like a responsible world sovereign is too ambitious, we can at least aim at something less muddled and absurd than the status quo. Something like the occasional, almost universally supported, humanitarian intervention plus obeying the admonition "do no harm." Let Latin America and the Middle East alone to deal with their problems without providing "roadmaps" and advice on "nation building" and killing lots of people through either economic sanctions or arms. Assume China is not out to conquer the world until there is clear proof to the contrary. Do not urge Japan (or anyone else) to arm. Stop selling weapons on the international market purely for profit.

(2) Military policy: Stop the charade of building "early warning systems" unless they are used as a symbol of US/Russian amity. Stop putting bases everywhere we can simply because it makes us feel powerful and safe. Stop talking about a "war on terror" in favor of "keeping America free from intimidation." Rationalize our efforts to deal with clandestine foes (rely mainly on infiltration) and do less to make other people hate us. Shift $200 billion from the

military budget to build a better society. Above all, recognize that any "liberal" who is unwilling to take on this fight is not serious.

(3) Domestic policy: That $200 billion should be used to tame and supplement the market. The market forces Americans to be less just to blacks than they would like and the state of black America is too dismal to be tolerated. If affirmative action is unwelcome, we have the resources needed to help all of those in distress. A thousand things can be done to allow people to develop excellences that the market does not reward. We can alleviate market tyranny in the form of coerced and wasteful competition (for the right neighborhood) by steps toward greater equality. A robust welfare state will counteract the market's tendency to erode civic virtue by maximizing personal security. We can cushion change for those who work in sociopathic corporations as those corporations are brought under control.

I have said little about preserving the environment because others can write with greater authority. Since the relevant steps will entail less affluence, Social Democracy is all the more necessary. The choice will be between a just society where hardships are shared and a coercive society where the powerful reserve them for the weak.

As for philosophy, the logic runs from clarifying humane-egalitarian ideals to providing them with a firm foundation to endowing ourselves with moral dignity.

(1) Clarification: Humane-egalitarian ideals go beyond justice as fairness. Although even that, taken in isolation, entails a robust welfare state and a departure from any notion that equal opportunity can be sustained by an open competition for wealth. A humane-egalitarian society is composed of people divided among a multitude of pursuits, each with its own excellence, and if market competition rewards some but not others, transfer payments will allow those others to be pursued. Such a society cannot evolve into a bastard "meritocracy." That requires a universal commitment to whatever narrow range of excellences the market rewards and will arise only among Carthaginians and not Athenians. Even Carthaginians would have to have a peculiar psychology: although seeking personal advan-

tage above all else they would have to divert huge resources to ensure fairness.

(2) Justification: There is no knowledge of the good and that includes attempts to base humane-egalitarian ideals on what we "know" of nature. Cultural relativism is logically incoherent and Rawls's attempt at justification, if that is what it was, is an evasion. The ancients can teach us much about the content of the good life but provide no justification. We should be satisfied with four consolations: lack of objectivity in ethics does not entail nihilism; objectivity would have a darker side; our ideals define who we are; and while that is also true of our opponents' ideals, we at least need not compromise logic or the truths of science. If we feel threatened by Nietzsche, we should note that he cannot make the same claim.

(3) Moral dignity: We have a license to endow ourselves with the free will that makes sense of moral praise and blame. I at least will blame my present self when I fall short of good behavior. However, we must be agnostic about whether we are really free. Even if we were not, our characters and our actions could still be assessed in the light of our ideals. In any event, struggling to do the right thing is our lot, and if we succeed the world will be better for it whether or not we deserve praise rather than mere commendation.

Since the inception of our nation, we have had a noble public philosophy, one always pursued if never fully actualized. If we lack intensity on behalf of our ideals, it is not because reason has banished faith. It is because indifference has cheated us of the use of our reason.

Appendix: tables with comments

Table 1 comment: The purpose is to show how few black males promising as spouses are available for every hundred black females, and to contrast this with other races.

Table 1 Whites, blacks, and Hispanics (ages 25–40): for each hundred women, the numbers of same-race men by category ("Other race husband" refers to women who have married out of their race)

Other race wife[a]	Prison & jail	Inadequate work[b]	Adequate work[c]	Military	Other race husband	Promising spouses
Non-Hispanic whites						
3.43	1.52	15.57	80.08	1.86	4.12	**86.06**
Non-Hispanic blacks						
5.12	9.58	24.00	53.04	2.14	2.19	**57.37**
Hispanics						
8.97	3.15	18.23	88.71	0.89	9.30	98.90
						95.81[d]

Notes:
[a] Men who have a wife of another race have been removed from all other categories to avoid overlap.
[b] Inadequate work means worked twenty-six weeks or less during the previous year.
[c] Adequate work means worked more than twenty-six weeks in the previous year.
[d] The second value (for the number of "promising spouses" for every hundred Hispanic women) has been adjusted for: foreign-born women with husbands abroad (as not seeking husbands); and foreign-born men with wives abroad (as unavailable for marriage). The former was subtracted from the denominator, the latter from the numerator.

Sources: Data in CPS, 2005; Harrison and Beck, 2005; Segal and Segal, 2004; Wikipedia, 2006.

Table 2 comment: Here we see the large number of black males we know exist but cannot be located by the census, at least from age 15 onwards.

Table 2 Male/female ratios: those estimated by birth/death certificates compared to those found in the census

Age	Black			White		
	Estimated	Census	E–C	Estimated	Census	E–C
0	104.15	104.15	—	105.02	105.02	—
1	103.82	103.80	—	104.88	104.99	−0.11
5	103.76	103.15	0.61	104.85	105.17	−0.32
15	103.66	101.63	2.03	104.80	104.87	−0.07
25	102.22	96.25	5.97	103.32	103.50	−0.18
35	98.83	90.26	8.57	102.20	101.41	0.79
45	97.73	87.87	9.86	100.85	100.04	0.81
55	95.21	82.98	12.23	96.50	96.54	−0.04
65	91.90	75.60	16.30	89.88	90.00	−0.12

Sources: Kochanek and Smith, 2004; US Health Statistics, 2006b.

Table 3 comment: By age 45, black women have lost an extra 9 percent of males from the pool of spouses or potential spouses because of differential death rates.

Table 3 Survival rates for black and white males

Age	Percentage of WM alive	Percentage of BM alive	Difference
25	96.29	95.51	0.78
35	93.77	87.32	6.45
45	90.07	81.06	9.01

Source: Arias, 2004.

Table 4 comment: This one, I think, is self-explanatory.

Table 4 Growing up as a black male in America: extra risk of death (by age 45) compared to percentages of deaths from combat in World War II

Embarked to a combat zone Unit	Number	Deaths	Percentage
Black males (total cohort)	315,241	28,403	9.01
Infantry	1,779,658	142,962	8.03
Air Corps	952,974	51,021	5.35
Field Artillery	437,066	9,585	2.19
Coast Artillery	322,478	4,311	1.34
Engineers	655,502	7,691	1.17
Armor	191,602	1,581	0.83
Other	2,563,383	17,723	0.69
All branches	6,902,663	234,874	3.40
The Western Front: original members of units who fought from the time their unit was committed to battle until the end[a]			
Troops with 66 tanks	14,400	1,665	11.56
Black males (no tanks)	—	—	9.01
Troops with 281 tanks	11,500	733	6.37

[a] Fought to the end means they were still there when combat ended or had died (from battle or other causes) or had been invalided out.

Sources: Rohlfs, 2005, p. 59; US Army AG, 1953, p. 48; US Army ASF, 1954, p. 12.

Table 5 comment: Here we estimate the total impact of "absent" men on the black population. At age 45, over 20 percent more black men are absent than white.

Table 5 Cohorts at age 45: black and white male percentages compared

	Dead	Missing	In prison	Total
Black	18.94	7.99	5.17	32.10
White	9.93	0.73	0.86	11.52
Difference	9.01	7.26	4.31	20.58

Note: The percentages of men missing and in prison have been adjusted to be percentages of the cohort rather than percentages of those still alive. *Sources:* Deaths, Table 3; missing, Table 2; in prison, Harrison and Karberg, 2003; cohort size, US Health Statistics, 2006a.

Table 6 comment: Note that the market concept of "good deals" predicts (P) the actual (A) percentage of solo-parents almost perfectly for both blacks and whites.

Table 6 Effects of marriage markets on percentage of solo-parents and children living with solo-parents

	Promising wives decimal	Number promising husbands	Product = no. of good deals	Percent solo-parents: P/A[a]	Percent children with solo-parent[b]
White	.89	86	76.5	23.5/22	23
Black	.74	57	42.2	57.8/59	63
Hispanic	.66	96	63.4	36.6/30	32

[a] P = Predicted percentage of solo-parents as calculated by subtracting the number of good marriage deals from 100. A = Actual percentage of solo-parents. The latter is calculated by dividing one-parent-family households (with children) by the total number of family households with children.
[b] The percentage of children living with a solo-parent excludes all children with two parents present, whether these are the natural parents (either married or cohabiting), a parent and a step-parent, or two adoptive parents. It includes those living with grandparents, which in a few cases may mean two grandparents. The data have been updated from 2001 to match the solo-parent data of 2003.

Source: US Census, 2001; 2004.

Table 7 comment: In Table 6, the concept of "good deals" interrelated the two factors of unpromising wives (children before age 20) and unpromising husbands. Here we isolate the latter and show that black men marrying out and having a criminal record are the major causes of the shortfall of promising husbands.

Table 7 Ultimate causes of the shortfall of promising male spouses

Race	Net effect of intermarriage	Prison inmate at some time	Total effects of prison + intermarriage	Shortfall of promising male spouses	Shortfall remaining
White	+0.69	−6	−5.31	14	8.69
Black	−2.93	−33	−35.93	43	7.07
Hisp	+0.33	−17	−16.67	5	—

Sources: "Net effect of intermarriage" and "Shortfall of promising male spouses" from Table 1; "Prison inmate at some time", Bonczar, 2003.

Table 8 comment: The first three rows of Table 8 refer to men living in households because this is a group for whom there exist comparable data. The last two rows include all men, which is important for appreciating the true state of the black marriage market. Black males have by far the largest prison population so counting that population makes a considerable difference.

Since the number of black males in prison who are married out is far smaller than the rate for other blacks, comparisons across the rows involving that estimate will be roughly correct. It is immediately evident that black women are vindicated in their impression that the black men marrying out are desirable spouses. Among black men who are married out (about 55 percent of them are married to white women), 83.31 percent were in steady work. This percentage is an almost perfect match for the black men who marry black women, and far above black men in general of whom only 63 percent are in steady work.

Table 8 Percentage of men in steady work: comparisons between married men, unmarried men, and men in general (for whites, blacks, and Hispanics)

	Whites	Blacks	Hispanics
Males married out of race (households)	90.32	83.31	90.56
Males married within race (households)	90.60	83.13	89.43
All males (households)	83.95	69.66	83.52
All males (households + M&P)[a]	82.96	63.09	81.28
Males unmarried (households + M&P)[a]	74.06	56.31	75.39

[a] Here military personnel have been included (as employed) and prison inmates included (as not employed) for reasons set out in the text.
Source: Data in CPS, 2005.

Table 9 comment: Black men are castigated as reluctant to commit. This table shows that the ratio of black to white in this regard is predictable: if one believes that men should not marry without steady work and a decent income; and takes into account the stress on marriage of owning few assets.

Table 9 Income, steady work, and family assets as predictors of differential marriage status of black and white males

	Married at present (2005)	Median income (2003)	Worked over 26 weeks (2005)	Median family net worth (2002)
Black	35.39%	$21,935	63.09	$5,988
White	57.56%	$32,331	82.96	$88,651
Ratio	0.615	0.678	0.760	0.068

Sources: Married, data in CPS, 2005; income, US Census, 2005; in work, Table 8; net worth, Kochhar, 2004.

Table 10 comment: Here we see that both race and gender differences about sex and marriage are a function of whether the marriage market favors males or females.

Table 10 Attitudes toward sex and marriage: race and gender comparisons in terms of percentages giving affirmative answers

	Love and sexual intercourse should be related	I think about marriage frequently	I would like to marry some day
1. Black females	76.3	29.5	82.17
2. Black males	29.2	3.3	79.18
3. F–M difference	**47.1**	**26.2**	**2.99**
4. White females	79.1	39.7	88.90
5. White males	61.7	20.2	87.77
6. F–M difference	**17.4**	**19.5**	**1.03**
7. Hispanic females	—	—	84.69
8. Hispanic males	—	—	93.28
9. F–M difference	**—**	**—**	**−8.59**
10. White females	79.1	39.7	88.90
11. Black females	76.3	29.5	82.17
12. W–B difference	**2.8**	**10.2**	**6.73**
13. White males	61.7	20.2	87.77
14. Black males	29.2	3.3	79.18
15. W–B difference	**32.5**	**16.9**	**8.59**
16. Hispanic males	—	—	93.28
17. Black males	—	—	79.18
18. H–B difference	**—**	**—**	**14.10**

Sources: Lynn, 2002; South, 1993.

Table 11 comment: Tracing white IQ gains from the WISC to the WISC-IV requires some adjustments. This is because the WISC standardization sample contained whites only and after that, beginning with the WISC-R, the standardization samples contained all races.

Therefore, I have converted WISC-R IQs into the "scoring against whites" convention by using the mean IQ and SD of the white members of its sample (Flynn, 1984). As for gains thereafter, since all succeeding standardization samples contained all races, we are measuring all races gains over time rather then white gains.

However, this is significant only if the former and the latter are much different. That is unlikely because whites numerically dominate the standardization samples. Moreover, the only group of any size that shows a faster rate of gain than whites are blacks. As we shall see, they have gained an extra 4.5 IQ points (measured at age 12) over a period of about 30 years. But since they are only 15 percent of the standardization samples, they would inflate the white rate of gain by only 0.0225 points per year. Over 30 years, this would amount to less than seven-tenths of an IQ point.

Table 11 White gains on WISC subtests and full-scale IQ: from 1947–48 to 2002

Subtests	Whites (1947–48) WISC	WISC to WISC-R (1972)	WISC-R to WISC-III (1989)	WISC-III to WISC-IV (2002)	Whites (2002) WISC
I	10	0.43	−0.3	0.3	10.43
A	10	0.36	0.3	−0.2	10.46
V	10	0.38	0.4	0.1	10.88
Cm	10	1.20	0.6	0.4	12.20
PC	10	0.74	0.9	0.7	12.34
BD	10	1.28	0.9	1.0	13.18
OA	10	1.34	1.2	[0.93]	13.47
Cd	10	2.20	0.7	0.7	13.60
PA	10	0.93	1.9	[1.47]	14.30
S	10	2.77	1.3	0.7	14.77
Total SS	100	11.63	7.9	6.1	125.63
Total IQ	100	+7.63 points	+5.37 points	+4.63 points	117.63

Notes:

(1) Subtests: Information, Arithmetic, Vocabulary, Comprehension, Picture Completion, Block Design, Object Assembly, Coding, Picture Arrangement, Similarities.

(2) Two values in col. 5 are in brackets. Some of the original subtests of the WISC were dropped in 2002 and gains on Object Assembly and Picture Arrangement had to be estimated. I assumed that their gains would have

made up the same proportion of the total gain in the 1989 to 2002 period as they did in the 1972 to 1989 period.

(3) "Total SS" refers to the standard scores used for each subtest. They have a mean of 10 and an SD of 3. "Total IQ" refers to the full-scale IQ score (with an SD of 15) that the SS total translates into when you use the WISC conversion table.

(4) The estimates of IQ gains in this table are a bit higher than those I have published in the past. My usual practice has been to use the conversion tables (of standard scores to IQ scores) of each test in turn as they appeared. But here, the purpose is to measure the total gain against the WISC sample, and therefore its conversion table has been used throughout (Wechsler, 1949, p. 26). The latter increases the estimates of IQ gains because the new standard score total rises higher and higher above the WISC mean – and the IQ-point bonus for each standard score point increases the higher you go.

Sources: Flynn, 2000b, table 1; The Psychological Corporation, 2003, table 5.8; Wechsler, 1992, table 6.8. Adapted from Table 1 of Flynn and Weiss, 2007.

Table 12 comment: As described in the text, given a comparison between the blacks and whites of 2002, you can now score the blacks of 2002 versus the whites of 1947–48.

Table 12 Blacks (2002) have mean IQ of 104.31 scored versus WISC whites (1947–48)

	Whites (1947–48) WISC	Whites[a] (2002) WISC	Black deficit[b] on WISC-IV	Blacks[c] (2002) WISC	B/W gap
I	10	10.43	10.70−8.72 = 1.98	10.43−1.98 = **8.45**	−1.55
V	10	10.88	10.71−8.59 = 2.12	10.88−2.12 = **8.76**	−1.24
A	10	10.46	10.49−8.87 = 1.62	10.46−1.62 = **8.84**	−1.16
PC	10	12.34	10.60−8.08 = 2.52	12.34−2.52 = **9.82**	−0.18
Cm	10	12.20	10.51−8.89 = 1.62	12.20−1.62 = **10.58**	+0.58
BD	10	13.18	10.55−7.98 = 2.57	13.18−2.57 = **10.61**	+0.61
OA	10	[13.47]	[1.96]	13.47−1.96 = [**11.51**]	+1.51
PA	10	[14.30]	[1.96]	14.30−1.96 = [**12.34**]	+2.34
S	10	14.77	10.64−8.45 = 2.19	14.77−2.19 = **12.58**	+2.58
Cd	10	13.60	10.09−9.31 = 0.78	13.60−0.78 = **12.82**	+2.82
Total	100	125.63	19.32	**106.31**	
FS-IQ	100	118.63	——	**104.31**	
V-IQ	100	110.74	——	**99.21**	
P-IQ	100	123.78	——		**110.10**

These scores are not directly comparable to the scores in which blacks have been scored against WISC-IV all races norms. For example, comparing 8.84 on Arithmetic with 8.87 might lead to the misapprehension that blacks lost ground between 1947–48 and 2002. In fact, they probably gained ground. Assuming that blacks were one SD below whites on Arithmetic in 1947–48, they were only 0.54 SDs below in 2002 (1.62 divided by 3.00 = 0.54).

Note: As noted in Table 11, the bracketed values for Object Assembly and Picture Arrangement are estimates. I assumed that the black versus white deficit on them was the average of the other Performance subtests.

Sources: Table 11; data on WISC-IV black and white subtest scores courtesy of The Psychological Corporation, copyright 2003, all rights reserved.

Table 13 comment: The text notes that even if the method of weighting to allow for SES and solo-parenthood differences between the races were appropriate, the weighting would be crude. However, on the face of the results, blacks in 2002 had an environment inferior to that whites enjoyed in 1947–48.

Table 13 Blacks (2002) scored versus WISC whites (1947–48): adjustments for inequalities in SES and solo-parent homes raise black IQ advantage to 7.51 points

Black IQ 2002:	104.31 (Table 12) + 4.97 (adjust solo-parents) = 109.28 adj	
White IQ 1947–48:	100.00 (Table 12) + 1.77 (adjust inferior SES) = 101.77 adj	
Difference:	+4.31	+7.51

Adjustment for SES of home occupational categories:

	1947–48	2002
(1)	Professional	Professional
(2)	Managers, officials, proprietors	Managers, executive, administrative

(3) Clerical, sales, kindred   Clerical, sales, technical
(4) Service, craft, foreman, kindred Service, craft, precision production, repair
(5) Operators, laborers, farmers   Operators, fabricators, laborers, farmers

Home	White/WISC Percentage	White/WISC Mean IQ		Black/WISC-IV Percentage		
(1)	8.33	109.2	(×)	11.98	(=)	1,308.22
(2)	12.08	105.1	(×)	9.88	(=)	1,038.39
(3)	13.23	104.1	(×)	29.32	(=)	3,052.21
(4)	24.38	99.2	(×)	29.24	(=)	2,910.53
(5)	41.98	95.9	(×)	19.48	(=)	1,868.13
Totals	100.00			100.00		10,177.48

So: 10,177.48 divided by 100 gives a white rise of 1.77 IQ points.

Adjustment for marital status of home:

Home	White/WISC-IV			Black/WISC-IV		
	N	%	IQ	N	%	IQ
Two-parent	342	78	102.32	36	40	93.39
One-parent	97	22	96.10	53	60	83.46
Difference			6.22			9.93

Correlations one parent and IQ: 0.241 (white); 0.411 (black)

Calculations:

(1) White children in one-parent homes 1947–48 are 10%

(2) So Black/WISC-IV must be weighted to reduce the percentage to 10%

(3) 90% × 93.39 = 8,405.1   9,239.7 divided by 100   = 92.40
    10% × 83.46 =   834.6   Mean of unweighted pop.   = 87.43
                  9,239.7   Difference (black handicap) = 4.97

Sources: Flynn, 2000c, p. 52; Rainwater and Yancey, 1967, pp. 108 and 111; Seashore, Wesman, and Doppelt, 1950, pp. 101 and 109; US Census, 2001, pp. 380–383; WISC-IV data from The Psychological Corporation, copyright 2003, all rights reserved.

Tables 14 and 15 comment: Together these tables demonstrate both the persistence of the "g pattern," that is, the persistence of the fact that the magnitude of the black–white score gap on the various WISC subtests correlates positively with the g loading of the subtests. But they also show that this does not really much increase the overall cognitive gap between blacks and whites.

Table 14 Correlations between WISC-R g loadings and racial score differences: the persistence of the g pattern over time

Data	WISC-R g loadings	WISC-R white (1972) minus black (1972)	WISC-IV white (2002) minus black (2002)	white (1947–48) minus black (2002)
I	.727	+2.32	+1.98	−1.55
V	.777	+2.56	+2.12	−1.24
A	.650	+1.74	+1.62	−1.16
PC	.581	+2.29	+2.52	−0.18
Cm	.684	+2.61	+1.62	+0.58
BD	.705	+2.69	+2.57	+0.61
OA	.597	+2.47	+1.96	+1.51
PA	.574	+2.27	+1.96	+2.34
S	.744	+2.39	+2.19	+2.58
Cd	.436	+1.35	+0.78	+2.82

Correlations with WISC-R g loadings:

	W–B gap WISC-R	W–B gap WISC-IV	W (1947–48) – B (2002) gap
Pearson	0.708	0.589	0.537
Spearman	0.636	0.488	0.491

Note: The g loading of each subtest has been corrected for attenuation by dividing by the square root of the subtest's reliability. Correlations are based on the standard score gap between white and black on the various subtests. I have not expressed this in standard deviation units because this is impossible for white (1947–48) and black (2002); and the whole point is to determine how robust the correlations are from their inception through that data set. However, the sizes of my correlations on the WISC-R are very close to Jensen's values using standard deviation units.

Sources: WISC-R subtest scores and g loadings from Jensen and Reynolds, 1982, pp. 425 and 431; WISC-R reliabilities from Rushton, 1995, p. 187; WISC-IV data courtesy of The Psychological Corporation, copyright 2003, all rights reserved.

Table 15 Blacks (2002) have a mean GQ of 103.53 scored versus
WISC whites (1947–48)

	Black (2002) minus white (1947–48)	(×) g loading	Preliminary (=) g values	Final (÷ .648) g values
I	−1.55	.727	−1.12685	−1.74
V	−1.24	.777	−0.96348	−1.49
A	−1.16	.650	−0.75400	−1.16
PC	−0.18	.581	−0.10458	−0.16
Cm	+0.58	.684	+0.39672	+0.61
BD	+0.61	.705	+0.43005	+0.66
OA	+1.51	.597	+0.90147	+1.39
PA	+2.34	.574	+1.34316	+2.07
S	+2.58	.744	+1.91952	+2.96
Cd	+2.82	.436	+1.22952	+1.90
Total (+100):	106.31	Ave: .648	Total (+100):	105.04
IQ:	104.42		GQ:	103.53

Sources: Black minus white score differences from Table 12; g loadings
Table 14.

Table 16 comment: Then we find that in Germany, an environment without a black subculture eliminated *both* the IQ gap and the GQ gaps between blacks and whites.

Table 16 German occupation children take the HAWIK: black and white are (almost) equal for IQ and GQ; and the g pattern disappears.

	Whites (−)	Blacks (=)	Difference	HAWIK	g values	
	(n = 69)	(n = 170)		g loading	W	B
A	8.865	8.625	+0.240	0.657	7.913	7.699
S	10.355	10.285	+0.070	0.691	9.722	9.656
BD	9.660	9.375	+0.285	0.716	9.398	9.120
PA	9.890	9.525	+0.365	0.730	9.809	9.447
PC	9.570	9.595	−0.025	0.753	9.791	9.817
V	10.075	9.930	+0.145	0.815	11.156	10.996
Cm	9.950	10.215	−0.265	0.817	11.045	11.339
OA	10.170	9.580	+0.590	0.829	11.455	10.791
I	9.040	9.105	−0.065	0.908	11.153	11.233
Cd	8.500	8.965	−0.465	[0.442]	5.105	5.384
Total:	96.075	95.200	Ave: 0.736	Total: 96.547		95.482
IQ:	97.00	96.50		GQ: 97.47		96.86

Correlations between score differences and HAWIK g:
Pearson without Coding: −0.245
Pearson with Coding: +0.418
Spearman without Coding: −0.267
Spearman with Coding: +0.079

Correlations between score differences and WISC-R g:
Pearson without Coding: −0.386
Pearson with Coding: +0.250
Spearman without Coding: −0.367
Spearman with Coding: +0.006

Note: From the intercorrelations, we can derive the g loading of each subtest of the German WISC (derivations courtesy of Bob Knight, Department of Psychology, University of Otago). Then, as Jensen (1980, pp. 217–218) points out, these must be corrected for attenuation by dividing them by the square root of the reliabilities. Strictly speaking, the corrected g loading for Coding is invalid because there are no reliabilities for the age groups for whom intercorrelations are provided (you cannot calculate split-half reliabilities for Coding). However, the HAWIK manual does give a reliability calculated from administering both the Coding subtest and an alternative version to fifty older children. The ten-subtest correlation assumes the applicability of that value, so we can get a result for all the subtests used to compare black and white for IQ.

Sources: The white versus black scores on the subtests are from Eyferth, 1960, p. 235. The HAWIK manual gives both the intercorrelations of the various subtests and their reliabilities (Hardesty and Priester, 1963, pp. 10–16).

References

PREFATORY NOTE ON CITATIONS FROM
PLATO, ARISTOTLE, HOBBES, KANT, AND
NIETZSCHE

The citations of these thinkers allow the reader to use any available current edition or translation. All citations of Plato and Aristotle refer to the relevant work and the pages of the standard medieval editions, whose page numbers are duplicated in every respectable current edition. They are always put in the margins of the text rather than at the top or bottom. The Akademie edition is the standard edition of Kant's works and my citations refer to its volumes and pages. These too are duplicated in every respectable current edition. Those who lack German, as I do, will easily find English translations of all of Kant's works.

When citing Nietzsche (*Beyond Good and Evil*, *The Genealogy of Morals*, *Thus Spoke Zarathustra*, *Twilight of the Idols*, and *Human, All-Too-Human*), I utilize his division of his books into sections. The sections range from a few lines to a few paragraphs, and they are either titled or numbered. Sometimes the number sequence runs throughout the work. Sometimes it terminates and begins again as you go from one larger unit to another, for example from the Preface of *The Genealogy of Morals* to the First Essay, to the Second Essay, to the Third Essay. I use Nietzsche's units of internal organization rather than citing pages because the latter would be peculiar to a particular edition. I follow the same procedure when citing Hobbes's *Leviathan*.

Arias, E. (2004). *United States Life Tables, 2002*. National Vital Statistics Reports, vol. 53 no. 6. Hyattsville, MD: National Center for Health Statistics.

Aristotle. *Ethics*; *Politics*. See Prefatory note to references.

Ayers, I., and Siegelman, P. (1995). Race and gender discrimination in bargaining for a new car. *American Economic Review*, 85: 304–321.

Benedict, R. (1934). *Patterns of Culture*. Boston: Houghton-Mifflin.

Bertrand, M., and Mullainathan, S. (2003). *Are Emily and Greg More Employable than Lakisha and Jamal? A Field Experiment on Labor Market Discrimination*. National Bureau of Economic Research, NBER Working Paper W 9873 (July 2003).

Bloom, A. (1987). *The Closing of the American Mind*. New York: Simon and Schuster.

Blum, W. (2002). *Rogue State: A Guide to the World's Superpower*. London: Zed Books.

Bonczar, T. P. (2003). *Bureau of Justice Statistics Special Report: Prevalence of Imprisonment in the U.S. Population, 1974–2001*. Washington, DC: NCJ 197976.

Brainerd, E. (2006). Uncounted cost of World War II: the effect of changing sex ratios on marriage and fertility of Russian women. http://web.gc.cuny.edu/economics/SeminarPapers/spring_2006_health_labor/rfwomen.pdf.

Breslau, N., Dickens, W. T., Flynn, J. R., Peterson, E. L., and Lucia, V. C. (2006). Low birthweight and social disadvantage: tracking their relationship with children's IQ during the period of school attendance. *Intelligence*, 34: 351–362.

Burt, C. (1959). Class differences in general intelligence: III. *British Journal of Statistical Psychology*, 12: 15–33.

(1961). Intelligence and social mobility. *British Journal of Statistical Psychology*, 14: 3–24.

Bush, G. W. (2002). State of the Union Address, January 29, 2002. See www.whitehouse.gov/news/releases/2002/01/20020129-11.html

(2003). Remarks to the Philippine Congress, October 18, 2003. See www.state.gov/p/eap/ris/rm/2003/25455/htm.

(2004). Letter from President Bush to Prime Minister Sharon, April 14, 2004. See www.whitehouse.gov/news/releases/2004/04/20040414-3.html.

Charles, N., and Coleman, C. (1995). Crime suspect. *Emerge*, 24–30.

Cole, W. S. (1962). *Senator Gerald P. Nye and American Foreign Relations*. Minneapolis: University of Minnesota Press.

Cook, P. J., and Ludwig, J. (1998). The burden of "acting white": do black adolescents disparage academic achievement? In C. Jencks and M. Phillips (eds.), *The Black–White Test Score Gap* (pp. 375–400.). Washington, DC: Brookings Institution Press.

CPS (2005). Data from The Annual Social and Economic Supplement (ASEC) to the Current Population Survey (CPS). US Census Bureau, March 2005.

Cunningham, N. E. (1987). *In Pursuit of Reason: The Life of Thomas Jefferson*. Baton Rouge: Louisiana State University Press.

Dennett, D. C. (2003). *Freedom Evolves*. London: Penguin.

Diamond, J. (1991). *The Rise and Fall of the Third Chimpanzee*. London: Radius.

(2005). *Collapse*. New York: Viking Penguin.

Dickens, W. T. (1999). Rebuilding urban labor markets: what community development can accomplish. In R. F. Ferguson and W. T. Dickens (eds.), *Urban Problems and Community Development* (pp. 381–485). Washington, DC: Brookings Institution Press.

Dickens, W. T., and Flynn, J. R. (2001a). Great leap forward: a new theory of intelligence. *New Scientist*, April 21, 2001, 44–47.

(2001b). Heritability estimates versus large environmental effects: the IQ paradox resolved. *Psychological Review*, 108: 346–369.

(2006). Black Americans reduce the racial IQ gap: evidence from standardization samples. *Psychological Science*, 17: 913–920.

Dilman, I. (1999). *Free Will: An Historical and Philosophical Introduction*. London: Routledge.

Downs, B. (2003). *Fertility of American Women: June 2002. Current Population Reports, P20–548*. Washington, DC: US Census Bureau.

Drucker, E. M. (2003). The impact of mass incarceration on public health in black communities. In L. E. Daniels (ed.), *The State of Black America 2003* (pp. 151–168). New York: The Urban League.

Dyer, G. (2002). UN goes along with charade, November 14, 2002. See www.aljazeerah.info/Opinion%20editorials/2002.

Eberhardt, J. L., Johnson, S., Davies, P. G., and Purdie-Vaughans, V. J. (2006). Looking deathworthy: perceived stereotypicality of black defendants predicts capital-sentencing outcomes. *Psychological Science*, 17: 383–386.

Eyferth, K. (1959). Eine Utersuchung der Neger-Mischingskinder in Westdeutschland [A study of black interracial children in West Germany]. *Vita Humana*, 2: 102–114.

(1961). Leistungen versschiedeneer Gruppen von Besatzungskinder im Hamburg-Wechsler Intelligenztest für Kinder (HAWIK) [Performance of various groups of occupation children on the Hamburg-Wechsler Intelligence Test for Children (HAWIK)]. *Archiv für die gesamte Psychologie*, 113: 222–241.

Eyferth, K., Brandt, U., and Hawel, W. (1960). *Farbige Kinder in Deutschland* [Colored children in Germany]. Munich: Juventa Verlag.

Eysenck, H. J. (1981). Special review: James R. Flynn, *Race, IQ and Jensen*. *Personality and Individual Differences*, 2: 259.

Ezorsky, G. (1991). *Racism and Justice: The Case for Affirmative Action*. Ithaca, NY: Cornell University Press.

Farley, R. (1995). *State of the Union: America in the 1990s*. New York: Russell Sage Foundation.

Feldman, S., and Shapir, Y. (eds.) (2004). *The Middle East Strategic Balance 2003–2004*. Brighton: Sussex Academic Press.

Ferguson, N. (2004). *Colossus*. London: Allen Lane.

Figlio, D. N. (2005). *Names, Expectations and the Black–White Test Score Gap. NBER Working Paper 11195*. Cambridge, MA: National Bureau of Economic Research.

Fitzgerald, F. Scott (1925). *The Great Gatsby*. New York: Charles Scribner's Sons.

Flynn, J. R. (1967). *American Politics: A Radical View*. Auckland: Blackwood and Janet Paul.

(1980). *Race, IQ, and Jensen*. London: Routledge.

(1984). Banishing the spectre of meritocracy. *Bulletin of the British Psychological Society*, 37: 256–259.

(1986). The logic of Kant's derivation of freedom from reason: an alternative reading to Paton. *Kant-Studien*, 77: 441–446.

(1991). *Asian Americans: Achievement beyond IQ*. Hillsdale, NJ: Erlbaum.

(1993). Derrida: what does he believe? *Political Theory Newsletter*, 5: 180–181.

Flynn, J. R. (2000a). *How To Defend Humane Ideals: Substitutes for Objectivity*. Lincoln: University of Nebraska Press.

(2000b). IQ gains, WISC subtests, and fluid g: g theory and the relevance of Spearman's hypothesis to race (followed by Discussion). In G. R. Bock, J. A. Goode, and K. Webb (eds.), *The Nature of Intelligence (Novartis Foundation Symposium 233)* (pp. 202–227). New York: Wiley.

(2000c). IQ trends over time: intelligence, race, and meritocracy. In K. Arrow, S. Bowles, and S. Durlauf (eds.), *Meritocracy and Economic Inequality* (pp. 35–60). Princeton, NJ: Princeton University Press.

(2007). *What Is Intelligence? Beyond the Flynn Effect.* Cambridge: Cambridge University Press.

Flynn, J. R., Dickens, W. T., and Breslau, N. (in preparation). The black–white IQ gap: massive expansion with age; signs of reduction between generations.

Flynn, J. R., and Weiss, L. (2007). American IQ gains from 1932 to 2002: the significance of the WISC subtests. *International Journal of Testing*, 7: 209–224.

Frankfurt, H. (1969). Alternate possibilities and moral responsibility. *Journal of Philosophy*, 66: 829–839.

Frier, R. G., and Levitt, S. D. (2006). *Testing for Racial Differences in the Mental Ability of Young Children.* NBER Working Paper 12066. Cambridge, MA: National Bureau of Economic Research.

Ginger, R. (1962). *Eugene V. Debs: A Biography.* New York: Collier Books.

Goldman, E. F. (1956). *Rendezvous with Destiny* (revised edn). New York: Vintage Books.

Gorman, J. R. (1971). *Kefauver: A Political Biography.* New York: Oxford University Press.

Gribben, J. (2005). *Deep Simplicity.* London: Penguin.

Haggis, J. (1992). The politics of difference. *Political Theory Newsletter*, 4: 70–78.

Halberstein, D. (2001). *War in a Time of Peace.* New York: Simon and Schuster.

Hamid, M. (2007). *The Reluctant Fundamentalist.* London: Hamish Hamilton.

Hanley, R. (1997). Black police groups denounce mistaken shooting of officer. *New York Times*, November 27, 1997.

Hardesty, F. P., and Priester, H. J. (1963, first published in 1956). *Handbuch für den Hamburg-Wechsler Intelligenztest für Kinder* [Manual for the

Hamburg-Wechsler Intelligence Test for Children]. Berne and Stuttgart: Verlag Hans Huber.

Harrison, P. M., and Beck, A. J. (2005). *Bureau of Justice Statistics Bulletin: Prison and Jail Inmates at Midyear 2004*. Washington, DC: NCJ 208801.

Harrison, P. M., and Karberg, J. C. (2003). *Bureau of Justice Statistics Bulletin: Prison and Jail Inmates at Midyear 2002*. Washington, DC: NCJ 198877.

Heckman, J. J., and Rubenstein, Y. (2001). The importance of non-cognitive skills: lessons from the GED testing program. *American Economic Review*, 91: 145–149.

Heckman, J. J., Stixrud, J., and Urzua, S. (2006). The effects of cognitive and non-cognitive abilities on labor market outcomes and social behavior. *Journal of Labor Economics*, 24: 411–481.

Herrnstein, R. J., and Murray, C. (1994). *The Bell Curve: Intelligence and Class Structure in American Life*. New York: The Free Press.

Hersch, Joni (2008). *Profiling the New Immigrant Worker: The Effects of Skin Color and Height*. Vanderbilt Law and Economics Research Paper No. 07–02, January 11, 2008.

Hewlett (2006). *Facts at a Glance*. Publication # 2006–03, April 2006, by the William and Flora Hewlett Foundation.

Hobbes, T. *Leviathan*. See Prefatory note to references.

Hofstadter, R. (1962). *The American Political Tradition*. London: Jonathan Cape.

Holton, R. (2008). Introduction to philosophy, Lecture 4, Handout IV. Online, January 26, 2008.

Houston, L. N. (1981). Romanticism and eroticism among black and white students. *Adolescence*, 16: 263–272.

Hymowitz, K. S. (2003). *Liberation's Children: Parents and Kids in a Postmodern Age*. Chicago: Ivan R. Dee.

Iwo Jima, Inc. (2006). U.S. invasion of Iwo Jima: the battle. www.iwojima.com/battle/battled.hym.

James, W. (1897). The moral philosophy and the moral life. In *The Will To Believe and Other Essays in Popular Philosophy* (pp. 184–215). New York: Longmans. (First published in *International Journal of Ethics*, April 1891.)

Jensen, A. R. (1973). *Educability and Group Differences*. London: Methuen. (1980). *Bias in Mental Testing*. London: Methuen.

(1998). *The g Factor: The Science of Mental Ability*. Westport, CT: Praeger.

Jensen, A. R., and Reynolds, C. R. (1982). Race, social class, and ability patterns on the WISC-R. *Personality and Individual Differences*, 3: 423–438.

Johnson, C. (2004). The arithmetic of America's military bases abroad: what does it all add up to? The Nation Institute: www.tomdispatch.com.

Jones, J. (2006). Marriage is for white people. *Washington Post*, Sunday, March 26, 2006.

Kane, T. J. (1998). Racial and ethnic preferences in college admissions. In C. Jencks and M. Phillips (eds.), *The Black–White Test Score Gap* (pp. 431–456). Washington, DC: Brookings Institution Press.

Kant, I. *Metaphysics of Morals*. See Prefatory note to references.

Kaufmann, W. (1954). Thus Spoke Zarathustra, First Part, Editor's Note No. 7, On Reading and Writing. In W. Kaufmann (ed.), *The Portable Nietzsche*. New York: Viking Press.

(1962). *Nietzsche: Philosopher, Psychologist, Antichrist* (7th edn). New York: World Publishing Company.

Kennedy, P. M. (1987). *The Rise and Fall of the Great Powers: Economic Change and Military Conflict from 1500 to 2000*. New York: Random House.

Kirschenman, J., and Neckerman, K. M. (1991). "We'd love to hire them, but . . .": the meaning of race for employers. In C. Jencks and P. E. Peterson (eds.), *The Urban Underclass* (pp. 203–233). Washington, DC: Brookings Institution Press.

Kirschenman, J., *et al.* (1996). Space as a signal, space as a barrier: how employers map and use space in four metropolitan labor markets. Unpublished paper prepared for the Social Science History Association Meetings, October 1996.

Kochanek, K. D., and Smith, B. L. (2004). *Deaths: Preliminary Data for 2002*. National Vital Statistics Reports, vol. 52 no. 13. Hyattsville, MD: National Center for Health Statistics.

Kochhar, R. (2004). *The Wealth of Hispanic Households: 1996 to 2002*. Washington, DC: Pew Hispanic Center Report, October 18, 2004.

Krock, T. J. (1992). *To End All Wars: Woodrow Wilson and the Quest for a New World Order*. New York: Oxford University Press.

References

Kurzweil, R. (2005). *The Singularity Is Near*. New York: Viking.

Lane, S., Keefe, R., Rubinstein, R., Levandowski, B., Freedman, M., Rosenthal, A., Cibula, D., and Czerwinski, M. (2004). Marriage promotion and missing men: African American women in a demographic double bind. *Medical Anthropology Quarterly*, 18: 405–428.

Levin, M. (c. 1991). Responses to race differences in crime. Unpublished manuscript.

Lippmann, Walter (1913). *Preface to Politics*. New York: Mitchell Kennerley.

Livingston, J. C. (1979). *Fair Game? Inequality and Affirmative Action*. San Francisco: Freeman.

Locke, John (1954). *Essays on the Law of Nature* (ed. and trans. W. von Leyden). Oxford: Clarendon Press.

Lynd, S. (1969). *Intellectual Origins of American Radicalism*. London: Faber and Faber.

Lynn, R. (1994). Some reinterpretations of the Minnesota Trans-racial Adoption Study. *Intelligence*, 19: 21–28.

  (2002). Racial and ethnic differences in psychopathic personality. *Personality and Individual Differences*, 32: 273–316.

Maher, M. (1940). *Psychology: Empirical and Rational* (9th edn). London: Longmans.

Martin, J. A., Hamilton, B. E., Sutton, P. D., Ventura, S. J., Menacker, F., and Munson, M. L. (2003). *Births: Final Data for 2002*. National Vital Statistics Reports, vol. 52. Hyatssville, MD: National Center for Health Statistics.

Martin, R. (2007). Commentary: Black men must reclaim our children. CNN Roland Martin black men (December 11, 2007).

Matthews, R. K. (1984). *The Radical Politics of Thomas Jefferson: A Revisionist View*. Lawrence: University Press of Kansas.

Mill, John Stuart (1958). *Nature and the Utility of Religion* (ed. George Nakhnikian). New York: Liberal Arts Press.

Moore, E. G. J. (1986). Family socialization and the IQ test performance of traditionally and transracially adopted black children. *Developmental Psychology*, 22: 317–326.

Morgan, G. A. (1965). *What Nietzsche Means*. New York: Harper and Row. (First published 1941.)

Morgenthau, Hans (1946). *Scientific Man versus Power Politics*. Chicago: University of Chicago Press.

Nagoshi, C. T., and Johnson, R. C. (1986). The ubiquity of g. *Personality and Individual Differences*, 7: 201–207.

Nielsen, K. (1985). *Equality and Liberty: A Defense of Radical Egalitarianism*. Totawa, NJ: Rowman and Allanhead.

(1994). How to proceed in social philosophy: contextual justice and wide reflective equilibrium. *Queen's Law Journal*, 70: 89–137.

Nietzsche, F. See Prefatory note to references.

Nisbett, R. E. (in press). *Intelligence and How To Get It: Why Schools and Cultures Count*. New York: Norton.

Nye, J. S. (2002). *The Paradox of American Power: Why the World's Superpower Can't Go It Alone*. New York: Oxford University Press.

Paine, L. S. (2002). *Value Shift: Why Companies Must Merge Social and Financial Imperatives to Achieve Superior Performance*. New York: McGraw-Hill.

Parker, D. (2007). Socialists for a bombed Baghdad. *Sunday Star–Times* (New Zealand), June 24, 2007.

Paton, H. J. (1967). *The Categorical Imperative* (6th edn). London: Hutchinson.

Patterson, O. (2006). A poverty of the mind. *New York Times*, op-ed, Sunday, March 26, 2006.

Persons, S. (ed.) (1963). *Social Darwinism: Selected Essays of William Graham Sumner*. Englewood Cliffs, NJ: Prentice Hall. All citations of Persons refer to Sumner's own words, not to editorial comment.

Peterson, M. D. (1998). *The Jeffersonian Image in the American Mind*. Charlottesville: University Press of Virginia.

Phillips, D. L. (2004). Turkey's dreams of accession. *Foreign Affairs*, 83: 86–97.

Pinker, S. (2002). *The Blank Slate: The Modern Denial of Human Nature*. New York: Viking.

Plato. *The Republic*. See Prefatory note to references.

Porter, A. N. (ed.) (1991). *Atlas of British Overseas Expansion*. New York and London: Simon and Schuster.

The Psychological Corporation (2003). *The WISC-IV Technical Manual*. San Antonio, TX: The Psychological Corporation.

Quandt, W. B. (1993). *Peace Process: American Diplomacy and the Arab–Israeli Conflict since 1967*. Berkeley: University of California Press.

Rainwater, L., and Yancey, W. L. (1967). *The Moynihan Report and the Politics of Controversy*. Cambridge, MA: MIT Press.

Rohlfs, C. (2005). How much did the US government value its troops' lives in World War II? Evidence from dollar–fatality tradeoffs in land battles. Unpublished paper, University of Chicago, Department of Economics.

Rushton, J. P. (1995). *Race, Evolution, and Behavior*. New Brunswick, NJ: Transaction Publishers.

Russell, B. (1946). *History of Western Philosophy*. London: Allen and Unwin.

Scarr, S., Weinberg, R. A., and Waldman, I. D. (1993). IQ correlations in transracial adoptive families. *Intelligence*, 17: 541–555.

Schull, W. J., and Neel, J. V. (1965). *The Effects of Inbreeding on Japanese Children*. New York: Harper and Row.

Seashore, H., Wesman, A., and Doppelt, J. (1950). The standardization of the Wechsler Intelligence Scale for Children. *Journal of Consulting Psychology*, 14: 99–110.

Segal, D. R., and Segal, M. W. (2004). America's military population. *Population Bulletin*, 59, no. 4: 1–40.

Shannon, D. A. (1960). *The Great Depression*. Englewood Cliffs, NJ: Prentice Hall.

South, S. S. (1993). Racial and ethnic differences in the desire to marry. *Journal of Marriage and the Family*, 55: 357–370.

Sowell, T. (1972). *Black Education: Myths and Tragedies*. New York: David McKay.

(1975). *Race and Economics*. New York: Longman.

(1994). *Race and Culture*. New York: Basic Books.

(1998). *Conquest and Cultures*. New York: Basic Books.

(2000). *A Personal Odyssey*. New York: The Free Press.

(2005). *Black Rednecks and White Liberals*. San Francisco: Encounter Books.

Stalenheim, P., Perdomo, C., and Skons, E. (2007). Military expenditure. In *SIPRI Yearbook 2007* (pp. 267–297).

Stove, D. (1995). *Cricket versus Republicanism and Other Essays*. Sydney: Quakers Hill Press.

Strawson, P. (1962). Freedom and resentment. *Proceedings of the British Academy*, 48: 204–205.

Strenze, T. (2007). Intelligence and economic success: a meta-analytic review of longitudinal research. *Intelligence*, 35: 401–426.

Sumner, William Graham (1899). The conquest of the United States by Spain. *Yale Law Journal*, 8, no. 4: 168–193.

Tawney, R. H. (1920). *The Acquisitive Society*. New York: Harcourt, Brace, and Howe.

(1931). *Equality*. London: Allen and Unwin.

Tessler, M. (1994). *A History of the Israeli–Palestinian Conflict*. Bloomington: University of Indiana Press.

Tuchman, B. W. (1978). *A Distant Mirror: The Calamitous 14th Century*. New York: Knopf.

US Army AG (1953). *Army Battle Casualties and Non-battle Deaths in World War II: Final Report, 7 December 1941–31 December 1946*. Washington, DC: Statistical and Accounting Branch, Office of the Adjutant General. Source: US National Archives II, National Archives Library Call No. 1954:4728.

US Army ASF (1954). *Statistical Review, World War II: A Summary of ASF Activities*. Washington, DC: Statistics Branch, Control Division, Headquarters, Army Service Forces, War Department. Source: US National Archives II, Record Group 160, Entry 94, Box 702.

US Census (2001). *POP6.B: Family Structure and Children's Living Arrangements: Detailed Living Arrangements of Children by Gender, Race, Hispanic Origin, Age, Parent's Education and Poverty Status, 2001*. US Census Bureau, Survey of Income and Program Participation (SIPP), 2001 Panel, Wave 2.

(2004). *Table FM-2: All Parent/Child Situations, by Type, Race, and Hispanic Origin of Householder or Reference Person: 1970 to Present* (internet release date September 15, 2004). Source: US Census Bureau, Annual Social and Economic Supplement: 2003 Current Population Survey, Current Population Reports, Series P20–553. (America's families and living arrangements: 2003, and earlier reports.)

(2005). *Table P-2: Race and Hispanic Origin of People by Median Income and Sex: 1947 to 2003*. US Census Bureau, Historical Income Table – People.

US Health Statistics (2006a). *Table 1–1: Live Births, Birth Rates, and Fertility Rates, by Race: United States, 1909–2001*. National Center for Health Statistics (US), Vital Statistics, Health, last modified May 26, 2006.

(2006b). *Table 1–24: Live Births by Place of Delivery, and Attendant, According to Race and Hispanic Origin: United States, Selected Years, 1975–2001*. National Center for Health Statistics (US), Vital Statistics, Health, last modified May 26, 2006.

US Navy (1950). *History of the Medical Department of the United States Navy in World War II: The Statistics of Disease and Injuries* (vol. 3). Washington, DC: Government Printing Office, OCLC 04067096.

Veblen, Thorstein (1899). *The Theory of the Leisure Class*. New York: Macmillan.

Wachter, K. W., and Freedman, D. A. (1999). *The Fifth Cell: Correlation Bias in U.S. Census Adjustment*. University of California, Berkeley, Department of Statistics, Technical Report 570, December 17, 1999.

Washington, H. A. (ed.) (1861). *The Writings of Thomas Jefferson*. New York: H. W. Derby.

Washington Report. See U.S. financial aid to Israel: figures, facts, and impact at www.Washington-report.org/htmls/US_Aid_To_Israel.htm.

Wechsler, D. (1949). *Wechsler Intelligence Scale for Children: Manual*. New York: The Psychological Corporation.

(1992). *Wechsler Intelligence Scale for Children – Third Edition: Manual (Australian Adaptation)*. San Antonio, TX: The Psychological Corporation.

Wicherts, J. M., Dolan, C. V., Hessen, D. J., Oosterveld, P., van Baal, G. C. M., Boomsma, D. I., and Span, M. M. (2004). Are intelligence tests measurement invariant over time? Investigating the Flynn effect. *Intelligence*, 32: 509–537.

Wikipedia (2006). Military of the United States (redirected from the United States Armed Forces). http://en.wikipedia.org/wiki/United_States_armed_forces. As retrieved on May 17, 2006.

Willerman, L., Naylor, A. F., and Myrianthopoulos, N. C. (1974). Intellectual development of children from interracial matings: performance in infancy and at 4 years. *Behavior Genetics*, 4: 83–90.

Wilson, D. S. (2002). *Darwin's Cathedral: Evolution, Religion, and the Nature of Society*. Chicago: University of Chicago Press.

Wittgenstein, L. (1989). A lecture on freedom of the will. *Philosophical Investigations*, 12: 85–100.

Wolff, K. H. (1955). *German Attempts at Picturing Germany: Texts*. Columbus: Ohio State University Press.

Wolff, T. (1998). *A Man in Full*. London: Jonathan Cape.

Woodham-Smith, C. (1991). *The Reason Why: The Story of the Fatal Charge of the Light Brigade*. Oxford: Penguin.

Yeatman, A. (1992). Minorities and the politics of difference. *Political Theory Newsletter*, 4: 1–10.

Young, I. M. (1992). Together in difference: transforming the logic of group political conflict. *Political Theory Newsletter*, 4: 11–26.

Zagorsky, J. L. (2007). Do you have to be smart to be rich? The impact of IQ on wealth, income, and financial success. *Intelligence*, 35: 489–501.

Zogby, J. (2004). Bush, Kerry fail leadership test on US Middle East policy. See www.aaiusa.org/pr/release04-19-04.htm.

Index of names

The following thinkers also appear in the index of subjects: Aristotle, Benedict, Debs, James, Jefferson, Kefauver, Nietzsche, Plato, Rawls, Sumner, and Strauss.

Index of names

Index of subjects

Many subjects appear under the main topics of the book, that is, under affirmative action, black Americans, free will and determinism, meritocracy thesis, race and IQ, Social Democracy, US foreign policy, and the thinkers listed (the last also appear in the index of names).